WHAT SHAKESPEARE READ—AND THOUGHT

WHAT SHAKESPEARE READ ~ AND THOUGHT

A. L. ROWSE

Coward, McCann & Geoghegan
New York

First American edition 1981

Library of Congress Cataloging in Publication Data
Rowse, Alfred Leslie, date.
  What Shakespeare read—and thought.
  Includes index.
  1. Shakespeare, William, 1564–1616—Knowledge and
learning. I. Title.
PR3000.R6   822.3′3   80-24459
ISBN 0-698-11077-3

Printed in the United States of America

TO

GEORGE WEIDENFELD

IN RECOGNITION

OF HIS ACHIEVEMENT

Contents

PREFACE   ix

1 Shakespeare's Education   1
2 Shakespeare and the Classics   14
3 The Theatre   35
4 History and Kingship   67
5 Comedy and Tragedy   80
6 Poetry, Language, Style   99
7 Shakespeare's Reading   124
8 Politics and Society   139
9 Contemporary Life   154
10 Ethics and Religion   180

INDEX   205

Preface

I owe this book entirely to Lord Weidenfeld whose idea it was: I should not have thought of it without his suggestion. I had, however, contemplated a book on the subject of Shakespeare's reading, and now I have been able to incorporate this into a larger framework. Something of my gratitude to my publisher for his enthusiasm and flair is indicated by my dedication.

Following up this suggestion offered me something new. Hitherto I had worked at Shakespeare's biography, his poems and plays in the light of their proper background, the life of his time, the Elizabethan age. It has been borne in upon me more and more that it is only along these lines that we can properly grasp his work. And more – purely literary criticism of Shakespeare has nothing more to say; neither has textual criticism; nor the pedantic search for 'sources'. They have all reached a dead end.

And all the while the obviously right and rewarding approach, the one that illuminates any writer's work – the life, circumstances and conditions of his time that enter so largely into it – has been neglected or ignored. It has, however, offered a glorious opportunity to the historian of the age, and has been rewarded with rich findings. The problems of Shakespeare's biography as revealed in the Sonnets – for so long open to every sort of uncertainty and absurd conjecture – have been solved, even (unexpectedly) that of the identity of the Dark Lady, who remained dark for so long. We can now view the leading Elizabethan writer, as I thought earlier we should with our added knowledge, in three dimensions. If my original solutions of the 'problems' of the Sonnets had not been right, I should never have got on the track of the Dark Lady – it was a bonus for sticking to my guns. Now we have the full picture – completely unanswerable, for it is the answer.

It is not only with regard to Shakespeare that a lifetime of research into his age has yielded significant new findings: it has also done so in regard to Sir Richard Grenville of the *Revenge*, Sir Walter Ralegh and Simon Forman (with something new yet to come about Sir John Harington of the *Epigrams*).

It takes about a generation for something really new and significant to sink into ordinary minds – those of the Shakespeare industry, for example. When Sir William Harvey found the answer to the problem of the circulation of the blood, not only was this leading authority in his field not credited, but his medical practice fell off sharply. Comic as this is in a way, its effects are not wholly laughable, when students of all kinds, who have so much to learn, are content to go on with the old dead lumber.

When I first began work on the leading writer in the age with which my research has been concerned all my working life, it was not so clear to me that I should be giving the study of Shakespeare a revolutionary new impetus. But that is how it has providentially worked out, and I am duly grateful.

ALR

1

Shakespeare's Education

EVERYTHING about William Shakespeare was surprisingly normal – except, of course, his genius. The point is worth making because genius so often goes with abnormality – the neurotic, eccentric or the odd. When one thinks of the idea of the poet incarnated in Shelley, Byron or Swinburne, let alone Baudelaire or Hölderlin; writers like Dostoievsky, Gogol or even Tolstoy, let alone a Strindberg or Nietzsche; a monument of common sense like Dr Johnson was decidedly eccentric; Beethoven outrageously so. The surprising thing about Shakespeare is that – like Churchill – he was so normal: a family man accepting the obligations (if not the restrictions) of family life, strongly heterosexual (no homosexual, like so many men of genius, his contemporaries, Marlowe and Bacon, for instance); a neighbourly man well grafted into the life of his home town, where he was determined to make good; a good fellow in his profession, as the tributes to him from his fellow actors show.

So too was his education. Everything shows that he had the normal grammar-school education of his age. Many market towns of the size of Stratford-upon-Avon, on its road- and river-routes, had their grammar school in the Elizabethan age; and what was taught was much the same all over the country: Latin accidence, grammar and the elementary classics were drilled into the boys. Lily's grammar – for Latin was the foundation and medium of grammar-school education – was virtually a national textbook; and the curriculum imposed did much towards forming the mentality of the age, a common universe of discourse. To change the image, it constituted the basic mental furniture.

Shakespeare was not a university man. But what matter? Neither was the scholarly Ben Jonson nor the laureate Drayton, Shakespeare's fellow Warwickshireman. Nor were other dramatists of note: Kyd or Dekker, Webster or Middleton or

Tourneur, or even the intellectual Chapman. Actually, for a budding dramatist, the university of life was a better school. True enough, when scouted by a university wit like Robert Greene later on (in 1592), and faced with the rivalry of another for Southampton's patronage in the shape of Marlowe, his inferiority in this unimportant respect was brought home. Southampton's eyes

> Have added feathers to the learned's wing,
> And given grace a double majesty.

But this was only a *façon de parler* expressed with Shakespeare's innate courtesy. The depreciation of himself was politeness, not to be taken too seriously:

> Thine eyes that taught the dumb on high to sing,
> And heavy ignorance aloft to fly –

for he was very far from being ignorant, heavy or dumb!

Amusingly enough, although his school education was almost entirely in Latin, his equipment in that respect was much like that of a modern grammar-school boy, not good enough for a colleger at Eton or Winchester, who has been kept to the grind till much later. At the same time, his classical background was fuller and richer, his knowledge of it ready at every moment to spring to mind; for it dominated an Elizabethan's education and was all round him not only in his reading, but in conversation, references, texts, depictions, wall paintings, pictures and tapestries. As I said, it provided much of one's mental furniture, and Shakespeare's plays, from beginning to end, are naturally full of it. There is no problem to those who know the age intimately and have given their lives to its study: he was not a university man, but a clever grammar-school boy.

And his plays are more full of grammar-school matter – the methods and modes of teaching, quips and phrases from the texts used, quotations and parodies, caricatures of schoolmasters and laughs at their expense – than those of any other dramatist of the time. This is a strong indication, but not the only one, that the old tradition, passed on by a member of Shakespeare's own company, that he had for a time taught school in the country (i.e. as an usher), is almost certainly correct.

2

Before going to the grammar school, at the age of about seven, an Elizabethan boy had to be able to read and write and be already 'fit' for grammar, i.e. Latin grammar. Most towns had some means of elementary instruction – before the Reformation it was a job for chantry priests – particularly for the sons of middle-class tradesmen or professional people, the upper crust, to which Shakespeare's family belonged. (Marlowe came from lower down, his father a shoemaker, and Ben Jonson's stepfather was a bricklayer; but the one went to King's School, Canterbury, the other to Westminster.) Shakespeare's background was superior, particularly on his mother's side, the Ardens – the family of Warwickshire gentry whose coat of arms he thought to impale with those he had taken out for his father, the motto: *Non sans droit!*

Stratford in fact had an elementary school, where small boys were taught their ABC, and to read and write. They learned from a hornbook, or ABC book, a brief primer printed on a board with a handle, like a hand-mirror. On it were printed the alphabet, in small and capital letters, the vowels and then the elementary syllables, the Grace and 'Our Father'. Before the first row is a cross, hence the name 'Christ cross-row'. Even this is made use of in the plays, in the way he had of making the utmost of everything.

Question and answer: here is the Bastard Faulconbridge in *King John* questioned as to his parentage:

And then comes answer like an Absey book.

The Two Gentlemen of Verona, an early play, has:

To sigh, like a schoolboy that had lost his ABC.

In *Richard III*, George, Duke of Clarence, says to Richard, Duke of Gloucester, of their brother, Edward IV:

He hearkens after prophecies and dreams,
And from the cross-row plucks the letter G ...

The first scene of Act v in *Love's Labour's Lost* is largely devoted to a caricature of a grammar-school lesson; but it draws on earlier experience, when Moth says of Holofernes, a schoolmaster:

He teaches boys the horn-book. What is a, b, spelt backward with the horn on his head?

Holofernes answers:

Ba, *pueritia* [boyhood], with a horn added.

Moth rejoins:

Ba, most silly sheep with a horn. You hear his learning!

This introduces the commonest (and most boring) of Elizabethan jokes about a cuckold's horns; a contemporary audience never seemed to tire of it – with bawdy gestures appropriate.

We are reminded that catechising was the mode of instruction from earliest years: 'What kind of catechising call you this?' Hero says in *Much Ado*. Claudio replies, 'To make you answer truly to your name.' The first question of the Church Catechism, which we still went through when I was a small boy, was: 'What is your name?' Elizabethan education was swaddled and suffused with religion at every stage: school opened and closed with prayers from the Book of Common Prayer, Bible readings and psalms, and in addition metrical psalms in the Genevan fashion were sometimes sung – all reflected in the plays, even the last. Attendance at church was compulsory on Sundays, and at the sermons, at the parish church of Holy Trinity or the Gild Chapel, which were frequent enough. Often children were required to write notes or memorise something from the sermon. There were also family events – christenings, weddings, funerals. Altogether the life was that of an intensely close community, in which everybody knew everybody else's business; there was little privacy; it was warm and tense, mercurial and temperamental, apt to be disorderly and explosive: a human beehive. Too communal for us today: we should find it suffocating.

The whole accent of education was on memorising; books were few and knowledge was drilled into one's head by endless repetition and rote. This is the foundation of Shakespeare's fabulous memory. Elizabethans in general must have had better memories than we moderns have, who load up our minds with too much, most of it rubbish, and read too many books, mostly of little value. Hence the extraordinary retentiveness of Elizabethan memories. But Shakespeare had a double, or even triple reason for his ability: not only his natural gift but, later, the trained memory of an actor. One

4

notices what a magpie mind he had: everything was picked up that might come in handy and it was made use of again and again; phrases from schooldays and attendance at church, from his wide reading, phrases and words with their associations from the poets and his fellow dramatists (especially from Marlowe).

Phrases from the Prayer Book used at church echo and re-echo through all the plays, chiefly ones from Matins and Evensong (especially from the Psalms), for those were the principal services. The Communion service was usual four times a year, and communicating at Easter was obligatory. Hamlet's phrase describing his hands as 'these pickers and stealers' reflects the phrase in the Catechism, and when Shakespeare cites the Commandments he does so in the Prayer Book version. There are scores of phrases which we need not go into in more detail here.* I would merely point to echoes of the Prayer Book in words like absolution and remission, amendment of our lives, labour in our vocation (from Falstaff!), grafted inwardly in our hearts; love, honour and obey; Good Lord, deliver us, grant us thy peace, world without end. These phrases had a different effect upon Elizabethans than upon us: to those of us who can remember them they are nostalgic and tired; to Elizabethans they were new-minted and stirring, and printed themselves freshly upon the mind.

No trace of the Roman missal or the Vulgate occurs in all his work; but the Anglican emphasis on charity is in keeping with the Catholic tradition of *caritas*. The complex association of love with charity appears in Berowne's

> For charity itself fulfils the law,
> And who can sever love from charity?

Here we go beyond the region of phrases to penetrate into Shakespeare's thought; for Berowne speaks for Shakespeare in *Love's Labour's Lost*, is in fact Shakespeare himself. Berowne's dark Rosaline is the Dark Lady of the Sonnets, described in practically the same words, and we know that the poet fell in love with her for her 'unworthiness', out of pity for her. Charity led to love.

---

* For more detail v. my 'Shakespeare and the Prayer Book', in *Ritual Murder*, ed. by Brian Morris.

We can see further how a moral outlook is built up and reflected in sentences from the Homilies, which were read in church much more frequently than sermons – for only a minority of the clergy could preach at all. Thus we are enjoined to 'have patience in adversity'. Shakespeare seems to have taken the lesson home to himself, for in his own life we encounter nothing of the restlessness and turbulence that marked the lives of Ben Jonson, Marlowe, or others of the dramatists frequently in trouble – killing or being killed in duels, in and out of prison – William Shakespeare never! Most revealing words are spoken in *Henry V*:

> In peace there's nothing so becomes a man
> As modest stillness and humility.

The writer is speaking for himself: it exactly describes Shakespeare's conduct of his own life.

The Homily against Swearing and Perjury is echoed again and again:

> It is great sin to swear unto a sin,
> But greater sin to swear a sinful oath.

The early plays have a good deal about oath-breaking, particularly in the political context. Still further reverberation is given throughout the plays to the overriding necessity for society of authority and due obedience, the prime virtue of a subject. In church everybody was told, 'Almighty God hath created and appointed all things in heaven, earth and waters, in a most excellent and perfect order.... In earth he hath assigned and appointed kings, princes, with other governors under them, in all good and necessary order. The sun, moon, stars, rainbow, thunder, lightning, clouds, and all the birds of the air do keep their order.' The consequences for society of the breakdown of order are fatal, both for the community and for the individual.

Shakespeare himself was not far away from the ghastly events of the Wars of the Roses he recorded in his early plays; and those were followed in the generation after him by the deplorable events of the odious Civil War. It fell to his daughter Susanna to entertain Charles I's unfortunate queen early on in it. As an intelligent and sensitive man Shakespeare felt to his finger-tips how thin is the crust of civilisation over what abysses of cruelty and misery for humans: anything can happen when order is shaken and breaks down. How right he was we have the worst of reasons for knowing, in the events of our own time. The civilised Victorian age could not understand it – a Victorian like Robert Bridges could not bear the brutality of life revealed in the plays; but William Shakespeare was right about life and humans, not Bridges. The point here is that Shakespeare's consistent attitude to society and political order and security was built up early, and corroborated all the way through from experience.

The Bible was as fundamental in the make-up of his mind as the Prayer Book; this also went back to schooling and early attendance at church, but he carried on with his reading of the Bible later. For it has been noticed that in his earlier work biblical phrases take shape from the Bishops' Bible, which was then that used in church. Later on he used the Geneva Bible, which came out in convenient forms – a man could even carry one in his pocket when jogging about the country. Most deeply stamped on his mind were the first book of the Old Testament, Genesis, and the first book of the New, the Gospel according to St Matthew – and, interestingly enough, the first book of Ovid's *Metamorphoses*. I think the fact is something of a pointer to the way of his mind.

It has been calculated that Shakespeare was five times more biblical in his references than any other dramatist of the time – some indication of his fundamental conformism. Of the hundred and seventy or so echoes from Genesis, most are from the first four chapters. I should suppose that this was what he had had enforced upon him earliest at school and church. What remained indelibly in his mind was the story of Cain and Abel: there are no less than twenty-five references. Others that recur hardly less frequently are Job and Judas; then, less frequently, John the Baptist, Samson, the Prodigal Son, Herod, Jephthah, and so on. Satan frequently crops up; 'to the teaching of Paul, and to the ministry of Christ, the references are multitudinous'.

We see that the *Bildung* that emerged was deeply Christian, Anglican, normally Protestant but conservative – just like the

Queen, or Elizabethans in general: a normal conforming subject of hers. No rebellious spirit, like Marlowe, or tumultuous temperament, like Jonson.

We have a realistic touch, probably from the usher observing rather than the boy himself, in

> the whining schoolboy, with his satchel
> And shining morning face, creeping like snail
> Unwillingly to school.

One does not see him as ever whining – too euphoric a temperament, or 'merry' as it was put; but there were times when he was unwilling enough to go to school, for everything shows that he was a 'sportive' youth, as he said of himself.

The grammar-school curriculum can be constructed pretty fully from his references to it and the use he made of it for caricature later. And this practically apart from our general knowledge of Elizabethan education. Drayton was brought up contemporaneously as a page in the household at Polesworth; his early steps at about ten would not have been different:

> And when that once *Pueriles* I'd read,
> And newly had my *Cato* construèd ...

he was at once fired by the idea of being a poet and asked his tutor to make him one:

> To it hard went I when shortly he began
> And first read to me honest Mantuan,
> Then Virgil's *Eclogues* ...

Drayton was citing the *Pueriles Sententiae*, or Sentences for Boys, copy-book maxims used in most schools; and the Distichs of Cato, another collection of moral sentiments in hexameter couplets. These were driven into one's head by much repetition. This was the method, so that a lot of phrases and quotations naturally came from the copy-books, not from wide reading in the authors quoted. Shakespeare makes this clear in probably his earliest play, *Titus Andronicus*, quoting the Horatian tag that fixed itself in my own head at school:

> Integer vitae, scelerisque purus
> Non eget Mauri jaculis nec arcu –
>
> O, 'tis a verse in Horace; I know it well
> I read it in the *Grammar* long ago.

8

Lily's Latin grammar is referred to again and again in the plays, and tag after tag is quoted from it: by characters in early plays like Demetrius and Chiron in *Titus*; by Tranio in *The Taming of the Shrew*; then by Holofernes, the schoolmaster in *Love's Labour's Lost*; thence on to Gadshill in *1 Henry IV*, and Sir Toby Belch in *Twelfth Night*; and lastly, Sir Hugh Evans, another schoolmaster caricatured, in *The Merry Wives of Windsor*. Evans, who was Welsh (the last of the grammar-school masters in Shakespeare's time was probably Welsh, a Jenkins), gives the boy William a long lesson in Latin grammar, which is a parody of Lily.

Another collection of phrases and maxims was the *Familiares Colloquendi*, or Colloquies. Holofernes, Armado, and Sir Nathaniel the curate make play out of this in a scene together. The next step was to confront poetry in the shape of Mantuan, the Renaissance Latin poet who was much used in schools, and whose first line (again) is quoted in the original. Then, 'Ah, good old Mantuan! Old Mantuan, old Mantuan! who understandeth thee not, loves thee not.' Shakespeare, as usual, is making the most of what he knows. From this one went on to passages from Caesar, Livy, Virgil, Horace and, above all, Ovid, which fixed themselves in the mind. All of these are cited in phrases or lines – sometimes a line in the original, in case anybody thought that Shakespeare didn't know his school-Latin. Selections from Plautus and Terence for comedy, and from Seneca for tragedy, were of more importance for the eventual dramatist. He knew no Greek, of course; not many Elizabethans did unless they were clerics with their knowledge of New Testament Greek.

We might emend Ben Jonson's 'small Latin and less Greek', of which far too much has been made – it has Ben's typical depreciation of anybody else – to read, more correctly: 'more Latin, and no Greek'.

From grammar one went on to logic and rhetoric, the latter of which was of great importance in Shakespeare's intellectual formation: one might well say that he was a rhetorical writer in the Renaissance sense of the term. The modes of logical discourse came in very handy for the dramatist early on, when closer to his school discipline. The first plays, particularly the *Henry VI* trilogy, are full of stichomythia, the line by line exchanges in antiphony which are artificial to our ears – as they are. Hair-splitting about words came naturally to him. He could not resist verbal conceits and fancies, double meaning and double-talk – not only bawdy *double entendre*, though that is present everywhere – and he gave us too much of them. However, this was in keeping with Elizabethan taste, which burgeoned, proliferated and floreated in every field. Such logical bouts helped to fill up the interstices of action, scenes in which nothing very much was doing.

Far more important was Renaissance rhetoric, a wide field. There it all is in the plays: the high, low and medium styles; the use of epithet and synonym for variation – and the 'varying' in this double mind sometimes goes on and on; then narration, comparison, amplification – a building-up upon a ground theme like a fa-burden in contemporary music. Shakespeare had only to look about him for the inspiration of the famous passage, 'All the world's a stage'; but the development of the theme of the seven ages of man comes from another textbook used in schools, Palingenius' *Zodiacus Vitae*, another Renaissance work. It is the combination of the two that is so characteristic. Again Aphthonius' textbook of rhetoric analysed Ovid's story of Venus and Adonis as an *exemplum* of narration. We see how that was taken up and given all too much narration later – for *Venus and Adonis* is inordinately elaborated.

Above all, there was *inventio*, or discoursing upon a theme. This was made the greatest use of in plays, until towards the end, when perhaps he tired of it or had no further need of it. We see how it worked in discourses on specific themes – like writing essays on a subject at school today: the Bastard Faulconbridge's famous discourse on Commodity, political convenience or expediency, to which all principle is sacrificed. Rumour is the subject of the Induction to *2 Henry IV*; we have an exordium on Reputation in *Othello*. Several such discourses on the burdens and obligations of kingship are developed, from *Henry VI* onwards. Hamlet not only goes into the mystery of existence, whether better to be or not to be, but reads us Shakespeare's own lesson on acting. Even Falstaff has a rhetorical discourse on what he thinks of honour.

Such history as was taught at school was classical, again in selections, from the point of view of enforcing and illustrating moral lessons. It included Caesar's *Commentaries* and the story of his life, certainly: Julius Caesar was always a living personality in Shakespeare's mind, much referred to in the early plays, quite apart from his later devoting a complete play to him. Some of Sallust and something of Livy appeared in the curriculum, and that was about all. Shakespeare's attitude to history was moralistic from beginning to end – he always enforces its lessons, as constantly as any schoolmaster could wish. This, like the excitement of the events themselves, serves also to bind a play together. But we should notice that, when he thinks of a historical parallel, it is a classical one that comes naturally and spontaneously to mind. English history was for him something of a discovery.

Plays were an important part of education both at school and at university, and these were again mainly Latin. Scholars were supposed to converse in Latin. (How much did they? I expect it was fairly elementary, though we know that a Stratford contemporary, a mere burgess, Abraham Sturley, could write a good letter in Latin.) Mulcaster, most famous of schoolmasters, makes the point in his *Elementarie* that taking part in plays was most useful in inculcating proper enunciation and training in elocution. His Merchant Taylors' boys often went to Court to perform – as did the boys of St Paul's, choir and school; Lyly's dramas were all performed by boys, and later the Boys' Companies for a time rivalled the Men's.

Visiting troupes of players regularly toured the towns – we have hundreds of references to them in surviving town accounts. Towns also had their own performances put on by the gilds or the corporation – these were in English and traditional – at Corpus Christi or Whitsuntide (the Prayer Book called it Pentecost). And this was additional to Christmas mummings, the old traditional folk-play of St George and the Dragon. Of this we have authentic recollection in a late play:

> Methinks I play as I have seen them do
> In Whitsun pastorals;

or an early one:

> At Pentecost,
> When all our pageants of delight were played,
> Our youth got me to play the woman's part,

> And I was trimmed in Madam Julia's gown ...
> And at that time I made her weep agood,
> For I did play a lamentable part.
> Madam, it was Ariadne passioning
> For Theseus' perjury and unjust flight:
> Which I so lively acted with my tears.

Need we doubt that that was a personal reminiscence? It bears that stamp upon it, and it comes from one of the earliest plays.

Titus Andronicus might be regarded as a school play, with its horrors, blood-shedding, revenges, according to the book. The suggestion came from Ovid, the manner is affected by Seneca, and Seneca is twice directly quoted in Latin, as if by a schoolmaster. Plautus is the main influence in *The Comedy of Errors*, the plot coming from the *Menaechmi* – as was recognised at the time by a young lawyer at Gray's Inn, who had been through the same curriculum at school. Traces of Terence are in the play too. It is rather suggestive that Shakespeare's earliest plays come out of this school background, reinforcing the tradition that for a time he taught school, however briefly, in his youth.*

Whatever books the schoolboy carried in his satchel, people in the neighbourhood possessed books, especially clerics. A curate in the parish had two copies of *Acolastus*, the Renaissance play on the subject of the Prodigal Son – and we have noticed how frequently he is referred to in the plays. The commonest dictionary used in schools was Withals', and there are traces of the illustrative phrases from that.† The big reference dictionary was Cooper's *Thesaurus* (for which he was rewarded with a bishopric); and Vicar Bretchgirdle left his copy of that expensive work to Stratford grammar school.

Shakespeare tells us that his blood was 'sportive'. Again we have the double sense so characteristic of him; he was implying, in regard to women, but it obviously applies to him also in terms of sport. He was an out-of-doors, country man; not an urban intellectual like Marlowe or Jonson. His early plays and poems are full of the sports he cared for. Most references are to bowls, which was then a rather upper-class game – and

*I owe this suggestion personally to the excellent Arden editor of the *Henry VI* plays, Andrew Cairncross.

†cf. H.M. Hulme, *Explorations in Shakespeare's Language*, 27–8.

that is like him too. Archery was practised even at school: the archery butts were on the big open space by the river, in front of the present theatre. Again we have the stamp of the personal in an early play:

> In my schooldays, when I had lost one shaft,
> I shot his fellow of the self-same flight
> The self-same way with more advisèd watch,
> To find the other forth; and by adventuring both,
> I oft found both.

I often think of this when looking over those spaces by the Avon at Stratford.

He knew all about coursing the hare on the bare stubbles in autumn to the north of the town, or further out upon the Cotswolds to the south. This is very familiar country, recognisable in several places, not only specifically in the Induction to *The Taming of the Shrew*. A poem devoted to hare-coursing, several stanzas of it, is sewn irrelevantly into *Venus and Adonis*. All his early work displays a perfect fixation on deer-hunting, with tell-tale references to deer-stealing. This was an irresistible, hardly disreputable, temptation to sportive young men without a deerpark of their own, to be disapproved of naturally by those who had one. The deer on Shotover were regular targets to the scholars of Oxford, for all the watch the keepers kept (Milton's grandfather was one):

> What, hast not thou full often struck a doe,
> And borne her clearly by the keeper's nose?

This comes from what is probably his earliest play. We have no reason whatever to doubt the ancient tradition that he left Stratford with some such amusing contretemps in the background.

2

Shakespeare and the Classics

SHAKESPEARE, like any educated Elizabethan, was
soused in the classics; it could not be otherwise, for the
classics provided their terms of reference. It is not easy for
a modern person to grasp the situation as it was four hundred
years ago; thus most discussions of the subject are anachronistic.
Classical scholars, like Professor J.A.K. Thomson – who gives
us our fullest description of the subject* – view it from the
point of view of modern classical scholarship. This is a mistake:
they do not know the Elizabethan age and fail to allow for the
difference. Elizabethan classical *scholarship*, as such, was not
exact or precise (and anyway was backward compared with
France or Holland); but classical *knowledge* was ubiquitous,
and all educated people shared its terms. To be educated was
to know Latin; to know Latin was to be a gentleman – and
William Shakespeare was very much set on being a gentleman.

So far we have only dealt with the foundations of his
schooling, and only the essentials of that; but I hope it is
sufficient to show what the essential grounding was. For the
flowering we must go further. We are what our education
makes us, but only in part: natural aptitudes come in, the
bent of our minds, as well as gifts – mathematical or linguistic,
scientific or literary. No doubt about Shakespeare's astonishing
gift for words, evident from the first. The education of a man
of genius is, even more than usual, self-education; and he was
very much a reading man, a quick reader too, who went on
with his own education.

Before he became successful he had plenty of time to lay in
a considerable stock of reading. What else need we suppose he
was doing in the so-called lost years people have made so much
needless fuss about, between Stratford and London? His twins,
Hamnet and Judith, were born in 1585; in 1587 he signed a

*J.A.K. Thomson, *Shakespeare and the Classics*, from which quotations come, unless
otherwise stated.

14

family legal document at Stratford; by 1590 he was already writing, and so successfully as to provoke Robert Greene's envious attack in 1592. Nothing singular about the course of events.

Classical knowledge is something different from the pedantry of scholarship; even today, when classical scholarship has almost faded from the land, educated discourse is full of its echoes. We may not be classical scholars but we have all heard of Julius Caesar or Nero, Aristotle (old country wives used to keep his book on midwifery in their chests) or Socrates, Alexander the Great or Augustus or Herod; numbers of people know of Hadrian by his Wall, or have lived by it. We may still talk of a Colossus or Pegasus or Hercules; we refer to Olympus (if not to Olympics) or Parnassus or Hades; we speak of Hymen or use clichés like cutting the Gordian knot; I have heard people use the phrase, piling Pelion upon Ossa. We can refer to hydra heads, or honey of Hymettus or Hybla; we know about Venus or Mercury, Europa and the bull, or Leda and the swan, Lethe or crossing the Styx, Marathon or Troy, Capua or the Rubicon. And usually, as with the Elizabethans, it is the Latin forms that are common, not Greek: we say 'By Jove!', not 'By Zeus!'

In the Elizabethan age – a Renaissance age – the classical world was all round one, in towns, streets, painted signs, heraldic arms, reliefs on chimney pieces, in furniture, even tombs; rendered in plaster-work, painted glass, wall paintings, tapestries, needlework, cushions, arras hangings; pictures, like that of Elizabeth I astounding the three Graces. The siege of Troy was depicted in a picture viewed by Lucrece; the story of Cyrus is told in a tapestry now at the Victoria and Albert Museum; representations of Venus were common. One sees classical subjects favoured in tapestry and needlework in Elizabethan houses like Hardwick or Hatfield, or in roundels with busts at Wollaton, or simply busts at Lumley Castle; caryatids everywhere and anywhere still. These are mere relics of what once was.

We find hundreds of classical references throughout Shakespeare's writing, from beginning to end. If a comparison is to be made, even in a contemporary context, it is a classical comparison that comes naturally to his mind. The matter goes much further, and more richly, than that. He was fascinated by the inexhaustible stories of classical mythology – some of which are still alive for us – and since Ovid's *Metamorphoses* was a chief repository of these in poetry, this was a favourite book with him. He resorted to it both in Latin and in Arthur Golding's rough but living translation. Most often Shakespeare relies on his memory; hence sometimes images, and even a story, may be confused – as with us, easily enough. In *Venus and Adonis* the wooing of Adonis is more like the pursuit of Hermaphroditus by the naiad Salmacis. In the original Adonis changes into a red flower, the colour of his blood; in Shakespeare,

> A purple flower sprung up, chequered with white,
> Resembling well his pale cheeks and the blood
> Which in round drops upon their whiteness stood.

One must allow for the use of amplification, and the needs of scansion and rhyme: a poem has to be made out of it. 'It looks as if Shakespeare had got mixed in his recollection,' says the scholar, 'at least he could not have been looking at the Latin here. Nor could he when he says that Venus "yokes her silver doves", for in Ovid the chariot is drawn not by doves but by swans. He was trusting to his memory, which told him that the sacred bird of Venus was the dove.' As a matter of fact her chariot is drawn by doves in a later book of the *Metamorphoses*.

What do these details matter? They lead us straight into the heart of the way he wrote. Even the classical scholar concludes, 'when he began to write *Venus and Adonis*, he shut his Golding and his Ovid and wrote out of his own mind. That was the right way to go to work.' Similarly when one comes to *The Rape of Lucrece*, which is based on Ovid's *Fasti*, since 'there was no English translation of the *Fasti* then existing or available, the inference would seem to be that he made direct use of the Latin original'. We are given several instances of phrases clearly suggested by Ovid's, with the rather grudging conclusion, 'we may suppose that Shakespeare did read it in a cursory way, lay it down and write *Lucrece*, as he had written *Venus*, entirely from his own resources'.

Exactly: the Professor has already told us that that is the right way to go to work (it was the way T.S. Eliot told me when young). Shakespeare looked up anything he needed, but relied mainly on his memory, and then wrote quickly. All the evidences are at one on that.

To go beyond words and phrases, the stories and suggestions from mythology, we have the plays influenced by classical drama, as *The Comedy of Errors* is by Plautus, *Titus Andronicus* by Ovid and Seneca, and the plays on classical subjects. Further than that, we have Shakespeare's conception of the classical as evidenced in *Julius Caesar* and *Coriolanus*, his own version of classical form (as against Ben Jonson's), and especially how he conceived Roman character to be – he had clearly given thought to that.

Titus Andronicus is a Senecan play, written while the author was still close to school experience. It is clearly written out of books, curiously mixed, considering the horror of the story, with pastoral and country passages, as if written at Stratford or not far away. The young author, anxious to outdo the horrors of popular drama like Kyd's *The Spanish Tragedy*, has fused the story of Tereus and the cutting out of Philomela's tongue, from Ovid, with the grisly feast of Thyestes, serving up human remains, from Seneca. Elizabethan Grand Guignol, we may say; and we must not take the horrors too seriously, though when the play was put on in London after World War II experiences, one person felt sick and had to go out. It is more relevant here to notice Shakespeare's *fusing* mind, as in the early *Comedy of Errors*, bringing plots together, no less than images and words. We already see the duplicity or triplicity of his mind at work.

Two passages from Seneca are quoted in the original Latin – rather like a schoolmaster turning author. 'The English poet has got the two passages mixed. True, but it is a mistake which could have been made only by a man who knew his Seneca well enough, or so he thought, not to bother about verifying his quotation.' Not to bother is like him. However, 'his familiarity with Seneca is indicated by many echoes and turns of phrase'. I have already mentioned the quotation of a couplet from Horace, with 'I read it in the grammar long ago.' The citation of Actaeon, a favourite with him in early work, is from Ovid:

> Had I the power that some say Dian had,
> Thy temples should be planted presently

With horns, as was Actaeon's; and the hounds
Should drive upon thy new-transformèd limbs.

Reading is specifically referred to:

I have read that Hecuba of Troy
Ran mad for sorrow;

and the beloved *Metamorphoses* actually appears upon the stage:

TITUS: Lucius, what book is that she tosseth so?
LUCIUS: Grandsire, 'tis Ovid's Metamorphoses.

Besides these authors the *Aeneid* of Virgil is reflected in several places – his acquaintance seems to run over the first six books, but more particularly Book I. We have an echo from Cicero. 'There are a good many passages drawn, directly or indirectly, from other classical authors, such as Herodotus and Livy. How much of it is first-hand knowledge it is impossible now to say.' Nor does it matter: the point is that it is absorbed into the system, and the range is wider than people recognise.

Along with *Titus* as his earliest work, 1590–1, came the three *Henry VI* plays, which also may in part be seen as Revenge plays, in the mode so popular at the time. They were inspired by the revelation of English history, and its possibilities for drama, made by the successful publication of Holinshed's *Chronicles* in the fuller second edition of 1587. This was all part of the national excitement about England's past and future, the patriotic fervour roused by the war with Spain reaching its peak in Armada year, 1588, another expression of which was Hakluyt's great sea-epic, the *Principal Navigations* of 1589. This spirit was the ground swell of much of Shakespeare's early work. Other aspiring dramatists were also alerted by the stories of England's past in Holinshed; but the newcomer who was also an actor was the most successful of them. This angered Robert Greene, who, for all his being a university wit and the leading literary journalist, was less successful. Somehow, we do not know how, he had been involved with the euphoric actor and felt that he had been let down; dying in poverty, he penned his bitter reproaches against Shakespeare, now coming to the fore with *Henry VI*, and warned his fellow writers against the players.

Shakespeare was not a university man, but he was prepared to challenge the university wits on their own ground, and he was to write just as if he were one. I do not think that this consideration has been sufficiently regarded – yet it is the point of the challenge he put forth to be recognised as a poet, a more serious literary claim when it came.

Here we are concerned only with the classical trappings of these plays, which – for all that they are about English history – are as much to the fore as in the work of the university men. Those best known were the Oxford men, John Lyly, grandson of the grammarian, and George Peele; and the Cambridge men, Robert Greene, Thomas Nashe, and Christopher Marlowe. The actor was most closely involved with and influenced by this last (there is abundant evidence not sufficiently brought out*), and they were connected briefly in Pembroke's Company for which Marlowe, not a mere actor, wrote. It is likely enough that in the First Part of *Henry VI* the actor was working over someone else's script, making adaptations and improvements; the Second and Third Parts are recognisably his own. Heming and Condell recognised his main claim to the First Part also by including it in his *Works*.

The classical background is written across all three Parts and, recognisably, the author is remembering, not looking up.

> A statelier pyramis to her I'll rear
> Than Rhodope's or Memphis' ever was.

Rhodope, we are told, should be Rhodopis, as in Herodotus. Perhaps Shakespeare's verbal tact told him that three endings in 'is' in two lines would not do. 'Our author at least knows that it was a lute on which Nero played, and not a fiddle.' Even classical scholars can err – surely it would not be a lute, but a lyre? We have a Roman triumph and Julius Caesar's star; Caesar was frequently present to Shakespeare's mind, and he seems to have had a definite image of him as a characteristic Roman, broad-browed with prominent nose. We have Hannibal, Astraea's daughter, Adonis' gardens; Daedalus and Icarus (as several times in his early work), Cyrus and Tomyris, Paris and Helen, Circe and Ariadne, the Minotaurs, and so on.

*Even in F.P. Wilson, *Marlowe and the Early Shakespeare*.

In the Second and Third Parts we find Althaea and Meleager more than once, Aeolus from the first book of the *Aeneid*, and references which show an acquaintance with classical folklore: the rumour that Brutus was a bastard son of Caesar, and the mistaken idea that Cicero was killed by a bandit-slave, when he was dispatched by an officer sent by Antony for the purpose. Roscius, who remained a name to play with in the theatre, is referred to as a tragic, when he was a comic, actor. In these plays Shakespeare is very fond of citing the 'basilisk', which comes from Pliny, as 'thou cacodaemon' in *Richard III* comes from Erasmus: he was evidently taken with the words. The north is sometimes referred to by its classical name, *Septentrio*.

A more tell-tale characteristic of his mind is that frequently he will use an English word in the classical meaning of its original. Only someone familiar with Latin, and who occasionally thought in Latin terms, would do this.

> Now am I like that proud insulting ship
> Which Caesar and his fortunes bare at once.

'Insulting' is used in its Latin sense of bounding along, leaping joyfully. The word 'indigest' he uses more than once.

> To set a form upon that indigest
> Which he hath left so shapeless and so rude:

evidently Ovid's 'rudis indigestaque moles', a rude and shapeless mass, had imprinted itself; it is the collocation of the two words together that makes it certain. Or he will use the word 'capricious' in its original sense of goat-like, from 'caper', a goat. With his double-mindedness, always seeing double meanings in words, he gives the audience a pun – though sometimes a pun is obscured by change of pronunciation. (I once elucidated an obscure Latin pun which had not been explained, the '*haud credo*' – the 'auld grey doe' – of *Love's Labour's Lost*.) Here we have:

I am here with thee and thy goats, as the most capricious poet, honest Ovid, was among the Goths –

and 'goat' and 'Goth' would have been closer in pronunciation then.

He was no less double-minded at plot-making: his earliest comedy, the *Errors*, fused two suggestions from Plautus, who had in any case got his from the Greek. Professor Thomson observes that he never seemed to weary of alluding to Hero and Leander. They are referred to twice in *The Two Gentlemen of Verona*, the theme of which is the conflict between love and friendship, in which friendship wins. The play belongs to 1592, when the conflict between his friendship with young Southampton, and his infatuation with Emilia Lanier was at its height. But the Professor was not aware of the reason why Hero and Leander were so much in Shakespeare's mind: it was the subject of the poem Marlowe was writing for Southampton's patronage in rivalry with *Venus and Adonis*. When *Hero and Leander* was eventually completed by Chapman and published in 1598, *As You Like It* which was written in that year has again two references to Hero and Leander, altogether three or four to Marlowe thus brought back to mind. These things are real: real writers write out of their experiences of life, unlike academic critics. (Shakespeare parodies the academics in *Love's Labour's Lost*, probably having Chapman partly in mind – as he certainly had him in mind in *Troilus and Cressida* – as well as Florio, Southampton's Italian tutor.)

The Taming of the Shrew, for all its Cotswold Induction, is full of classical allusions. Written 1592–3 it has Venus (Cytherea) and Adonis, much in his mind with the poem written 1592–3 and the charming, naughty sonnet in *The Passionate Pilgrim*, which is indubitably his. This ends with Adonis naked on the brook's bank and with Venus watching and taking in all his parts:

> He, spying her, bounced in, whereas he stood:
> 'O Jove,' quoth she, 'why was not I a flood?'

('Whereas' is a form he frequently uses for 'whereat'.) Thomson corroborates with two different points: 'We have the same confusion between Venus and Adonis on the one hand, and Salmacis and Hermaphroditus on the other. Again in both, Ovid's "stagnum", which means a pool or lake, is called a brook. Since it is a canon of textual criticism that community of error normally implies community of origin, I believe that the sonnet was in fact written by Shakespeare.' Well, of course, there never was any reason for doubt, any more than with his prentice poem for Southampton's patronage, *A Lover's Complaint*. Superfluous doubt is as unreasonable as superfluous credulity.

Among many other allusions we have Dido and Europa. We all know who they were, but only one brought up in the classics would know that Dido had a sister, Anna, and that Europa was the daughter of Agenor. We have all heard of Socrates and his shrew of a wife, Xanthippe; but Shakespeare knew that

> Aeacides
> Was Ajax, called so from his grandfather.

Once more we have a specific reference to a book of Ovid, the *Ars Amandi*:

> I read that I profess, the Art to Love.

The following lines go further, into the matter of classical ethics, which was largely Stoic (we do get later a reference to Epicurus):

> while we do admire
> This virtue and this moral discipline,
> Let's be no stoics nor no stocks, I pray;
> Or so devote to Aristotle's checks
> As Ovid be an outcast quite abjured.

How much is implied in this short passage! Aristotle's 'checks' means the self-control he urged upon the passions, the discipline of moderation in everything. This was contrary to Shakespeare's belief in the passion of love, which he put forward at this time in *Love's Labour's Lost* and the *Sonnets*, and his romantic view that it was irresistible, useless to try to check it. Ovid stood for Love, and was an outcast for it; let him not be quite 'abjured' – once more the Latinised word, the English for it is 'forsworn'.

Our classical scholar is perceptive about *Love's Labour's Lost* of 1593, about which so many people have been in the dark, and now unnecessarily have remained in it. Everyone can tell that it was written for a select audience; he sees that it was written for an audience of young men who had much the same kind of classical and literary education to appreciate the exceptional number of quotations and allusions of both kinds, as well as the specific caricatures of pedants, dons, writers. These brisk young men thought that they could abjure the society of women. Nature took its revenge on them and made them fall in love.

This was precisely what happened to the adolescent Southampton, who was homo-erotic and would not marry or respond to women (until he was seduced by Shakespeare's Dark Lady). The play is a skit on him and his circle by his poet, good-humoured about the young men and their ladies. Don Armado, Holofernes and Moth are treated more sharply: they are caricatures. The classical scholar grasps that 'there is little doubt that Armado and Moth and Holofernes, these three at least, are satirical portraits of living contemporaries. But the portraits of a great artist are never mere caricatures.' We must agree. A creative writer mixes the traits and creates something new; but there is no doubt whatever that Don Armado is Don Antonio Perez, at this time an *habitué* of the Essex–Southampton circle, outstaying his welcome at Essex House. The portrait is very near the bone. Holofernes less clearly represents Florio, an intimate of the circle as Southampton's Italian tutor, resident with him at Southampton House and at Titchfield. Florio was touchy and resented something of this at the time (though there may be a few hits at Chapman's portentous style, too). Even without an intimate knowledge of the circle, Thomson thought that Holofernes was sometimes Florio and sometimes Chapman. Chapman was obviously replying to Shakespeare the following year, 1594, with

> Presume not then, ye flesh-confounded souls,
> That cannot bear the full Castalian bowls,
> Which sever mounting spirits from the senses,
> To look in this deep fount for thy pretences.

Shakespeare's 'pretence' was his challenge to be taken for a poet, with the confident epigraph to *Venus and Adonis* from Ovid: 'Let the populace admire base things: to me let divine Apollo minister water from full Castalian bowls.' Shakespeare was certainly sensual, and held by nature and the flesh; the unsuccessful Chapman prided himself on being an intellectual, his spirit mounting above and beyond the senses. Shakespeare's challenging epigraph on the 'first heir' of his invention came from the passage where Ovid claims to be a great poet. William Shakespeare was *not* one to hide his light under a bushel – as Robert Greene had noticed.* It is thought that Moth, 'tender Juvenal', was young Nashe. Everyone recognises that Berowne was Shakespeare himself, the King of Navarre Southampton, and Berowne's Rosaline the Dark Lady.

The play is crammed with classical allusions and school quotations, with its caricature of a lesson in Latin grammar, the absurdities of teaching and of some people's writing. Of the schoolboy Latin jokes, we are to conclude, 'apparently Shakespeare's audience was young enough to enjoy them'. We now know that it was. We learn that when Don Armado greets Holofernes with 'Chirrah!' – Antonio Perez was fantastically conceited and pretentious – it is his pronunciation of ' "Chaere!", the Latin form of the regular Greek salutation'. The play exhibits all kinds of 'odds and ends of classical scholarship, very brilliantly used, mostly for a satirical purpose'. That very well sums up that aspect of it; and that is the point, the use made of it – the end being to write a play – not getting bogged down in sources or even explanations of jokes that have become esoteric to us, not so to them.

We need hardly go in detail into the classical colouring given to *A Midsummer Night's Dream*, produced privately the following year, 1594, for the marriage of Southampton's mother to Sir Thomas Heneage, Vice-Chamberlain of Queen Elizabeth's Household. The elderly couple, Theseus and Hippolyta – a nod to the elderly couple married on 2 May 1594 – are given Greek names from Sir Thomas North's Plutarch. The venue is Athens. Theseus–Heneage is complimented by being made the kinsman of Hercules, a figure that came frequently to mind.

We have Pyramus and Thisbe again – this time caricatured at length for the rude mechanicals' play – Actaeon's hunting dogs also; Amazons and Bacchanals, Aurora, Ariadne and Cynthia. All these and others are familiar enough references to us; not so with

> Didst thou not lead him through the glimmering night
> From Perigenia, whom he ravishèd?

*cf. more fully my *Shakespeare the Man*, 59–61.

24

And make him with fair Aegle break his faith,
With Ariadne and Antiopa?

We have the Centaurs, an Athenian harpist and a Thracian singer, Cadmus and Nestor, a wood of Sparta, Thebes, Crete. More moving to us is

The thrice three Muses mourning for the death
Of Learning, late deceased in beggary.

This is fairly clearly a reference to Greene's recent death in 1592; it is respectfully phrased. Greene always made a point of claiming 'learning', though he lived the life of literary bohemia (Shakespeare not: he preferred the company of the Earl of Southampton). And the non-university man, who yet challenged an equality with them, respected 'learning': he applies the same phrase to his rival for Southampton's favour, Marlowe.

Romeo and Juliet, of 1594, belongs to this group of plays by its Southampton association. Placing the theme of youthful infatuation in the perspective of family feud, duelling and death, was clearly inspired by the recent events of 1593. There was the feud of the young Earl's friends, the Danvers brothers, with the Longs, and their killing of the heir, Henry Long, with Southampton helping them to make their get-away from Titchfield to Henry of Navarre, 'Signor Florio' taking part. Then Marlowe got himself killed after several affrays in which he had been involved. Some have seen flecks of Marlowe, reasonably enough, in Mercutio.

Shakespeare found a Renaissance story suitable to answer to these occurrences, not a classical one, and classical allusions are fewer. But Mercutio holds forth, not inappropriately for a Marlowe, who had written about some of them:

Dido, a dowdy; Cleopatra a gipsy; Helen and Hero hildings [good-for-nothings] and harlots; Thisbe a grey eye or so, but not to the purpose.

To return to English history. Professor Thomson regards *Richard III* – which we place about 1592–3 – as 'for a large part of it a markedly Senecan play, and so far classical. The ghosts in the last act are altogether in the vein of Roman tragedy; so is the dream of Clarence in Act I, Scene iv, although a romantic imagination has been at work upon it. Richard himself has a good deal of the Senecan tyrant, made human and convincing by Shakespeare, who gives him a distinguishing quality of cynical humour.'

Richard II of 1595 is close to *Romeo and Juliet* in its lyrical character: it is the most lyrical of the history plays, with a good deal of rhyme in it. On the other side it obviously belongs with *King John* of 1596, especially in the patriotic speeches of John of Gaunt in the one and of Richard Cœur de Lion's bastard, Faulconbridge, in the other. These expressed the mood of the early 1590s, the boastfulness of an up-and-coming people – to our ears rather brash. The Elizabethans, however, had reason to be proud of their country; we have had none since the heroic years 1940–5, when the long proud history went out in flames.

The difference between these two plays is that *Richard II* is an inspired play; *King John* is not, except in the characters of Faulconbridge, Hubert and Arthur, and to some extent Arthur's mother, Constance. Shakespeare was working over an earlier play, *The Troublesome Reign of King John*, and keeping too close to it; this results in *longueurs* in the text.

Classical comparisons come easily to mind though the action is remote. The Duke of Austria apparently wears a lion's skin, for Faulconbridge says,

> It lies as sightly on the back of him
> As great Alcides' shows upon an ass.

'Alcides is Hercules, about whom Shakespeare knows a great deal, including this alternative name of the hero. The skin worn by Hercules was that of a lion – the Nemean lion. There is however another allusion here, namely to the fable of the Ass in the Lion's skin. This too an audience familiar from schooldays with the chief fables in Aesop would have no difficulty in grasping.' Aesop lasted to my early elementary school days, though in English. Reference occurs, as frequently, to Mercury, usually as Jove's messenger. A line and a half,

> this pale faint swan,
> Who chants a doleful hymn to his own death,

virtually translates Ovid's line:

carmina iam moriens canit exsequialia cygnus.

One hardly expects the reigns of Henry IV and Henry V to give much scope for classical lore, but it is there all the same, and actually dominates the talk of two characters, Pistol and Fluellen. Pistol's talk is very odd; one gets the impression that he is always tight, and yet that is not it. It is bombastic, swaggering, would-be-impressive with its quotations, sometimes from current plays, often with classical allusions and senseless phrases:

'Tis 'semper idem' for 'obsque hoc nihil est'.

What did he mean? '*Semper eadem*' was the Queen's personal motto; did he mean that without her nothing is? It looks as if Shakespeare uses him to ridicule the prating style of the earlier drama; lines from Peele are burlesqued twice. Pistol's Latin, like everything about him, is comic. Shakespeare must have had some such ridiculous person in mind. People have realised that he had some individual in view in portraying Fluellen – possibly Sir Roger Williams; for he was a strongly marked character in himself and well known in the Essex circle. He was well read in the 'disciplines' of war – as Fluellen was – and wrote about it.

We need not specify any more the classical allusions we have seen to constitute the regular furniture of Shakespeare's mind, but we note yet another reference going back to school and Lily's grammar:

'Homo' is a common name to all men.

When Falstaff proposes to parody the King interviewing his son, 'I will do it in King Cambyses' vein,' this refers to Thomas Preston's early tragedy written in the kind of bombast Pistol talks. How much more there is in Shakespeare than meets the eye – especially when one is familiar with what was going on in his time, his proper background!

The Induction to the Second Part fulfils the role of the Prologue in ancient drama; and since it is on the theme of 'Rumour painted full of tongues' the suggestion may have come from the passage on Fame in the *Aeneid*, Book IV. When

Falstaff describes the symptoms of the King's illness he says, 'I have read the cause of his [i.e. its] effects in Galen.' This Greek writer dominated Renaissance medicine. A little later, in *The Merry Wives of Windsor*, we find Hippocrates added; and, 'What says my Aesculapius?', who was the god of medicine. What we note is that Falstaff's remark is the third or fourth time that someone refers to classical reading. Shakespeare was in fact very much a reading man, though he read quickly – as he wrote.

As You Like It, of 1598, has a number of tell-tale autobiographical touches. The old displaced Duke has taken to the Forest of Arden, and 'there they live like the old Robin Hood of England. They say many young gentlemen flock to him every day, and fleet the time carelessly, as they did in the golden world.' This takes us within the bounds of Shakespeare's imagination, if not yet into the heart of it. For though the forest may be supposed to be in France, we cannot doubt that it was the Forest of Arden he had in mind, whence his people came; Stratford was on the threshold of it. His imagination was moved by the memories of an older England, of Robin Hood and similar folklore; his education speaks in 'the golden world', for it comes from Ovid, the beginning of the *Metamorphoses*. Here, in this fusion, we have him.

In 1598 the dead Marlowe came back to mind when *Hero and Leander* was at last published. The specific references in the play are well known, including that to the manner of Marlowe's death, over the big reckoning in the little tavern-room.

> I'll have no worse a page than Jove's own page,
> And therefore look you call me Ganymede.

This may be regarded as a fourth reverberation in that echoing mind, for Marlowe's *Dido* began with a naughty scene between Jove, Ganymede and Juno. Nor indeed is the thought of Juno far away:

> And whereso'er we went, like Juno's swans ...

Actually Juno's bird was the peacock, swans were Venus's. What does it matter? We see how Shakespeare's mind worked. Even in next year's play, *Much Ado* of 1599, though the

28

story was a Renaissance not a classical one, the heroine is given the classical name of Hero. I think we can now see why.

We come now to a turning-point, with *Julius Caesar* in 1599, for it is this play that led him to explore the depths of tragedy proper. It is the first of several plays devoted to classical subjects, followed by *Troilus and Cressida*, a very different kind of work and not based on North's Plutarch, as were *Antony and Cleopatra, Coriolanus* and *Timon of Athens. Cymbeline* is supposed to be taking place in the reign of Augustus, but it is not classical at all; it is a wandering romance, rather experimental. Shakespeare was always experimenting, and it is noteworthy how varied even the Roman plays are – except always for their wonderful poetry and eloquent prose.

Julius Caesar gives us Shakespeare's idea of classicism. It does not cohere with Ben Jonson's more academic idea, and he was critical of it; but *Julius Caesar* is alive and thrilling, where Ben's *Sejanus* and even *Catiline* are really dead, works for the study. Shakespeare constructed and wrote *Julius Caesar* carefully, giving thought to what was something new for him, though Caesar was a character who had long inhabited his mind. He deliberately abnegated any comic relief, to which his mind had always been given. He had wallowed in the rollicking with Falstaff and his boon companions, and one can see how naturally this proliferating naughtiness came to his mind. The evidences indicate that his was a merry, euphoric nature – so unlike the obsessed Marlowe or the gloomy Chapman.

Now Shakespeare sacrificed all this for a plain, noble style, without any comic relief or his usual flashes of gentleness, except in the exchanges of Brutus with his wife or his page, Lucius. Clearly he had 'formed for himself the notion of a style corresponding to the Renaissance conception of the Roman character'. (Montherlant, in *La Guerre civile*, approximates even more closely, and with more exact scholarship, to what Romans were really like.) Shakespeare came closer to this with the bare, positively *raide*, style of *Coriolanus* with its disillusioned tone. The most rhetorical, almost florid, thing in *Julius Caesar* is Antony's great speech over Caesar's body; this is Shakespeare's own, since it is not in Plutarch. Altogether, *pace* Ben Jonson, Shakespeare had his own considered ideas about style and aesthetic decorum, as we see from the full dramatic criticism delivered by Hamlet to the players. *Hamlet* was written immediately after *Julius Caesar*: he must have been giving thought to style at that time.

No less classical is the conception of Caesar's ghost (it is interesting that the ghost in *Hamlet* played a similarly decisive role, but that is a Gothic ghost, not a classical one). Ghosts were common stock-in-trade in Elizabethan plays, as they were to the contemporary mind; but Caesar's was different. His was his *daemon*, or the spirit that dominated him in life, liberated by death; in the Latin word, his *genius*, which overshadows the conspirators in the second half of the play and decides their fate. Shakespeare held to this classical conception. It is referred to in *Macbeth*:

> under him [Banquo]
> My Genius is rebuked: as, it is said,
> Mark Antony's was by Caesar.

This concept was developed further in *Antony and Cleopatra*, where Antony's spirit was always daunted by that of Octavius Caesar, whenever he came in competition with it, at games or whatever. A soothsayer told Antony how it would be:

> Thy demon – that's thy spirit which keeps thee – is
> Noble, courageous, high, unmatchable,
> Where Caesar's is not. But near him thy angel
> Becomes a fear, as being o'erpowered ...
>
> thy lustre thickens
> When he shines by. I say again, thy spirit
> Is all afraid to govern thee near him.

Each has a daemon; it is the classical conception. Daemon – genius – spirit – angel (the Christian concept of guardian angel): we note the syncretism of a Renaissance mind.

It is curious that Shakespeare did not quote Plutarch's story that, when all was lost at Philippi, Brutus repeated a couplet from a lost Greek tragedy: 'Poor Virtue, I find you now a fable; yet I practised you as if you were real.' He missed a good point there: it provides the epitaph on all victims of liberal illusions. Perhaps he thought the point sufficiently made by Brutus' career. Certainly Shakespeare made him nobler than he was in real life, and Caesar less noble, to maintain a dramatic balance, when the action of Brutus and the conspirators was dastardly.

Cicero's weak points are also brought out, and rather satirised: his vanity – he would not take part in anything 'that other men begin' – and his timidity. He has the failings, the ineffectiveness, of an intellectual; when Caesar was offered the crown, all he did was to talk Greek. He was 'a Grecian and scholar'; we may take it from Professor Thomson that he was 'of the best kind, but a scholar; and, since Cicero was that, Shakespeare could not refrain from having a dig at him'.

How very different a play is *Antony and Cleopatra* of some years later, 1607; though based on Plutarch with a classical subject, it is not classical in style. It is the richest of all the plays, with the Renaissance colouring of a Veronese. Ovid was in mind once more: 'the sevenfold shield of Ajax' is Ovid's 'clipei dominus septemplicis Aiax'. And Cleopatra's 'none but Antony should conquer Antony' echoes

> ne quisquam Aiacem possit superare nisi Aiax.

One might almost say that the *Metamorphoses* was the dramatist's bedside book, either in the original or in Golding's translation, for he used both.

Professor Thomson wonders whether Shakespeare had met such a person as Cleopatra in real life, so striking is the sheer forcefulness of her personality. Agatha Christie was convinced that he was remembering, and rendering, someone he had known. What we now know about the Dark Lady shows her to have been extremely temperamental and variable; passionate and sensual; tyrannical and dominating, but seductive; given to sudden changes and withdrawals; ultimately not to be relied on; her chief characteristic the very forcefulness of her personality.

The two plays, bitter in subject and atmosphere, *Coriolanus* and *Timon*, belong together, 1608–9. The Professor guesses, 'It would be strange if Shakespeare was never depressed or ill, or even (like Swift or Carlyle) angry with the world. It is hardly possible to explain *Troilus and Cressida* or *Timon* unless one allows for that. If he felt an impulse to express himself on the subject of the "vulgar" and their political guides he could not have chosen a better subject than Coriolanus.' This is apt: after all he *chose* the subject he wanted to write about at the time, what suited his mood, or the circumstances. This is evident from the beginning with his choice of *Henry VI* and the war in France to chime with the popular mood.

Shakespeare had always held a contemptuous, if good-humoured, view of the people; this was usual with Elizabethans, for the people at large were uneducated, less monochrome and more colourful, with more 'characters', released and unabashed – as in Dickens. In 1608 there were riots and risings in the Midlands, notably in Northamptonshire and extending into Warwickshire, against the enclosures of land by the gentry and on account of dearth, want of corn. The successful dramatist so bent on being a gentleman was now a landowner in the vicinity, his ear quick to social disturbance. These themes appear in *Coriolanus*. Professor Thomson considers that Shakespeare, 'though taking all his information from Plutarch, sees deeper. One consequence is that *Coriolanus* is still a political force and awakens political passions.' It is indeed: it awoke a riot when performed in Paris in 1939 – much too near the bone. I do not suppose that, with its view of the people, it is given many performances in Soviet Russia; though the assumptions as to the people are common to both and are those acted on there in practice. It would be too revealing; a plain and severe classic drama, it is bleakly truthful.

Timon is a play of bitter disillusionment; perhaps this is why it was never finished – too unpalatable. This play too was made mainly, though not wholly, out of Plutarch; something of Lucian was drawn upon. The Elizabethans had no such clear idea of the Greeks, but Timon was the type for misanthropy in Renaissance literature. To my mind the play is both Renaissance and topical in atmosphere, fascinating in both aspects.

What then are we to think of *Troilus and Cressida* with its Greek theme? Again, not a popular play but written for a select audience, I find it one of the most brilliant and suggestive of them all, with suggestions that go far beyond the play. Shakespeare's mind was always impressed by the fall of Troy, there are many allusions to it in the course of his work. With the Elizabethans it was the medieval view that prevailed: sympathies were with the Trojans, from whom the ancient British were supposed to be descended. Not much sympathy was wasted on Helen, who was the cause of it all; Cressida was a whore, Ajax a blockhead, Achilles not much of a hero. Shakespeare takes over this view of the matter, mainly from Caxton's *Recuyel of the Histories of Troy*.

For many of the events that occur and for illustrative detail he had near at hand Chapman's translation of the *Iliad*, coming out at the time, from 1598 onwards. Shakespeare had no objection to making use of what opponents or critics had to offer. He used poor Robert Greene's *Pandosto* later on for *A Winter's Tale*; he drew on Jonson's *Every Man in his Humour* for his jokes about humours in *2 Henry IV* and *Henry V* (that is the point of the repeated refrain, 'And that's the humour of it.'). He corrected 'Caesar doth no wrong but with just cause', in accordance with Ben's criticism.

Chapman's *Iliad* had been dedicated to Essex as an English Achilles, 'the most honoured instance of the Achilleian virtues'. Much had happened since the high expectations of Essex's campaign in Ireland, expressed in *Henry V* in 1599. He had made an appalling fiasco and was running, with Southampton as his aide, on a collision course with the government. The satire of *Troilus* also levelled mockery at Chapman's inflated heroics. The language of this supposedly Greek play is the most highly Latinised of all.

Of the great tragedies, we need not repeat the allusions we have seen to be regular, in phrase or citation of names. More important, *Macbeth* exhibits certain classical aspects. It has compact, classic form; only one bit of comic relief; it employs tragic irony, working on the foreknowledge of the audience; the murder of Duncan takes place off stage as in Greek tragedy, all the more terrifying – unlike the killings with which the stage is littered through the naif early chronicle-plays.

The Gothic *Hamlet, Prince of Denmark*, has its classic flecks, as every play has. The long Pyrrhus speech, which Hamlet begins and the First Player continues – it sounds like a parody of earlier Elizabethan writing – is full of classical gear: the fight with Priam before Ilium, Mars and the Cyclops, and the goddess Fortune envisaged as Elizabethans saw her in pageants and processions.

> What's Hecuba to him, or he to Hecuba,
> That he should weep for her?

It is hard to say why those words should so affect one. How mysteriously some words, or collocation of words, operate! Shakespeare noticed somewhere in Plutarch that a Greek tyrant had wept to see the sorrows of Hecuba displayed on the stage – and then this magical formula comes out of it.

A more important matter is Hamlet's wrestling with himself on the subject of suicide; for, though he sets his life 'at no more than a pin's fee', his conscience is against it. Christianity forbade suicide; Roman stoicism allowed it in some circumstances. When he reaches his end Hamlet concludes,

> I am more an antique Roman than a Dane.

We hardly need cite Dr Johnson's famous, authoritative, 'I always thought Shakespeare had enough Latin to latinise his grammar', for today we know more of the subject and that *he* knew more. Shakespeare was not a classicist at heart, as Dr Johnson was. It was not the marrow of his brain – still less of his heart – which was romantic; but it was more than the trimmings. It gave him much of his education; it contributed to the shaping of his plays and their contents, besides providing subjects for some of them. We might say that he loved classical mythology, as much as he loved the folklore of an older England.

Altogether, Francis Meres was not far wrong in thinking of Shakespeare as the English Ovid: 'So the sweet, witty [i.e. clever] soul of Ovid lives in mellifluous and honey-tongued Shakespeare; witness his *Venus and Adonis*, his *Lucrece*, his sugared sonnets among his private friends, etc.' This was written in 1598, with the best of his work yet to come; but though this was only one aspect of it even then, others thought of him in similar terms.

3

The Theatre

WILLIAM Shakespeare was one of the most fortunate
writers that ever lived, in that the circumstances of
his work and writing turned out to be the most
propitious possible for him – unlike writers today. For us the
whole current of the time is contrary; we have constantly to
battle against it; nothing helps, everything discourages. He
was borne up on a wave, in the historic circumstances of his
country on the upgrade; everything was inspiring, everything
chimed together: the new poetry of Spenser and Sidney began,
with the madrigals also, the oceanic voyages, the war with
Spain, the palaces to house the paladins of the time.

In nothing was he ultimately so fortunate, after a strenuous
apprenticeship, as in the Elizabethan theatre: he was on a
moving escalator that bore him upwards. Playing, play-acting
of every kind and variety was a national activity. It had an
important part in education, at school and at the university;
it flourished from parish and town to great houses, London
and the Court. A play of Shakespeare's was even performed
on shipboard – an East Indiaman on its long voyage, off the
coast of Africa. Troupes of strolling players constantly toured
the country and have left their evidences in unnumbered town
accounts, Stratford among them. They were welcomed and
remunerated in the Elizabethan age; not until the sour Puritan
bourgeois got the upper hand in the towns were they paid to
go away. And when the Puritans achieved their Revolution
they put an end to the theatres and the stage. By then
Shakespeare had been twenty-six years in his grave.

His life coincided with the peak reached by the Elizabethan
stage, when the theatres in London were a prime attraction
for visitors from abroad. They were a product of the expansive
eighties. The Burbages built the first Theatre and the Curtain
just outside the City walls in the fields of Shoreditch; this was
followed in 1599 by their move to the South Bank to build the

Globe. The Swan and the Rose were already there. Before that, playing places in the City were the galleried courtyards of big inns, like the Cross Keys. The halls of great houses and colleges were available, and in the country playing places have left their names in town and village.

The building of a specific Theatre by James Burbage marked a turning-point: it led to the maturing of the stage and everything connected with it, acting and writing, the increasing sophistication which nurtured a new epoch in the world's drama. James Burbage had been an actor in his youth, in Lord Hunsdon's troupe, and later, as Lord Chamberlain, Hunsdon was to be responsible for entertainments at Court. He also became patron of the company of which Shakespeare was a leading figure, both as actor and dramatist.

The land in Holywell where the Theatre and the Curtain lay (this name referred to the curtain-wall, nothing to do with stage-curtains) was owned by the Earls of Rutland. Shakespeare's last activity, of which we have record, is the making of an *impresa* or device for the young Earl of Rutland's shield at a tilt; Richard Burbage painted it, Shakespeare supplied the words.

In the end it consoled him that he made a fortune by the theatre. It had not always been so. Earlier, to be a player had been the least honourable of the professions, and Shakespeare insisted on being regarded as a gentleman. The Ardens, his mother's family, were gentlefolk; his father's not – though a leading burgess in Stratford, his affairs had not prospered. It was more gentlemanly to be a poet – a university man was *ipso facto* gentled, however badly he behaved (like a Greene, or a Marlowe) – than to pen plays; to be a player was to be no gentleman at all. In 1592, in spite of having achieved the patronage and friendship of a young earl, the actor was still resenting it:

> Alas! 'tis true I have gone here and there,
> And made myself a motley to the view.

Then follows the famous outburst:

> O! for my sake do you with Fortune chide...
> That did not better for my life provide
> Than public means which public manners breeds.

36

The result:

> Thence comes it that my name receives a brand,
> And almost thence my nature is subdued
> To what it works in, like the dyer's hand –

evidently a rather dirty hand.

In fact his name had been branded by the insulting remarks about him as a plagiarising-player-playwright by the most popular literary journalist in London, Robert Greene. This was 'the vulgar scandal stamped upon my brow', which Southampton's favour helped him to overcome:

> So you o'er-Greene my bad, my good allow.

That this was much resented we know from the apology of Henry Chettle, who was prevailed on to testify not only to 'his facetious grace in writing' and his excellence 'in the quality he professes', i.e. as an actor, but, what was more important to him, that 'divers of worship [i.e. gentlemen] have reported his uprightness of dealing, which argues his honesty'. In the Elizabethan age the word meant honourableness; Ben Jonson was to use the same word of him later. In other words it meant a gentleman – unlike Robert Greene, or so many denizens of the theatre. His own career and that of his fellows of the Lord Chamberlain's Company – their prestige still further increased when James I took over patronage and they became the King's Men, grooms of the royal household – put the stamp upon the profession as respectable, even meritorious. Just as William Shakespeare was for a time a companion of Southampton's, so Richard Burbage later became a friend of the more youthful Pembroke.

Shakespeare became a founder-member of the Lord Chamberlain's Company in 1594, a sharer in its profits. They became the most successful company in London, and with these partners, his 'fellows' – almost like a college – he remained for the rest of his life. He thus attained security and independence; freed from patronage, no longer depending on the whims and humours of anybody else, his only aim was to do his best and please the public. In this he stood out, popular as an actor, and the most popular playwright of his time. This must have reconciled him to his profession. It is rather paradoxical that

37

Ben Jonson, who was always asserting his independence, in fact continued to be largely dependent on patronage. Shakespeare did not need to assert his independence; after 1594 he achieved it.

Of all our writers he was the most professional man of the theatre – not a semi-professional like Jonson or Chapman, but wholly: actor, dramatist and producer; sharer in the company's profits, who sometimes received the moneys, ultimately part-owner of the Blackfriars Theatre. This makes him unique among all our great poets, many of whom have written plays – like Shelley, Wordsworth, Coleridge, Byron, Browning, Tennyson, Matthew Arnold, Robert Bridges, Hardy – but how many of them are actable? They had not his unique advantages for writing plays. A deeper consideration remains: it was drama that extended his faculties the farthest, that gave the fullest scope to his genius, especially for words, and so drew the best poetry out of him. His long narrative poems distinguished him as a poet and won recognition for his claim to be regarded as such; his more personal, autobiographical sonnets contain much fine poetry. His voice is always recognisable, even in the least thing he wrote, but, when one thinks of the unparalleled poetry of *Hamlet* or *Antony and Cleopatra* or *The Tempest* ... no one in the language has surpassed it, and few have equalled it.

Thus our leading authority on the Jacobean theatre, Professor G. E. Bentley, gives us a salutary warning that most academic criticism of Shakespeare is beside the mark that does not hear the verse or see the play in the conditions for which it was written. 'To understand any artist his work must be considered in the historical environment in which his genius operated.'* Of course – and in this case the *professional* environment in which he worked. For though the genius matched the hour, the man took the opportunities opening up as few have had the luck to do; he worked within the conditions of his profession, as Bach or Mozart did. He did not work in solitude, 'preparing ideal plays for an ideal company performing in an ideal theatre', still less writing closet plays for the study, to be read not acted. Hence his lifelong experience of acting and the

* G.E. Bentley, *Shakespeare and his Theatre*, 21, 22, 46.

stage, particularly his own experience as an actor, turned out to be a heaven-sent qualification for the dramatist.

The conditions of the Elizabethan stage and of acting were very different from the modern, dating back to the Restoration – and this makes a stumbling-block for critics not intimately acquainted with Elizabethan conditions. The stage itself was not the modern picture-stage but jutted out into the midst of the audience, so that one virtually saw the performance in the round, a three-dimensional affair, like life itself. Thus an intimate contact was created between actors and audience. Bad actors were hissed, good actors applauded; the audience itself, emotional and mercurial, were practically part of the performance, expressing their delight at any 'notable act of cozening' and their enthusiasm at love-making. The theatre was very much a place for assignations – between actors and attractive members of the audience too, as we know from stories about assignations made by Burbage and Shakespeare.

Relations between actors and audience were something of a love-affair; we can see that in Shakespeare's ingratiating prologues and epilogues. The actor was paramount in such circumstances, his personality dominant, as we can appreciate from the cult of Edward Alleyn or Burbage, Tarleton or Kemp. Little scenery distracted the attention from him or the action; the action itself was essentially placeless, except for an occasional direction as to the scene. The modern acts and scenes division of his plays mostly come from eighteenth-century editors. The Elizabethans were attuned to much speedier action – 'the two-hours traffic of the stage'; scene following swiftly upon scene, or in exciting contrast; the end of the scene snapped by a concluding rhymed couplet, and straight away off again. The impact must have been double what *we* get in the theatre; everything was for excitement – drama – like the age itself.

The conditions to which he was accustomed and which he made the most of were very different also. Earlier, conditions were rather shiftless, aggravated by the disastrous circumstance of two successive plague years, 1592 and 1593. The formation of the Lord Chamberlain's Company in 1594 achieved exceptional solidity and permanence: Burbage, Shakespeare,

Augustine Phillips, Pope, Heming, Condell, Kemp or Armin, worked together, with some variation, for years. It was a close fellowship and a hard-working one. They did not have consecutive runs with a play as today; they operated like repertory, with several plays running or rehearsing in the course of a week. And what memories they had we can realise from what happened when the Essex conspirators, shortly before the rising in 1601, called on them to put on *Richard II*. Though it was then an 'old play' they could do it, and did. They worked and ate together, remembered each other in their wills, left each other their musical instruments or their clothes, an expensive item; some of them, we know, lodged together. Shakespeare – with his family at Stratford, to which he returned for a time each year, according to Aubrey – seems to have lodged in London on his own, as a writer pre-eminently would need to do for his writing. John Aubrey tells us that he was not 'a company-keeper', as we might have guessed, but very much of an observer, watching every kind of human with his humours and his follies, from a Dogberry at Long Crendon to the glittering assemblage at Court.

People have asked where he got his knowledge of Courts and kings, nobles and high society, from. Superfluous to ask, when he and his company were constantly performing at Court, at Whitehall or Windsor or Greenwich: an actor had a fine view from his own place of the denizens of Courts. And, from his friendship with Southampton and his circle, he had an inside view as to personalities, their likes and dislikes, their promise and shortcomings, their groupings and partisanships. Anyone who knows the goings-on at Elizabeth I's Court can recognise the flecks of Essex's character in Bolingbroke, the dangerous cult of 'popularity', his sulking in his tent as Achilles in *Troilus*; or his fatal indecision and self-questioning in *Hamlet*, apart from the direct reference to his leaving London for the Irish campaign in *Henry V*. Those who know old Burghley well can recognise the touches of him in Polonius – it was safe to make them, for Burghley had died a couple of years before, in 1598. The Essex–Southampton group detested Burghley, immovable as he was so long as he lived, at the right hand of the Queen; and Southampton had a double reason for it, for he had been the old man's ward, broke his promise to marry his granddaughter and was made to pay heavily for it. Those who do not know the life and circumstances of the age should be content to be told.

During his prentice years the actor would have been one of a troupe of strolling players such as he depicts in *The Taming of the Shrew* or in *Hamlet*. Touring the country on horseback – as he describes himself in the Sonnets – gave plenty of opportunity for observing characters and humours, along with 'bare ruined choirs', when so many were to be seen after the ruin of the monasteries; or again monuments with their effigies, tombs and upripped brasses, for which he had an observant eye: many references to such things witness his interest.

> Why should a man whose blood is warm within
> Sit like his grandsire cut in alabaster?

> By the honourable tomb he swears
> That stands upon your royal grandsire's bones.

> And brass eternal slave to mortal rage.

The Chamberlain's Company itself toured the country, and this is registered in town accounts – as at Dover, for instance. No reason to suppose he had not seen the beetling cliff at Dover, of *King Lear*, now known by his name – Shakespeare Cliff; or that, when at the end of the Sonnets he says,

> I, sick withal, the help of bath desired,
> And *thither* hied, a sad distempered guest,

he did not know Bath, which the touring companies regularly visited.

The leading companies – the Lord Chamberlain's and the Lord Admiral's supplied the model – had a regular organisation, firm though flexible. Sometimes a member of it left, as when Will Kemp, Shakespeare's principal comedian, left in 1599, to be succeeded by Robert Armin. The dramatist's characterisation of the Fool in subsequent plays changed in consequence: from an extrovert, rumbustious character such as Falstaff, he became the rather melancholy, reflective Feste of *Twelfth Night* or the philosophic Fool in *King Lear*. The number of full members of the company, the 'fellows' or sharers of the profits, was not large – seven or eight; then came the hired men, the waged servants of the company; lastly there were three or four boys to play the women's parts. The long list of characters in a play is not to be taken at face value, for many parts could be doubled – one can tell which, when some characters never appear on the stage together. The boys were apprentices, and sang; Burbage had no singing voice, and his parts are given no songs. The plays written during the years 1594 to 1601 had two excellent boy-actors to provide for, one tall, the other short, and they were duly provided with paired parts: Helena and Hermia in *A Midsummer Night's Dream* in 1594; Portia and Nerissa in *The Merchant of Venice* of 1596; Rosalind and Celia in *As You Like It* in 1598, Beatrice and Hero in *Much Ado* of next year; Olivia and Viola of *Twelfth Night* in 1601. Then that couple of boys grew up and the paired couples ceased. How talented and well trained they must have been!

With few boys to play in the company, 'the major female roles in Shakespeare's plays are few, generally two to four large enough for the characters to have names'.* Tributes to the excellence of the boy actors were made, though they were hardly necessary when we reflect how successful the boys' companies were, at one point challenging the men's. One Elizabethan visitor to Venice was surprised to find that women actors could be as good as the boys at home. Unimaginative people underestimate the emotional potentialities of boys and how many of them enjoy feminine characteristics, though knowledge of English public schools might instruct them. (And not only English schools: Montherlant's *La Ville dont le prince est un enfant* is based on his own experience at school, as is his novel, *Les Garçons*.) All the same, one would like to meet the boy who could play the part of Cleopatra: I have never yet seen an actress encompass it.

The actor-dramatist conceived his plays in terms of the resources he had to operate with, and was content like any good craftsman to work within the conditions available. After 1594 he makes no further complaint about his profession: he makes instead the admission that he was neglecting Southampton for it. Needs must: it was a very demanding profession and he was determined, no longer young, to make a success

* G. E. Bentley, *op. cit.*, 42.

42

of it. All the patronage he needed now was that of the public – and we shall see how he made up to it.

The year 1594 was then the firm new starting-point for his career, with the reorganisation of the companies into two paramount ones, the Lord Chamberlain's and the Lord Admiral's. These two played together for a short season of ten days out at Newington Butts in June, but never again. They were rivals, inspired by healthy competition. The Admiral's Men had their own permanent playhouse on the South Bank in Henslowe's the Rose; but they were hit by Marlowe's death in 1593 (he wrote his later plays for them), and then by the retirement of Edward Alleyn, hitherto the foremost tragic actor. The field was favourable for the Chamberlain's Men, with its competitive dramatist, to take the lead – which it proceeded to do.

They continued to occupy Burbage's old playhouses, the Theatre and the Curtain; but it seems that in the autumn of 1596 they played at the Swan.* This was a new venture of Francis Langley, which he built on his manor of Paris Garden, the manorial rights of which he bought from Lord Chamberlain Hunsdon. The reason for thinking that his players were there briefly comes from a legal document in which Shakespeare is named along with Langley – a formality, and that is all there is to it (though Hotson built a crazy edifice of conjecture upon it). Far more important is the fact that a drawing of the interior of the Swan is the only representation of what the inside of a contemporary playhouse looked like – with the usual fabric of argumentation about that.

In July Hunsdon died; the patronage of his company was immediately assumed by his son, though he was disappointed of his hope of succeeding at once as Lord Chamberlain. This office fell to Lord Cobham, of the Cecil grouping, to which Essex and Southampton were opposed. Lord Cobham's ancestor had married the Lollard knight, Sir John Oldcastle, the original name Falstaff carried – hence the joke about the 'old knight of the castle'. Shakespeare had to change the name and explain at the end of the Epilogue to 2 *Henry IV*:

* cf. W. Ingram, *A London Life in the Brazen Age, Francis Langley, 1548–1602*, cc. VII and IX.

'for Oldcastle died a martyr, and this is not the man'. Subsequently, with *The Merry Wives of Windsor*, Shakespeare had to change to Broome the name Brooke, the family name of the Cobhams, which they objected to having made fun of. We glimpse something of the dramatist's closeness to the feuding at Court through his familiarity with the Southampton circle.

An inhibition of all playing within the City was enforced from July to late October, on the excuse of recurrence of plague. The City authorities were always hostile to the players, on grounds of moral as well as physical infection. Tom Nashe wrote that 'the players are now piteously persecuted by the Lord Mayor and the aldermen and, however in their old Lord's [Hunsdon's] time they thought their state settled, it is now so uncertain they cannot build upon it'. With the old Lord – Emilia Bassano's protector – the players had a friend on the Privy Council. However, under the new Lord Hunsdon's name and patronage, his players gave all six performances at Court that Christmas season – which lasted from Christmas eve to Twelfth-night. That was a record. Shortly Lord Cobham was dead, and the new Hunsdon became Lord Chamberlain, his company resuming their title.

That summer a group of theatre folk were in trouble – as Shakespeare never was – for their part in a topical play, *The Isle of Dogs*, which satirised some political person or theme. Ben Jonson and Nashe had written some of it; Nashe fled to Yarmouth, Ben was arrested with the actors, Gabriel Spencer and Robert Shaw. Next September we find Philip Henslowe lamenting the death of Gabriel Spencer at the hands of Ben Jonson, bricklayer. A few months before, Spencer had killed his man. Both these events took place in the parish of St Leonard's Shoreditch, where so many of the theatre folk and foreign musicians belonging to the Court, like the numerous Bassanos, lived. Gabriel Spencer lived in Hog Lane, the venue of Marlowe's affray with William Bradley, who was killed by Marlowe's friend, the poet Thomas Watson. Watson and Marlowe, close friends, were both living then on the edge of Shoreditch. We see how tempestuous these theatre people were – the Bassanos were quarrelling, duelling folk too. Aubrey heard that Shakespeare had lived earlier in Shoreditch; we note that the conduct of his life is in some contrast with that of his colleagues and friends.

In this very year 1598 the agreeable William invited his rumbustious junior to contribute a play to the repertory of the company. Ben responded with one of the best of his comedies, *Every Man in his Humour*, and Shakespeare acted in it. For Ben published a list of the 'principal comedians' in two groups: one headed by Shakespeare, followed by Phillips, Condell, Sly, Kemp; the other by Burbage, Heming, Pope, Beeston, Duke. Here is the famous Company as it stood in that year of grace. Shakespeare did not play in Ben's play next year, *Every Man out of his Humour* – too busy presumably with his own work, writing *Henry V* and *Much Ado*. But he had taken Ben's point about humours, and made jokes of it in his own plays at the time. We recall Aubrey's 'Ben Jonson and he did gather humours of men daily wherever they came', and a confused recollection of the Constable, presumably Dogberry, 'he happened to take at Grendon [Long Crendon] in Bucks, which is the road from London to Stratford ... Mr Josias Howe is of that parish, and knew him'.

The year 1599 was indeed a busy year – when the Burbages plucked down the timbers of their old Theatre and transported them across the Thames, to build their grand new playhouse, the Globe, on the South Bank. This had become the fashionable theatre area, with the Rose and the Swan, and was yet conveniently outside the jurisdiction of the City. Who thought of the rather grandiloquent name for the new venture, reported to have 'Hercules and his load', i.e. the globe, for its sign? Under the contract the Burbages had one moiety of the interest, the other was shared by the five chief actors; so Shakespeare originally owned a one-tenth share in the profits and, when Kemp left, a part of his.

The Globe opened with *Henry V*. We hear Shakespeare's personal voice, courteous, almost obsequious, appealing to the audience to use their imagination for the historic events to be represented:

> But pardon, gentles all,
> The flat unraisèd spirits that hath dared
> On this unworthy scaffold to bring forth
> So great an object. Can this cockpit hold

45

> The vasty fields of France? Or may we cram
> Within this wooden O the very casques
> That did affright the air at Agincourt?

Self-deprecation always flatters other people's vanity, and they are invariably simple enough to fall for it. Shakespeare knew that well, and was never ashamed to play on it (like Betjeman today); Ben Jonson thought himself above it. However, Shakespeare's appeal to the imagination was sincere enough:

> For 'tis your thoughts that now must deck our kings,
> Carry them here and there, jumping o'er times,
> Turning the accomplishment of many years
> Into an hour-glass. For the which supply,
> Admit me Chorus to this history:
> Who Prologue-like your humble patience pray,
> Gently to hear, kindly to judge, our play.

This is his authentic personal voice – the usage of 'which' as a noun, 'the which', is, by the way, regular with him. And no doubt he played the part of Chorus, which is exceptionally personal in character, and practically carries his signature.

A later Chorus, that to Act IV, continues the note of deprecation and corroborates the comparatively small resources of the company:

> And so our scene must to the battle fly;
> Where – O for pity – we shall much disgrace,
> With four or five most vile and ragged foils [swords],
> Right ill-disposed in brawl ridiculous,
> The name of Agincourt. Yet sit and see,
> Minding true things by what their mockeries be.

We note that the appeal is addressed to that part of the audience which is seated in the galleries, not the groundlings.

It did not take Ben Jonson long to get out of step with his new-found colleagues, who had given him his opportunity to win public acclaim with *Every Man in his Humour*. His quarrel with them occurred next year, after their production of *Every Man out of his Humour*, in which Shakespeare did not play. A young admirer of Jonson's, Marston, portrayed him in a light which the touchy Ben regarded as a caricature. Jonson replied in a satire, the *Poetaster*, performed by the Children of the Queen's Chapel at the private theatre within Blackfriars. This held up to ridicule the men's company at the Globe and some of its actors. Dekker then took up the cudgels on behalf of the Chamberlain's Men, with his *Satiromastix*, performed at the Globe. For a couple of years the world was enlivened by what has become known as the War of the Theatres, i.e. the private theatre of the boys, much given to satire and topicality, against the 'common' stage of the 'common' players, as Ben called it derogatorily. Shakespeare took up the phrase and replied to it in *Hamlet*. The quarrel aroused much public interest and called attention to players and playwrights – no bad thing for the box-office; libels and abuse passed to and fro – as Shakespeare said, 'there has been much throwing about of brains'.

Jonson resented something about Shakespeare, as Greene had done – no doubt his success, inspired by envy. Referring to his own work, '*they* say you have nothing but *humours*, revels [i.e. *Cynthia's Revels*], and *satires*, that gird and fart at the time,' the reply is made: 'No, not we. *They* are on the other side of Tiber' – Blackfriars being on the north bank of the Thames, the Globe on the South Bank. 'I hear you'll bring me on the stage there; you'll play me, they say. I shall be presented by a sort of copper-laced scoundrels of you ... your mansions [i.e. on the stage] shall sweat for't, your tabernacles, varlets, your Globes and your Triumphs.' Two professions are satirised, lawyers and players. Remember that Ben regarded himself as a poet not as a player; he was not a professional.

> Are there no players here? no poet-apes,
> That come with basilisks' eyes, whose forkèd tongues
> Are steeped in venom, as their hearts in gall?

We may recognise Shakespeare's addiction to the phrases about basilisks and forkèd tongues here, and there is no doubt that he was aimed at. 'They are grown licentious, the rogues; libertines, flat libertines. They forget they are in the *statute* [i.e. as vagrants, earlier], the rascals; they are blazoned there, there they are tricked, they and their pedigrees: they need no other heralds, I wiss.'

The actor-dramatist, with his proper ambition, had signalised his success not only by buying the best property in his native town, New Place, but by taking out a coat-of-arms in his father's name – so that he would have been born a gentleman – with crest and proud motto, *Non sans droit* (Not without right). Ben had devoted a whole scene to this theme in *Every Man out of his Humour* – in which Shakespeare had not chosen to act – all about a boar's head as crest, with or without head, rampant or not. (The Boar's Head scenes of *2 Henry IV* were quite recent.) Ben ends the scene by suggesting for coat-of-arms, 'a hog's cheek and puddings in a pewter field'; for motto, *Not without Mustard*. Shakespeare's crest was a knightly helmet; Ben suggested for crest a frying-pan. It really is good fun.

Another fleck – or flick of the whip – may well be: 'He is a gent'man, parcel-poet, you slave; his father was a man of worship, I tell thee. Go, he pens high, lofty, in a new stalking strain: bigger than half the rhymers in the town again ... he will teach thee to tear and rant.' Jonson in the play is Horace, who lays down the law how one should write, of course. Shakespeare might be Ovid: 'Ovid, whom I thought to see the pleader, become Ovid the play-maker.' 'I hear of a tragedy of yours coming forth for the common players.' On saying farewell, 'Commend me to seven-shares and a half' – a good joke on what Shakespeare's share in the Globe amounted to after Kemp's departure. In *Cynthia's Revels* Jonson pointedly aligned himself on the side of the Queen for her severe treatment of Essex. This, though well justified, was unpopular with the mob. Shakespeare was aligned with Essex – and was always popular.

This was what jarred on Jonson: he could never be popular himself. In his preface to *The Alchemist* we read:

> I deny not but that these men, who always seek to do more than enough, may some time happen on something that is good and great; but very seldom. And when it comes it doth not recompense the rest of their ill. .... I speak not this out of a hope to do good on any man against his will; for I know, if it were put to the question of theirs and mine, the worse would find more suffrages: because the most favour common errors.

There was the rub: like many writers, a touchy race, Jonson was jealous of one who was more successful and, the more irritating because it went against *his* rules, the better scholar. Shakespeare *was* facile and prolific, and wrote many lines that

48

could well have been blotted – Ben said he could well have blotted a thousand. He himself worked more slowly and carefully: he was known to be a rather constipated writer. As for the *Poetaster*, I find it a bore.

Good-humoured as he was, Shakespeare did not leave the matter without a reply. In the Cambridge *Parnassus* play, Kemp of the Chamberlain's Men says: 'O that Ben Jonson is a pestilent fellow: he brought up Horace giving the poets a pill; but our fellow Shakespeare hath given him a purge that made him bewray [i.e. expose] his credit.' People have wondered since what the pill was. Part of the reply comes in *Hamlet*. 'There is an eyrie of children, little eyasses [note the bawdy pun], that cry out on the top of question, and are most tyrannically clapped for 't.' Note again Shakespeare's lofty way of putting it.

These are now the fashion, and so berattle the common stages – so they call them – that many wearing rapiers are afraid of goose quills and dare scarce come thither.... What, are they children? Who maintains 'em?... Will they pursue the quality no longer than they can sing? Will they not say afterwards, if they should grow themselves to common players – as it is most like, if their means are no better – their writers do them wrong, to make them exclaim against their own succession [i.e. their own future].

'If their means are no better' – there is a backward look at his own earlier resentment at having to fall back on 'public means which public manners breeds'. He goes on, 'Faith, there has been much to-do on both sides; and the nation holds it no sin to tarre [spur] them to controversy. There was for a while no money bid for argument, unless the poet and the player went to cuffs in the question.' Hamlet asks: 'Do the boys carry it away?' Answer: 'Ay, that they do: Hercules and his load too', i.e. over the Globe.

This was written in 1600, in the middle of the War of the Theatres. Shakespeare had not quite finished with the matter. In the Prologue to *Troilus and Cressida* next year he has a reference back to the 'armed Prologue' Jonson brought on for the *Poetaster*:

> And hither am I come
> A Prologue armed, but not in confidence
> Of author's pen or actor's voice...

> To tell you, fair beholders, that our play
> Leaps o'er the vaunt and firstlings of those broils –

i.e. the Trojan War,

> Beginning in the middle; starting thence away
> To what may be digested in a play.

When the play was published in 1609 it was furnished with a curious puff by way of Preface, from 'a never writer, to an ever reader'. 'You should see all those grand censors ... flock especially to this author's comedies, that are so framed to the life that they serve for the most common commentaries of all the actions of our lives, showing such a dexterity and power of wit that the most displeased with plays are pleased with his comedies.' Dull and heavy-witted worldlings, 'have found that wit there that they never found in themselves' – it sharpened their brains for them. Such is the salt of that wit one would think it 'born in that sea that brought forth Venus'. It deserves study as much as 'the best comedy in Terence or Plautus. And believe this, that when he is gone and his comedies out of sale, you will scramble for them.'

Who ever wrote this puff for a piece 'never clapper-clawed with the palms of the vulgar', i.e. written for a select, private audience? Curiously enough, the rare expression 'clapper-clawed' occurs in the play, and again in *The Merry Wives of Windsor*. Shakespeare's young acquaintance, Nashe, seems to be the only other writer to use it. The text of the play is a remarkably good one, close to the author's manuscript. Did he write the puff himself? We know that he could turn his hand to anything.

The War of the Theatres seems to have left no permanent bad blood. Jonson later wrote,

> Now for the players, it is true, I taxed 'em,
> And yet but some; and those so sparingly,
> As all the rest might have sat still, unquestioned,
> Had they but had the wit, or conscience
> To think well of themselves –

as he certainly did of himself. And then, rather ruefully:

> Only among them, I am sorry for
> Some better natures, by the rest so drawn
> To run in that vile line.

50

He continued to have his reservations about his senior whose work ran on such different lines from his own; and some of his criticisms are much to the point. He did not care for improbabilities:

> To make a child now swaddled to proceed
> Man, and then shoot up in one beard and weed
> Past three-score years; or with three rusty swords,
> And help of some few foot-and-half-foot words
> Fight over York and Lancaster's long jars.

However, if he did not like it, the public did. He wished for plays

> Where neither Chorus wafts you o'er the seas,
> Nor creaking throne comes down, the boys to please.

The reference to Shakespeare's historical plays is obvious. Nor did he approve of Calibans, 'nor a nest of antics'; he did not wish to compete with 'those that beget *Tales*, *Tempests*, and such-like drolleries'; *Pericles* was to him a 'mouldy tale'. Actually, all these were successful, especially *Pericles*, which made the pill harder to swallow.

However, Ben found William personally irresistible: 'I loved the man, and do honour his memory – on this side idolatry – as much as any. He was indeed honest [i.e. honourable], and of an open and free nature. Had an excellent fancy, brave notions and gentle expressions: wherein he flowed with that facility that sometimes it was necessary he should be stopped. His wit was in his own power: would the rule of it had been so too.' This was just: Shakespeare simply could not stop the fertility of his mind, the inventiveness and verbal play bursting the bounds. In the end, Ben could not help bursting the bounds with the most generous of all tributes from one writer to another, in the verses prefaced to the First Folio: 'To the Memory of my beloved, the Author.'

The rivalry with the boys' companies had an important consequence in the long run. The Burbages were owners of the private theatre in Blackfriars where they performed. By 1608 their vogue was coming to an end, and the Burbages found themselves with the lease on their hands. Here was a grand opportunity for the most experienced and successful company in London to try something new: to run a small enclosed theatre, with a more select clientèle – as such it would be more profitable – along with the big public Globe, with its capacity for holding an audience of perhaps two thousand.

This was a challenge to be met by new developments, new kinds of plays, new faces and recruits from a younger generation of writers. The leading playwright of the company had always been ready for experiments: he must have welcomed Ben Jonson with his realistic kind of play in 1598. That the inner group of fellows who ran the company agreed upon the new venture is clear from the contract made that summer to the new lessees: the two Burbages and Thomas Evans, Shakespeare, Heming, Condell and Sly. These became in effect part-owners, with all the more incentive to make a success of it.

Shakespeare, putting a lump sum down and paying a rent with the rest, could be trusted to do his best. He had always been one for making the most of his opportunities, moving upwards with the escalator; the future was with Blackfriars, with its more opulent, upper-class audience. Also he could be trusted to straddle the two, and appeal to both; no one knew better than he did the capabilities of the men with whom he was associated for so long. And there was his 'fabulously acute sense of the theatre'.

Ben Jonson was recruited to write for the new venture – a pointer to its nature, with Ben's more specialised intellectual appeal. Nearly all the rest of his plays were written for it. Two promising young gentlemen of good family, Francis Beaumont and John Fletcher – who so far had not had success with their new kind of plays – were given their chance, made the most of it and more than fulfilled expectations. Beaumont died early, but Fletcher remained, to step into the eldering master's shoes as chief dramatist of the company. Shakespeare could afford to take things more easily now: he had a collaborator in his eventual successor. *Henry VIII*, his last play – written for the Globe audience – may have had some collaboration from Fletcher; it is thought that Fletcher's play, *The Two Noble Kinsmen*, shows some touches of the old master. The elaborate stage directions of the last plays are taken to mean that he was more often away at home in Stratford, as other evidences show that he was.

The effect of this new development on his writing is evident: *Cymbeline* of 1609 is experimental and not wholly successful. But the next two plays for Blackfriars, *The Winter's Tale* and *The Tempest*, triumph: romantic and pastoral, a world of fancy and imagination, with the opportunities they gave for masque, such as an aristocratic audience appreciated and had then become the craze at Court. Ben responded to this with his numerous masques. His senior stuck to plays, with masques incorporated.

Thus the King's Men had far and away the lead with their plays at Court. In Queen Elizabeth's time they netted an average of £35 a year; in James I's over £130 a year in addition to their allowances as royal servants. In the winter of 1612–13, in the Court festivities for the wedding of Princess Elizabeth to the German Prince Palatine of the Rhine – from which the present royal family are descended – of the fourteen plays, six were by the one eldering dramatist. The Blackfriars audience always expected something new; the Globe remained faithful to old favourites. But it was in the course of the new play, *Henry VIII* – a significant return to well-trodden history for that audience – that the Globe burned down. It was a considerable loss to the fellows, in those days when there was no insurance; however, their solid resources enabled them to rebuild it even better than before.

It was time for Shakespeare to retire: the most respected citizen of his native town, the gentleman of New Place, Master Shakespeare. He is thus respectfully referred to in the legal documents and evidences – *not*, be it noted, Esquire, a step up in the social hierarchy. (Jonson attained to neither, and he did not have a coat-of-arms.)

Blackfriars became henceforward more important to the King's Men. Shakespeare's continuing interest in their business is witnessed by his last purchase of property, a half-share in the gatehouse there, convenient for visits to London from Stratford, where he was now a leading property-owner.

Times, and the atmosphere, were changing from the old rampaging, glorious days of Elizabeth. Under the pressure, and the challenge, of the war with Spain, the nation was united (as again in the heroic years, 1940–5). With peace, things began to fall apart: social divisions became more acute;

cracks began to appear; the old confidence between Crown and people – the Stuarts, after all, were aliens – broke down. Something of this is reflected in the more questioning and disturbed drama from *Troilus and Cressida*, even *Hamlet*, onwards. The widening social split is witnessed too in the theatre audiences: the people went to the Globe, the upper classes to Blackfriars. One sees the upper-class taste in the boredom with rant and reality, the preference for escape into the world of fairy-tale and pastoral enchantment. It was the integrated society of the Armada years that gave its drama a universal appeal; and Shakespeare could manage both.

The mimetic genius of an actor was an immense qualification to this end. An actor has to put himself into so many characters that it gives him something of a Protean nature. When one reflects that one has seen superb and utterly convincing performances by Laurence Olivier in one season of such differing characters as Henry IV, Prince Hal, and Justice Shallow, while Edith Evans had an even wider range (and she *became* in private life something of the part she was acting at the time), there is no mystery whatever in Shakespeare's knowledge of the society he had a privileged position for viewing, from top to bottom. Nor is there any mystery in his understanding of it; he was a very clever man. But others have understood society as well as he. The miracle is in his rendering of it – the miracle of genius. When one thinks of the achievements of genius – of a Beethoven, a Newton or Einstein – and the achievements of, say, a shop-steward or any ordinary trade-unionist! ... But, of course, the natural inequalities between one man and another are immeasurably greater than any in the animal kingdom – and Shakespeare well understood that too.

A conservatively-minded conformist, he remained faithful to his family at Stratford. Ben Jonson sat loosely to family ties, his marriage not happy; the volatile Marlowe had no family ties, for obvious reasons. We can trace Shakespeare in London, from his obscure early lodging in Shoreditch mentioned by Aubrey. From 1596–8 he was assessed for taxes, for which he was in arrears (good for him!), in the parish of St Helen, Bishopsgate. This was still convenient for the Theatre and the Curtain – just out along Bishopsgate Street past Bedlam to

Holywell Priory. Moorfields and Moor-ditch, a very unsavoury gutter, full of refuse, were just behind Bedlam: 'Is this Moorfields to muster in?' and '... the melancholy of Moor-ditch! Thou hast the most unsavoury similes.' It is all very real to anyone who knows Elizabethan London. Within the City wall was the parish church of St Helen's, with its fine array of monuments, and next to it Richard III's Crosby Place (in our time moved to Chelsea).

With the move to the South Bank, where the Globe was established, Shakespeare was taxed there in 1599–1600. The Globe was next door to the stews on Bankside, Winchester House, and St Mary Overy (now Southwark Cathedral). 'Winchester goose', referred to in *1 Henry VI* and *Troilus and Cressida*, means the pox one could so conveniently catch next door to the theatre. The church was then dominated by the big monument to the poet John Gower: no wonder he dominates the telling of *Pericles*. Edmund, Shakespeare's young actor-brother, was buried in the church in 1607.

We learn, from the Bellot–Montjoy case of 1612, that some ten years before or less, 'Master' Shakespeare was lodging with the French family of Montjoie or Montjoy, on terms of confidence with Madame Montjoy, for he negotiated the betrothal of her daughter to Bellot and actually betrothed them.* We do not know how long he had known this family. *Henry V*, with its scenes in French, was written in 1599; the French herald in it, who is given a speaking part, has the name Montjoy. The Montjoys were tire-makers, wig or head-dress makers – a subject of which the writer was very conscious – in Silver Street by Cripplegate: a short step down Wood Street to St Paul's Churchyard, where the booksellers had their stalls with the latest books, pamphlets, and plays at 6d a time. Wood Street led into Cheapside; the Boar's Head of Mistress Quickly and Falstaff being in East Cheap.

Shakespeare had been familiar with Blackfriars from earlier days, when his Stratford schoolfellow, Richard Field, printed *Venus and Adonis* and *Lucrece* there. Blackfriars was also familiar territory to both Lord Chamberlain Hunsdons. The old Lord, who kept Emilia, owned a house there; his son, the second

* For Madame Montjoy, v. my *Simon Forman: Sex and Society in Shakespeare's Age*, 96–8.

Lord, lived there. William Strachey, who had been constantly in and out, sent thither his letter home, which described the tempest that wrecked the *Sea Venture* on Bermuda in 1609, and that sparked off the play of 1611.

The more intimately one knows the events of the time – year by year and, if possible, month by month – the more intimately one can distinguish them interwoven into the plays, as with any writer's work, reflecting his experience of life and his observance of its flow. Not to have this knowledge is a disqualification for understanding any writer, especially Shakespeare of four hundred and more years ago.

The Elizabethan theatre, then, is the proper background in which to see and understand Shakespeare; and this is reflected over and over, in scores of references – not only in the plays – from the beginning to the end of his work.

His earliest work, *1 Henry VI*, opens with, 'Hung be the heavens with black': the 'heavens' were the canopy over the stage proper, and *Lucrece* refers to the regular custom:

> Black stage for tragedies and murders fell.

In the Second Part, the Duchess of Gloucester, though a woman, 'will not be slack to play my part in Fortune's pageant'. Pageants are not infrequently mentioned, both directly, and as a simile: from the early 'pageants of delight', the Whitsun pastorals of *The Two Gentlemen of Verona*, to 'this insubstantial pageant faded' of *The Tempest*. Let us have 'Some delightful ostentation, or show, or pageant'; or 'Shall we their fond pageant see?' – the play of Pyramus and Thisbe presented by Bottom the weaver and his mates. The sympathetic Abbot of Westminster considers Richard II's theatrical abdication 'a woeful pageant'. Queen Margaret described her supplanter, Edward IV's Queen, in terms of the theatre:

> I called thee then poor shadow, painted queen,
> The presentation of but what I was,
> The flattering index of a direful pageant.

'What pageantry, what feats, what shows' are always ready to mind for a comparison, like the pageant of Ajax's blockhead behaviour, or the curiously tell-tale phrase in *Othello*, ' 'Tis a pageant to keep us in false gaze' – the dramatist's subconscious foretelling the falsity that is to be the theme of the play.

The Third Part of *Henry VI* is a revenge play of the type made popular by Kyd. At the battle of Towton, in the war between York and Lancaster, Richard of Gloucester speaks of it as such:

> Warwick, revenge! Brother, revenge my death!

i.e. Clifford's killing of Warwick's brother; and

> Why stand we, like soft-hearted women here...
> And look upon, as if the tragedy
> Were played in jest by counterfeiting actors?

Many are the references to actors and acting, from the personal comment in Sonnet 23:

> As an unperfect actor on the stage
> Who, with his fear, is put beside his part;

to the similar observation in *Coriolanus*, 'like a dull actor now, I have forgot my part, and I am out'; or Coriolanus' confession, 'It is a part that I shall blush in acting.' On the other hand,

> ...in a theatre the eyes of men
> After a well-graced actor leaves the stage
> Are idly bent on him that enters next.

How often he must have observed just this: in it speaks personal experience. He was himself a good actor, as Aubrey tells us, and we may infer his prestige from the first place he is accorded in the list of actors presenting Ben's play. 'Now Ben Jonson was never a good actor, but an excellent instructor' – this is in keeping with character too. William had the further advantage of being 'a handsome, well-shaped man, very good company, and of a very ready and pleasant smooth wit'. His wit was the first thing one noticed about him. We need not doubt the tradition that he played 'kingly parts', and Adam in *As You Like It*; it is obvious that he himself spoke the Choruses in *Henry V*.

> Vouchsafe to those that have not read the story
> That I may prompt them; and of such as have,
> I humbly pray them to admit the excuse

57

Of time, of numbers, and due course of things,
Which cannot in their huge and proper life
Be here presented.

Once more we have the graceful excuse, the intimate relationship between actor-author and the audience: he appeals to
their imagination to transport the King to France:

There must we bring him; and myself have played
The interim, by remembering you 'tis past.

And at the end:

Thus far, with rough and all-unable pen,
Our bending author hath pursued the story.

In all performances of *Henry V* the Chorus should be
represented as the 'bending author'.

Players themselves are spoken of with easy familiarity in
every respect, critically, dismissively, with inner sympathy,
with the authority of a master of the stage. In the amateur
performance of Bottom's mates, 'there is not one word apt,
one player fitted'. All the same, the Duke has a kind word for
them: 'The best in this kind are but shadows; and the worst
are no worse, if imagination amend them.' And at the end,
'No epilogue, I pray you; for your play needs no excuse. Never
excuse; for when the players are all dead there need none to
be blamed.' Again, we have the dismissive 'strutting player',
of *Troilus and Cressida*, 'whose conceit [conception] lies in his
hamstring'; or the sympathy in, 'A poor player that struts and
frets his hour upon the stage' – like Shakespeare's youngest
brother, dead at twenty-six.

Many characters see themselves as playing a part in life as
on a stage – like Shakespeare's linguistic use of the double-
reflexive – their lives falling into scenes and acts. Brutus
recommends his fellow conspirators:

Let not our looks put on our purposes,
But bear it as our Roman actors do,
With untired spirits and formal constancy.

When Caesar was offered the crown, Casca reports, 'If the
tag-rag people did not clap him and hiss him, according as he

pleased and displeased them, as they use to do [i.e. are accustomed to do] the players in the theatre ...' After all,

> All the world's a stage,
> And all the men and women merely players:
> They have their exits and their entrances.

And their cue – the figure is frequently used:

> Were it my cue to fight, I should have known it
> Without a prompter.

> Had you not come upon your cue, my lord,
> William, Lord Hastings, had pronounced your part.

Henry V speaks:

> Now we speak upon our cue, and our voice is imperial;

Hamlet:

> What would he do,
> Had he the motive and the cue for passion
> That I have?

Here again we have the double-mirror effect, for Hamlet the actor is speaking as if in real life about one of the players performing for him. No wonder Shakespeare is so conscious of the thin partition between being and seeming, the duplicity in people and of life itself. It must be constantly borne in upon an actor, and this is an actor-dramatist's vision of life.

Antonio in *The Merchant of Venice* sees the world as 'A stage where every man must play a part, And mine a sad one'. The dispossessed Duke in *As You Like It* reflects on the world:

> This wide and universal theatre
> Presents more woeful pageants than the scene
> Wherein we play in.

Rosalind is inspired by the thought of lovers love-making:

> I'll prove a busy actor in their play.

Henry IV reflects on his experience, 'All my reign hath been but as a scene, acting that argument' – the burden of anxiety, guilt and fear that came from compassing the crown. Richard II is conscious of himself as acting a part, even as king: 'Thus play I in one person many people – and none contented.'

59

What means this scene of rude impatience?

asks the Duchess of York; to receive from Edward IV's Queen the answer:

To make an act of tragic violence.

The Bastard Faulconbridge describes the men of Angers standing on their battlements,

As in a theatre, whence they gape and point
At your industrious scenes and acts of death.

Again we have somewhat of a mirror effect, for the actors would be standing up aloft, on the gallery above the stage. Indeed, the playhouse itself receives mention: the Prologue which sets the scene for Act II of *Henry V*, transporting the action to Southampton, thence to France, indicates:

There is the playhouse now, there must you sit;

while the groundlings are described in *Henry VIII*: 'Youths that thunder at a playhouse, and fight for bitten apples.'

The device of making up a scene extempore for fun makes one of Falstaff's amusing japes: 'What, shall we be merry? Shall we have a play extempore?' This takes place at one of those merry meetings at the Boar's Head, to Mistress Quickly's delight: 'O Jesu, this is excellent sport, i' faith.' Falstaff plays the part of the King, Henry IV, carpeting his errant son, Prince Hal, for his pranks and the company he keeps. Dame Quickly: 'O, the father, how he holds his countenance!' And then, with enthusiasm: 'O Jesu, he doth it as like one of these harlotry players as ever I see!' There is a note of affection in that remark.

The Taming of the Shrew is presented as a play within a play, performed for the benefit of Christopher Sly, the Cotswold tinker. A lord commends one of the players he has recognised:

This fellow I remember
Since once he played a farmer's eldest son:
'Twas where you wooed the gentlewoman so well.
I have forgot your name; but, sure, that part
Was aptly fitted and naturally performed.

The approach of the players was heralded by a trumpet, which was the regular thing for a travelling troupe. Robert Cecil's querulous old aunt, Lady Russell, was much annoyed by the trumpets and drums of the players in Blackfriars, where she lived.

When Hamlet received such a travelling troupe at the Court of Elsinore, he inquired, 'How chances it they travel? Their residence, both in reputation and profit, was better both ways.' Shakespeare knew that from his own early touring days. The answer came: 'I think their inhibition comes by means of the late innovation.' This would refer to a temporary restriction upon playing, perhaps occasioned by the War of the Theatres, or that occasioned by *The Isle of Dogs* affair.

Shakespeare makes use of these players, within the play, to give us his mature reflections on acting: here we have the best dramatic criticism of the age, from the person best qualified to speak. He begins by showing how foolish all the fuss about categorising different dramatic *genres* can be – a salutary restriction upon a lot of critical palaver. He himself straddled all the conventional boundaries, as a man of genius would do, accepting none of the limitations laid down by the second-rate. He parodies these in the foolish, prosy mouth of old Polonius, who lays down the law as having acted himself when a youth at the university. 'The best actors in the world, either for tragedy, comedy, history, pastoral, pastoral-comical, historical-pastoral, tragical-historical, tragical-comical-historical-pastoral, scene individable, or poem unlimited. Seneca cannot be too heavy nor Plautus too light.' What an ass! – as indeed Hamlet calls him.

From fairly early on, about 1592, with his entry into the Southampton circle, Shakespeare had come to insist on naturalness in acting – getting away from the orating and prating of earlier Elizabethan drama, in which he had himself been brought up, witness his first historical plays, the contrast between the *Henry VI* trilogy and *Richard II*. Now he imparts his ideas fully in Hamlet's instructions to the actors: 'Speak the speech, as I pronounced it to you, trippingly on the tongue; but if you mouth it, as many of our players do, I had as lief the town-crier spoke my lines. Nor do not saw the air too much with your hand – thus! – but use all gently; for in the

61

very torrent ... of your passion, you must acquire and beget*
a temperance that it may give it smoothness.'

There follows Shakespeare's opinion of fools among actors
– and audience. 'O it offends me to the soul to hear a
robustious, periwig-pated fellow tear a passion to tatters, to
very rags, to split the ears of the groundlings – who, for the
most part, are capable of nothing but inexplicable dumb shows
and noise. I would have such a fellow whipped for o'erdoing
Termagant; it out-herods Herod. Pray you, avoid it.'

On the other hand,

Be not too tame neither, but let your own discretion be your tutor.
Suit the action to the word, the word to the action; with this special
observance, that you o'erstep not the modesty of nature. For anything
so o'erdone is [away] from the purpose of playing: whose end ... is
to hold, as 'twere, the mirror up to nature. To show virtue her own
feature, scorn her own image, and the very age and body of the time
his form and pressure.

This is indeed a lofty and comprehensive conception of the
purpose and ideal of drama: to express the age and time in
all its features. And this is precisely what Shakespeare accomplished in his own body of drama. The whole of the Elizabethan
age is there, with one large and significant exception: the
idiotic religious disputes which filled so much of it with rancour
and turmoil. It was not only that this nonsense was not
permitted on the stage, mercifully, but that Shakespeare had
not the least interest in it, any more than Elizabeth I, who
well knew how ulcerated it was, and how dangerous to peace
and order.

Back to what he disapproved of in acting. 'Now, this
overdone or come tardy off, though it makes the unskilful
laugh, cannot but make the judicious grieve; the censure
[opinion] of the which one must o'erweigh a whole theatre of
others.' One sees his contempt for ordinary fools, the masses,
in every mortal thing he wrote. Here they are on the stage:
'O, there have been players that I have seen play – and heard

* Note the use of the word 'beget' to mean merely 'get'. The comparable use in the
phrase of Thorpe's dedication of the Sonnets, 'the only begetter', the one person who
had got the manuscript, has caused endless confusion. Even the foremost Shakespearean
scholars have failed to notice the significance of the fact that the dedication is the
publisher's, and Mr W.H. his man, not Shakespeare's.

others praise, and that highly – that, neither having the accent of Christians, nor the gait of Christian, pagan, nor man, have so strutted and bellowed that I have thought some of Nature's journeymen [tradesmen] had made men, and not made them well, they imitated humanity so abominably.' Anger speaks in that, more than irritation: one can see that, as a producer, he would be as authoritative as his view of society was authoritarian. No wonder Shakespeare's company was the best in London.

The player answers: 'I hope we have reformed that indifferently with us, sir.' To which is replied, shortly: 'O, reform it altogether.' And then, for the clowns: 'And let those that play your clowns speak no more than is set down for them.' Here speaks the author, irritated by having his text held up by some fool gagging, to appeal to nitwits in the audience. 'For there be of them that will themselves laugh, to set on some quantity of barren spectators to laugh too – though in the meantime some necessary question of the play be then to be considered. That's villainous, and shows a most pitiful ambition in the fool that uses it.'

One wonders how the audience at the Globe took that straight talk! It does not seem to have militated against his popularity, any more than the constant contempt for the people expressed in his plays. I expect they were too stupid to take it in – or recognised its truth, as some even do.

All that said, we come to a proud expression of belief in his own profession, at last. Let the players be well bestowed, i.e. well looked after. 'Do you hear? Let them be well used; for they are the abstract and brief chronicles of the time.' That is, they record it. 'After your death you were better have a bad epitaph than their ill report while you live.'

How providentially this has been fulfilled – just like Cassius' prophecy after the assassination of Julius Caesar:

> How many ages hence
> Shall this our lofty scene be acted over
> In states unborn and accents yet unknown!

Or Cleopatra's forecast that the comedians would 'extemporally stage' her and Antony's revels in the streets.

In fact, William Shakespeare has largely imposed his

conception of his historic characters upon subsequent ages – it is a good thing that his extraordinary insight into human character got them largely right, better than many historians. The great Duke of Marlborough said that all that he knew of English history came from Shakespeare's plays – and he did not do badly: it did not put him far out. An academic historian who knew more about the fifteenth century and the Wars of the Roses than anyone alive, K.B. McFarlane, called Shakespeare the greatest of our historians. And he pointed out that Shakespeare was nearer the truth about Henry V than the Victorians knew: Shakespeare was closer to the traditions as to Prince Hal's spirited misdoings before his accession to the throne and the real conversion he underwent at that. And of course he penetrated to the neurasthenic essence of Richard II's personality, and to the murderous quality of Richard III's, conscience-stricken and desperate at the end.

The Prologues and Epilogues illustrate fully the actor-dramatist's intimate relation to his audience, his constant playing up to them (whatever he thought of the groundlings), his patience and polite seductiveness. Sometimes the Prologue forecasts the story or sets the scene – all that the Elizabethan stage thought necessary. The intervention of eighteenth-century editors, which is religiously observed in modern texts, giving the Fourth Act of *Antony and Cleopatra* no less than fifteen scenes, is patently absurd – when the action was intended to be played swiftly with no scene changes. The Prologue to *Romeo and Juliet* tells us all that is necessary:

> Two households, both alike in dignity,
> In fair Verona, where we lay our scene.

The story

> Is now the two-hours' traffic of our stage;
> The which if you with patient ears attend
> What here shall miss, our toil shall strive to mend.

The intent is always to please the audience, principally, one gathers – from several mentions to those seated – 'the judicious' in the galleries. Gower, the antique Chorus of *Pericles*: 'Please you, *sit* and hark.' Apology is regularly made for the inadequacy of the stage; the appeal is to the judicious to use their

imagination: 'In your imagination hold this stage the ship.'
Each of the several Choruses of *Henry V* makes this appeal.
The last of them has the corroborative reference to the success
of the *Henry VI* trilogy which first won the actor acclaim as a
dramatist: the story of the king,

> Whose state so many had the managing
> That they lost France and made his England bleed:
> Which oft our stage hath shown. And, for their sake,
> In your fair minds let this acceptance take.

Observing the success of Maria's and Sir Toby's plans to
make a fool of Malvolio, in *Twelfth Night*, a servant of the
Countess comments: 'If this were played upon a stage now,
I could condemn it as an improbable fiction' – once more the
double-reflexive in action. At the end of that most beautiful
play, there is a nostalgic return to folklore with the folksong,
'When that I was and a little tiny boy':

> A great while ago the world begun,
>   With hey, ho, the wind and the rain,
> But that's all one, our play is done,
>   And we'll strive to please you every day.

Often enough a play displeased – never one of Shakespeare's
so far as we know. But the Epilogue to *2 Henry IV* says, 'Be it
known to you' – a laugh, for this was the familiar way royal
pronouncements began – 'as it is very well, I was lately here
in the end of a displeasing play, to pray your patience for it
and to promise you a better.' We cannot now know what that
play was, nor does it matter. He goes on: 'I meant indeed to
pay you with this: which, if like an ill venture it come unluckily
home, I break and you, my gentle [i.e. gentlemanly] creditors,
lose. Here I promised you I would be, and here I commit my
body to your mercies.' It is his authentic voice; still more as
he goes on: 'All the gentlewomen here have forgiven me. If
the gentlemen will not, then the gentlemen do not agree with
the gentlewomen, which was never seen before in such an
assembly.'

So too in the last words the old master was to address to his
faithful audience in the long love-affair between them:

> I come no more to make you laugh; things now
> That bear a weighty and a serious brow,

> Sad, high, and working, full of state and woe,
> Such noble scenes as draw the eye to flow,
> We now present.

Henry VIII was presented with exceptional magnificence.

> Those that come to see
> Only a show or two and so agree
> The play may pass, if they be still and willing,
> I'll undertake may see away their shilling
> Richly in two short hours.

Once more, it is the sixpenny sitters who are appealed to, not the groundlings who paid their penny to stand. And at the end, his last words:

> 'Tis ten to one this play can never please
> All that are here. Some come to take their ease
> And sleep an act or two...

As always, he relied on 'the merciful construction' of the ladies:

> If they smile
> And say 'twill do, I know within a while
> All the best men are ours; for 'tis ill hap
> If they hold when their ladies bid them clap.

Anyone who cannot see that the author of the plays was himself an actor must be a great fool. But then ordinary people, as he knew, cannot think; they can mend a fuse, but, when it comes to real thinking, they cannot do it – and do not know it.

4

History and Kingship

ENGLISH history came with the excitement of discovery to Shakespeare, as to other dramatists at the time. We have seen that such history as they learned at school was classical, almost entirely Roman, principally from Caesar, with bits of Livy, Sallust or Suetonius. Julius Caesar was much more real to Shakespeare all his life than William the Conqueror was, let alone Alfred of Wessex. We must not, however, forget the importance of tradition in a largely aural, or oral, society; memories carried back, in such societies, not far beyond one's grandfather. Traditions of a grand noble family were more tenacious – Lord Henry Howard's, for example, as to Richard III's 'heinous crime'.

The application for the Shakespeare coat-of-arms gave a hint of ancestral service to the crown: it may be that his grandfather had fought at Bosworth – the battlefield is only some thirty miles away from Snitterfield. It was the grand-daughter only of the victor there who occupied the throne; her father, Henry VIII, was the grandson of the Yorkist Edward IV, whose characteristics he inherited: large-made, fat, an out-of-doors man; handsome when young, a womaniser; capricious and cruel. Nothing much could be said about him while his daughter was on the throne, for he had killed her mother – as his grandfather had killed his brother, Clarence, and his great-uncle, Richard III, had killed his nephews. Such was the Yorkist family. The Lancastrian family tradition was transmitted through the Lady Margaret, heiress-general of John of Gaunt, who was as pious as she was politic. These qualities were inherited by her son, Henry VII: his grand-daughter turned after him, inheriting his brains and humanity, if not his piety.

These events, the conclusion of the Wars of the Roses, were fairly close to the Elizabethans, only a couple of generations away. Hence the anxiety about the succession to the throne, the fear of intestine divisions leading to civil war, the insistence of every thinking person on unity around the throne, the national support the Tudors enjoyed (such as the alien Stuarts could not command). Shakespeare did not need the history books, the chroniclers, to bring that home to him: the theme is insisted on from the beginning to the end of his work, as in all the political thought of the time. It was self-evident, its urgent message brought home again in the disastrous Civil War that racked the country while his daughter still ruled at New Place.

What Shakespeare needed books for was the facts, the events and characters, the stories out of which plays could be made – plenty of drama in the raw history, especially of the previous century which provided so much exciting material. The book that came so usefully to hand on the threshold of his career was the enlarged edition of Holinshed's *Chronicles*, of 1587. Holinshed, another Warwickshireman, was the compiler bringing together others' work; the great advantage of his book was its comprehensiveness, its disparate mass of material, a quarry. A book with an impact of its own was Edward Hall's chronicle, which had a message, adumbrated in its title, *The Union of the Two Noble and Illustre Families of Lancaster and York*. Hall was a Henrician gentleman, one of the great majority who went along with Henry's doings, the Reformation and the strident patriotism of a new, up-and-coming people. A rhetorician who depended on other chronicles up to the reign of Henry VII, Hall depended on Polydore Virgil for that, the Renaissance historian who set a higher standard than native writers and had the benefit of information from the King himself. For Henry VIII's reign Hall could rely on his own knowledge and experience; the result is vivid and racy, moving with the current.

Another noteworthy, popular work, but in verse, was the *Mirror for Magistrates*, which had five or six editions during Shakespeare's lifetime. This was another co-operative work, containing the moral tales of the rise and fall of prominent figures of the past. History, as opposed to pure annalistic chronicle, was a moralistic exercise to the Elizabethans and was taught pithily as such at school. They were not shy of drawing lessons from the past, the mistakes people make and the crimes they commit – a perfectly valid, and even salutary, aspect of its study, lost sight of in the academic treatment of the subject today. The greatest of our historians, Gibbon, thought history 'little more than the register of the crimes, follies, and misfortunes of mankind'. At any rate, the moral aspect of it and the lessons to be drawn, both for society and the individual, were of prime importance to Shakespeare, along with its drama.

These obvious works provided regular staple fare which he could always look up for his English history plays – as he regularly relied on North's translation of Plutarch, more closely, for his Roman plays. Anything else that was markedly relevant and convenient he called into use, for example, Daniel's *Civil Wars*, which came out in 1595. For *Richard III* he used Sir Thomas More's account of the usurpation – and More was not only close to those events but had several authoritative sources of information as to what had happened. A considerable common stock of historical subjects existed, with the mounting interest in England's past that went along with increased national self-consciousness and pride. For *King John* Shakespeare had an earlier play to work over, *The Troublesome Reign of King John*; *The Famous Victories* contributed something to *Henry V*. And so on it went.

The long broils of Lancaster and York – which bored Ben Jonson, but not the public – were due to the feebleness, incompetence and ultimate breakdown of Henry VI. If it had not been for that, the claim of York to the throne would never have become practical politics. Henry VI, who was not a fool but a *fainéant*, knew the validity of his occupancy of the throne: he said once that he, his father before him, and his grandfather had all been recognised as king by country and Parliament in three generations; they had all been anointed and crowned, they had the sacred aura of kingship. To this Henry VI added that of a saint – which people also recognised; it was long before anyone raised a hand against him. Succeeding to the throne as a baby, he had a long minority, which opened the way to ulcerated faction-fighting. To this was added the equally disastrous struggle to hold on to Henry V's conquests in France. The two factions were headed, the one by Cardinal Beaufort, who favoured a peace-policy, the other, the patriotic war-party, by the popular Humphrey, Duke of Gloucester.

The chief theme of Part 1 of *Henry VI* is the war in France, with 'fighting Talbot' as the popular hero – the utmost sentimental effect is made of the argument between father and son as to which shall sacrifice himself, overwhelmed by superior forces, fly or die. This kind of thing made for the play's success with the public – and much of it is as naif as the public was. So is the treatment of the Pucelle, Joan of Arc, in accordance with English prejudice against her, as something of a witch and more of a strumpet. A subsidiary theme is Henry's unfortunate marriage to Margaret of Anjou, without dowry or alliance, brought about by Suffolk. We note unmistakable touches of Shakespeare in this first play, though he may have been revising another's text.

No doubt whatever with regard to Parts 2 and 3, which have firmness and consistency of language from the first scene. A great deal of history is intelligibly traversed, and diverse conflicting characters brought out: notably, the ineffective character of Henry is sympathetically developed, overborne by his passionate and vengeful Queen Margaret. The curious episode of Humphrey of Gloucester's wife's sorcery is transcribed from the chronicles – authentically medieval; so too is Suffolk's fall and murder at sea. York advances his claim to the throne, with support from Ireland, and has underhand dealings to raise the commons in the shape of Jack Cade. It is in the Cade scenes – which are invented – that we hear not only the voice of the people but Shakespeare's; his authentic voice is most obvious in the touches of humour – not much elsewhere in this fratricidal record of mutual killings. It is a relief to hear Cade: 'Is not this a lamentable thing, that of the skin of an innocent lamb should be made parchment? that parchment, being scribbled o'er, should undo a man? Some say the bee stings, but I say 'tis the bees' wax; for I did but seal once to a thing, and I was never mine own man since.'

The most moving poetry is given to poor Henry VI in his long soliloquy on the cares of kingship – at which he was no good – and his affecting contrast with the simplicity and content of the shepherd's life. This is a theme of which Shakespeare would make more with Henry IV and Henry V.

But it was historically true of the martyred Henry VI, who could not bear the trappings of royalty and would wear a hair shirt under his ceremonial robes; he was never happier than when staying in a monastic house with the religious. Yet even he could comment to the keepers who found him wandering on the Borders:

> Look, as I blow this feather from my face,
> And as the air blows it to me again,
> Obeying with my wind when I do blow,
> And yielding to another when it blows,
> Commanded always by the greater gust –
> Such is the lightness of you common men.

So the Wars of the Roses swayed to and fro, with the tale of their mutual killings mounting up, each side charging the other with reason enough. It ends with Richard of Gloucester's stabbing the King in the Tower. There is no reason to doubt that he did it: one chronicle actually said so, and it is known independently that he was at the Tower the night the King died. The moral of it all was clear enough.

The Third Part of the trilogy was a revenge play, so was its sequel, *Richard III*. The play as such must not detain us; suffice it to say that it is roughly true to the actual history. Shakespeare made Richard more human by giving him a cynical turn of humour, which he is not otherwise known to have possessed. The dramatist had the authority of More's truth-telling book behind him, and More was a friend of Surrey, who had been in the council-chamber on the fatal day of Richard's *coup d'état*, and of Fitz James, bishop of London at the time; More's father had been a barrister in the City – and the City knew what had happened, if not the details, which More ferreted out.

Actually, there was a case for Richard's usurpation: no one wanted a royal minority again, and his nephews were thirteen and ten respectively. Richard began by bastardising them. Buckingham helped him to the crown, but the murder of the boys that summer, in August 1483, turned his stomach. Next year Richard's own son died; he could have rehabilitated his nephews had they been alive. The fact that they were already dead brought forward their sister Elizabeth as the Yorkist heiress; the rumour that Richard meant to marry her, his wife having died, horrified the City, which made it impossible for Richard, driven to desperate straits, to do so. The way was now clear for a union of the houses by her marrying Henry VII. This ended the blood-feud. Never was there a more striking example of historical – and dramatic – Nemesis than Richard III's.

The dissension within the royal family went back to the deposition of Richard II and the assumption of the crown by John of Gaunt's son as Henry IV. The rights and wrongs of this need not be disputed; the plain fact is that Richard II had failed as king, alienated the governing class, the nobility, and could not be trusted: he was not only neurasthenic but psychotic. Bolingbroke may not have intended to take the crown when he returned to claim his rights as Duke of Lancaster; but events forced him to do so. And he could never have trusted Richard with his life: at the next turn of the wheel the King would have had him by the neck.

All the same Richard was the legitimate, rightful, anointed king; and

> Not all the water in the rough, rude sea
> Can wash the balm off from an anointed king.

The stain upon Henry IV's accession disturbed his reign, filled it with challenges to his authority, conspiracy, rebellion – and, perhaps, himself with guilt. For, upon the first conspiracy to replace Richard on the throne, he died within gloomy Pontefract castle, no one knows how. Shakespeare adopts Holinshed's account of Richard's death, from a blow by an otherwise unknown Sir Piers of Exton; but when Richard's tomb was opened, his skull was found to be undamaged. It is more likely that the tradition is true that he starved himself to death – or was starved: he was neurotic enough for anything. When the body was brought to Westminster for burial, Henry helped to carry the pall.

So long as his uncle John of Gaunt was alive, Richard had kept on the rails; but in his last two years he certainly left them for a personal tyranny which was as irresponsible as self-destructive. He then departed for Ireland, leaving England open to his opponents and supplanters. This was not very sensible of him. Shakespeare's portrayal gets the essence of his personality: a spoiled child, king from his boyhood, adolescent rather than adult; emotional, temperamental, unstable. He is sympathetic to the man, candid in his revelation that he was no good as king. Kings who were no good at the job rode for a fall in the Middle Ages (as even in our time).

In addition to Holinshed, Shakespeare had Samuel Daniel's *Civil Wars*, just come to hand in 1595. He was a congenial spirit, besides personally known to Shakespeare, for he was Florio's brother-in-law. He derived some touches from Froissart, whom Lord Berners had translated. No reason to suppose that he consulted much else, there was no need to – and the search for *recherché* sources for what he wrote goes beyond common sense. Common sense tells us that his experience in the theatre was more important. He had Marlowe's *Edward II* for a pacemaker, as his own *Henry VI* plays exerted an influence on Marlowe's.

The prime source was Shakespeare's own imagination, playing on the past: he makes John of Gaunt more attractive than he is known to have been historically, and gives him the splendid patriotic speeches that have stirred Englishmen up to their recent past (not today!). The theme of the play, adumbrated in *3 Henry VI* and given fuller development in both parts of *Henry IV* and *Henry V*, is that of kingship. In *Richard II* the scales of justice are held fairly. There is a dual responsibility, that of subjects towards their rulers, but also of rulers, if not to the ruled, then to their office. There is the sacrament of their anointing and coronation: they have to fulfil their duty to God. The oaths taken at the coronation have been held to be binding all through our history. Richard II fell down on them, and was (rightly) displaced; nevertheless his displacement did wrong. Here was the kind of inextricable dilemma history places rulers and leaders in: it faced Oliver Cromwell with Charles I, a comparable tragedy in which nothing right could be achieved and wrong was done.

This issue is not the theme of the next history play, *King John*: the patriotic theme of Gaunt is further expounded in the invented character of Cœur-de-Lion's bastard Faulconbridge. The scenes where Shakespeare's imagination was free to invent are, as usually the case, the best. Again the conflict is with France, and rude things are said about the French –

73

popular with an English audience, particularly after Henri IV let his ally Elizabeth I down by becoming a Catholic and then making a separate peace with Spain. The second conflict is King John's with the papacy. This rehabilitated that monarch's reputation with Protestants – the ex-friar John Bale's play is full of anti-papal rant. Shakespeare's is not; it is simply patriotic. The Pope's Legate, Cardinal Pandulph, is not abused but delineated as a scheming prelate – Shakespeare's usual line with ecclesiastics. He portrays Cardinal Beaufort, Bishop of Winchester, unfavourably in *Henry VI*. Archbishop Chichele, founder of All Souls College, is given the discredit for prompting Henry V to embark on his French war – for which there is no historical warrant. Wolsey is given unfriendly depiction – until his downfall, then the floodgates open.

In fact, Shakespeare's was the view of the normal, middle-of-the-road, secular Englishman: by no means fond of clerics; Protestant, but the reverse of a Puritan; conservative, carrying on the phrases of an older England, 'By our Lady', 'By the mass', 'priests' not 'ministers', a proper respect for saints and saints' days. In truth, he stood precisely where the Queen stood: no trouble from him.

The growing sophistication of his political understanding may be seen in the disingenuous political exchanges of Cardinal Pandulph, and the insincerities of politics, against which Arthur's mother, Constance, and Faulconbridge protest in their different ways. Pandulph argues like a politician, to persuade King Philip:

> For that which thou hast sworn to do amiss
> Is not amiss when it is truly done;
> And being not done, where doing tends to ill,
> The truth is then most done not doing it.
> The better act of purposes mistook
> Is to mistake again: though indirect,
> Yet indirection grows direct,
> And falsehood falsehood cures. . . .

There is much more to the same effect – the dramatist seeing both sides, as a dramatist should. Still more in the Bastard's famous outburst about political expediency:

> That smooth-faced gentleman, tickling Commodity,
> Commodity, the bias of the world . . .

> That broker that still breaks the pate of faith,
> That daily break-vow, he that wins of all,

that makes politicians take people in, break their word, change sides, jump on the band-waggon: the way the world goes.

We can observe the maturing of Shakespeare's understanding of politics with his observation of the 1590s, the growth of Essex's favour with Queen and people, the expectations of him, the partisanship and faction-fighting at Court, in the growing political sophistication of his plays. *Henry IV* and *Henry V* are essentially about kingship and the burden of the crown upon him that wears it. *1 Henry IV* begins:

> So shaken as we are, so wan with care,

Henry longing for a period of internal peace, a respite. He specifically claimed that he had not sought the crown:

> Though then, God knows, I had no such intent,
> But that necessity so bowed the state
> That I and greatness were compelled to kiss.

He had cultivated popularity – as Essex was doing, to Elizabeth's distrust – and flecks of Essex appear in Bolingbroke as later in Hamlet.

> And then I stole all courtesy from heaven,
> And dressed myself in such humility
> That I did pluck allegiance from men's hearts.

Richard II had thrown his crown away:

> The skipping king, he ambled up and down
> With shallow jesters and rash bavin wits,
> Soon kindled and soon burnt; carded his state;
> Mingled his royalty with capering fools.

And so he fell. Moral: kings must do their duty, keep their state – as George V's Queen Mary used to say privately, 'We are set apart.' (Their son, Edward VIII, kept neither state nor dignity, and so he fell.)

The cares of state, continual rebellions, anxiety, mistrust wore out Henry IV, a strong man, long before he died at only forty-five. When he had a series of strokes that incapacitated him his son thought to take over, then his father would temporarily recover. Shakespeare is roughly right in his presentation.

> How many thousand of my poorest subjects
> Are at this hour asleep ...

while the King wakes and watches. The chops and changes of politics get him down:

> O God! that one might read the book of fate,
> And see the revolution of the times.

A few years before, Richard and Northumberland had been feasting together, friends; and 'in two years after were they at wars'.

> It is but eight years since
> This Percy was the man nearest my soul,
> Who like a brother toiled in my affairs.

Now he was betraying him, trying to drive him from the throne where he had placed him. Politics!

Elizabeth I once spoke out on this theme: 'To wear a crown is a thing more glorious to them that see it than it is pleasant to them that bear it.' She had certainly seen these plays (witness her command to see Sir John Falstaff in love, and hence *The Merry Wives of Windsor*). She was quite capable of making such a reflection from her own experience; but one wonders whether the prevailing theme of these plays had not had its effect.

The last scene, where Prince Henry takes the crown from his dying father's pillow, and the King rouses himself to confide to his son all his inward grief of heart, is true to the spirit. I find Henry IV intensely moving – more so than his son, the popular choice; literary people, especially critics, hardly ever understand the inner strains of politics, the exigencies that force themselves upon their actors:

> God knows, my son,
> By what bypaths and indirect crooked ways
> I met this crown. And I myself know well
> How troublesome it sat upon my head.

Things would be easier for his son,

> For all the soil of the achievement goes
> With me into the earth.

And so it was: Henry V inherited a united kingdom, able to lead his country into France to renew his family's claim, descending from Edward III, to the French throne. We must remember that these people were more than half-French, joint members of the French military aristocracy that ruled in Western Europe. In the course of these wars the nationalist spirit was aroused in both England and France, where Joan of Arc was its incarnation and became its patron saint; the militant St George became England's patron, replacing the peaceful Edward the Confessor.

To the Elizabethans Henry V was the ideal hero-king, and so in many ways he was, upright and just, a most remarkable ruler, and a reformed man from Prince Hal, who even so was an expert soldier. Shakespeare may not have known that the night he succeeded to the throne, his father lying dead in Jerusalem Chamber, his son spent the whole night in the Abbey in confession with an anchorite and rose to confront his duty, a new dedicated man. But he did know that Henry underwent a conversion on his accession:

> The tide of blood in me
> Hath proudly flowed in vanity till now.
> Now doth it turn and ebb back to the sea,
> Where it shall mingle with the state of floods
> And flow henceforth in formal majesty.

In *Henry V* Shakespeare, always experimenting and developing, confronts another aspect of kingship, not the trials of internal dissension but the external test of leadership in foreign war. We take for granted all the asseverations of patriotism, living as they were right up to the Second German war, when their capacity to renew courage and inspire were again proved. It is the responsibility of the ruler, or leader. That is the special theme here, highlighted in a remarkable discussion between the disguised king, prowling in the camp the night before Agincourt, and an ordinary soldier, Williams, who is ready enough to question the action. 'If the cause be not good,'

Williams argues, then 'the King himself hath a heavy reckoning to make' for all the lives that have been sacrificed. Henry's reply is to accept responsibility; the subject's duty is to obey, though 'every subject's soul is his own'.

Here is the real equality, not in responsibility – that of the leader is so much greater. The argument is a fascinating one – Shakespeare is always clever at arguing, putting both sides of the case – and it takes us right into the heart of moral and social responsibility, that of the individual to society, not without urgent relevance today. When Henry is alone with himself that night, baring his conscience in prayer, he prays that his father's sin in compassing the crown may not be laid against him; otherwise, he is prepared to bear all:

> Let us our lives, our souls,
> Our debts, our careful wives,
> Our children, and our sins, lay on the King!

Then follows a wonderful example of *oratio* (if we wish to be academic): Henry's soliloquy on ceremony, probing into what constitutes the difference between the ordinary man and a king or ruler:

> Art thou aught else but place, degree, and form,
> Creating awe and fear in other men? ...
> And what have kings that privates have not too,
> Save ceremony – save general ceremony?

Here we see the sceptical side of Shakespeare's mind, seeing through everything. Nothing is claimed for the sacramental aura that surrounds kingship, the anthropological relic that still remains in civilised societies, and even the sacrificial element that republics impose upon their presidents – as ancient kings were ritually sacrificed (see Frazer's *Golden Bough.* Human affairs, with the mass of men, do not change much.) The speech goes back to the familiar theme of the peace of mind the ordinary citizen can enjoy, the ruler never, for 'the tide of pomp beats upon the high shore of this world' – or, as we should say in our degenerate days, the ceaseless light of publicity beats on him, so that even the leader's private life is no longer his own.

The speech ends somewhat ironically with,

What watch the King keeps to maintain the peace,

when in fact Henry had made the war. And Henry V was such an able soldier and ruler that he conquered the succession to the throne of France. Dead at thirty-five, he left these thrones to the infant Henry VI, a child one year old – with the eventual impossibility of holding on to the conquests in France, once the French were united. To what point had it all been? We are back where we began.

5

Comedy and Tragedy

WE MUST make our point of departure Dr Johnson's insight that what came naturally to Shakespeare was comedy, that he had to work towards tragedy – along with his deepening experience of life, we may add. This is in keeping with his portrait of himself as Berowne:

> A merrier man ...
> I never spent an hour's talk withal.
> His eye begets occasion for his wit;
> For every object that the one doth catch
> The other turns to a mirth-moving jest.

This is already a pointer to the source of the comic spirit in him: his extraordinary verbal facility, running over with high spirits so that he could hardly stop making puns, endless quibbles, innuendoes, and double talk – to such a degree that the classic taste of Dr Johnson could not but disapprove. However, it was highly to the taste of the Elizabethans. His tongue was indeed 'conceit's expositor', the expounder of fancies, often 'merry' in the contemporary sense, meaning bawdy. He could hardly use the verb 'prick' without thinking of the naughty noun; or such words as 'stand' or 'come' without sexual connotations – let alone senile Shallow's reminiscence of the little quiver-fellow drilling at Mile End Green who 'would manage you his piece thus ... and come you in, and come you in'.

The continual bawdy appeal – he is one of the bawdiest of our writers – is a considerable element in the humour and a salty preservative that is part of his work's vivacity and livingness. The better one knows the language of the time, the more one finds of it – sometimes a *recherché* suggestiveness that needs working out today, like the conundrum about 'brakes of ice'. A strait-laced Victorian like Robert Bridges was much put off by this, and considered that Shakespeare put it in largely to amuse the groundlings. No doubt this was a motive, and a proper one for a dramatist – as we can see from Hamlet's comment on the players' play, that it had little appeal since 'there were no sallets in the lines to make the matter savoury'. Shakespeare's plays do not suffer from a want of that element.

Though it appealed to the audience, it also arose out of his own nature. He was a natural, bawdy heterosexual. It is not characteristic of homosexuals to go in for that sort of thing; they are more refined, or anyway not interested in the parts of the opposite sex. Everything about women excited William Shakespeare – he reminds me of a Cornish miner to whom the sight of a woman's bloomers on a clothes-line would give an erection. The first thing Shakespeare, as Berowne, objects to in the ordinances laid down by the King of Navarre for the young men's three-year term of study – as at an (Elizabethan) university – is '... not to see a woman in that term!' Berowne–Shakespeare finds that insupportable for a good fellow. He has a skit on others of his characteristics, such as liking his food and plenty of sleep. His was a euphoric, happy, self-confident nature, as Robert Greene had noticed.

In any case Berowne thought abjuring the society of women to shut oneself up in academic study was nonsense:

> From women's eyes this doctrine I derive:
> They are the ground, the books, the academes,
> From whence doth spring the true Promethean fire.

Women offer inspiration to a natural man – they did not to Marlowe or Francis Bacon, or Ben Jonson (though he was not a homosexual, as they were). And

> ... love, first learnèd in a lady's eyes ...
> Courses as swift as thought in every power,
> And gives to every power a double power ...
> A lover's eyes will gaze an eagle blind;
> A lover's ear will hear the lowest sound ...
> Love's feeling is more soft and sensible
> Than are the tender horns of cockled snails.

This is William Shakespeare at twenty-nine – the image and the phrase are, consciously or subconsciously, expressive of his overmastering urge.

Love is the predominant subject of romantic comedy, and

Shakespeare was well equipped for it. His comedies, and other works, deal with love from every aspect and in every light; he rings all the changes possible on the subject, one would have thought, until the flame of life burned low. And yet quite late, in the improbable ambience of *Coriolanus*, is an image of married love:

> O, let me clip [embrace] ye
> In arms as sound as when I wooed, in heart
> As merry as when our nuptial day was done,
> And tapers burned to bedward.

We should ask in what respect his differed from others' comedy at the time. John Lyly was the earlier master; but his was an artificial comedy, really adolescent, written entirely for the boys' companies. Shakespeare's was adult and natural, for all its romantic quality.

The theme of *The Two Gentlemen of Verona* of 1592 is the conflict between love and friendship. This was natural enough, for it was dominant in his mind at the time in the conflict between his attachment to his young patron, to whom he owed so much – encouragement, inspiration, love – and his infatuation for the temperamental Emilia. All the critics have found the dénouement of the play unsatisfactory, a casual dismissal:

> ... that my love may appear plain and free,
> All that was mine in Silvia I give thee.

They have failed to notice that this was exactly what happened in life, as recorded contemporaneously in the Sonnets. The naughty Emilia made a pass at the young Earl, whom his poet reproaches with

> Ay me! but yet thou mightst my seat forbear ...

And then, with a generous outburst:

> Take all my loves, my love – yea, take them all.

A mistake that is often made with *The Taming of the Shrew* is not to realise that the fanciful hero is really in love with the contrary and contradictious Kate: he reduces her to submission and coaches her in her much-needed lesson by his assertion of love combined with his absurd treatment of her, teaching her

82

to behave properly, and know her place as wife. The upshot has also been much questioned, by people who do not know what the accepted Elizabethan view was as to the respective spheres of husband and wife. This was the traditional one of the Christian Church: 'Let women be subject to their husbands, as to the Lord,' quoth St Paul. No likelihood that the conforming family man wished to depart from that formula:

> Thy husband is thy lord, thy life, thy keeper,
> Thy head, thy sovereign....

This did not mean any lack of sympathy for women: quite the contrary. It is obvious throughout the plays that Shakespeare's sympathies are much with the women; he holds the scales tilted in their favour. A woman critic says, that his 'sympathy with and almost uncanny understanding of women characters is one of the distinguishing features of his comedy, as opposed to that of most of his contemporaries'. He had the advantage of being exceptionally interested in the subject.

Thus, at the heart of a highly artificial comedy, *Love's Labour's Lost* (1593), is a real theme. It was important that his young patron should marry and do his duty by his family; but he was ambivalent, and for long would not respond to women. The play's proposition that these young men should withdraw from their society to give themselves up to study was patently absurd, and the play is a skit on the circle by its ebullient, euphoric poet. Dr Johnson had the insight to understand that Shakespeare drew real characters from life, more than can be recognised hundreds of years after. But an intimate knowledge of just those years – revealed in the Sonnets, corroborated by the play and externally by Southampton's biography and Simon Forman's valuable information – has revealed the obvious characters of this topical play: Southampton, Shakespeare, his dark mistress Emilia, Don Antonio Perez, and fairly certainly Florio and Nashe.

It is topical, concerned with oath-breaking, much to the fore with Henry of Navarre's imminent breaking of his oaths to the Protestant cause to win Catholic support in France. (This much upset Elizabeth I.) The French atmosphere is clear in the names of Navarre and his circle, Berowne (Biron), Longueville, Dumaine, and the visiting Princess of France and her ladies, who topple the young men over. Perez is twice recognisably described:

> This Armado is a Spaniard, that keeps here in Court,
> A phantasm, a Monarcho, and one that makes sport
> To the prince and his book-mates.

Monarcho was the name of Elizabeth I's dwarf. Perez was maintained by Essex at Essex House, until everybody tired of him and his inflated, pretentious airs. His attempt on the virtue of the country girl was all the more comic because he was well known to be homosexual. His letter is a full parody of the fantastic rhetorical style for which Perez was noted.

We see how much more fun this comedy provided for those alive at the time – and Southampton's concern in it is attested by its being the first play he offered for James I's entertainment, reviving it after more than a decade. It gives full play to Shakespeare's mania for verbal quips, quibbles and puns, which the Elizabethans delighted in. Some of the fun is lost to us; nor do we care so much for the formal wit-combats of such as Beatrice and Benedick in *Much Ado* – so popular still with the Victorians – the sparring between enthusiastically heterosexual lovers. Still less do we appreciate the fun provided by official Fools and jesters. They were then a feature in great houses, to help to fill up the empty spaces of winter nights; the last such kept Fool I know of is as late as the reign of Queen Anne, kept by the Arscotts of Tetcott on the remote borders of Devon and Cornwall. So all this professional fooling of clowns, the Fool in *Twelfth Night* and so on, was real to the Elizabethans, though less so to us.

However, we must consider what Shakespeare himself thought of the role of Fool:

> This fellow is wise enough to play the fool,
> And to do that well craves a kind of wit [i.e. intelligence].
> He must observe their mood on whom he jests,
> The quality of persons, and the time,
> And, like the haggard [hawk], check at every feather
> That comes before his eye. This is a practice
> As full of labour as a wise man's art.

That is, his job is to comment on the quirks and absurdities of people's behaviour, point out its folly – a sufficiently large universe of discourse in itself. Then, too, in an aristocratic or courtly society, where formality was of the first importance and many things could not be said too openly, the Fool provided an outlet and release. He could say things to grandees which no one else could, and they could be free with him. They could lower themselves to his level without loss of dignity – compare the truth-telling exchanges between the Countess and the Clown in *All's Well*. Whipping the Fool, when he went too far (or as a scapegoat), was customary enough in the life of the time and is often referred to in Shakespeare's plays – hardly intelligible to us, and no less distasteful.

The Fool further serves to counterpoint the action, scoring its ironies, drawing the moral, bringing home, for example to King Lear the consequences of his lack of grasp on reality. We see the further irony here that it is left to the Fool to make people face the reality of their situation; we may say, the hard facts of life.

Most appealing to the modern mind are the comic touches from lower-class life, sometimes rude in their realism, like Lance and his dog, or Bottom and his workmates. We have in the artificial, courtly skit of *Love's Labour's Lost* more fun at the expense of country swains, in Costard (meaning Pate) and his sweetheart Jacquenetta, and the masque of the Nine Worthies which the rustics put on. One of them falls down on his part. 'There, an 't please you: a foolish mild man; an honest man, look you, and soon dashed! He is a marvellous good neighbour, faith, and a very good bowler; but for Alisander [Alexander the Great] – alas! you see how 'tis – a little o'er-parted', i.e. the part is too much for him.

Plenty of bawdy as usual, to amuse the young men, or indeed any Elizabethans: they were not squeamish, not even the Queen (unlike Queen Victoria, who couldn't bear such talk). Here we have a lot about pricks and shooting at the mark, which is a 'clout'. 'Let the mark have a prick in 't, to mete at', i.e. to measure. Costard: 'Indeed a' must shoot nearer, or he'll ne'er hit the clout.' 'An if my hand be out, then belike your hand is in.' 'Then she will get the upshoot by cleaving the pin.' 'She's too hard for you at pricks, sir: challenge her to bowl.' 'I fear too much rubbing.' They talk 'greasily'.

The Merchant of Venice (1596) – a favourite with the Victorians – is more seemly; naturally, for though it ends happily, as a comedy should, its action comes close to tragedy until the end. The theme of friendship between two men, Antonio and Bassanio, is once more to the fore. *As You Like It* of 1598 has three or four references to Marlowe; but how different this is from his sense of the comic – the rather cruel slapstick of browbeating and tormenting Barabas. This play is pure comedy, with a pastoral background and a few serious touches; the theme the contrast between Court sophistication and rural simplicity. Touchstone, the clown in this play, claims to be a courtier: 'I have trod a measure [dance]; I have flattered a lady; I have been politic [insincere] with my friend, smooth with mine enemy; I have undone three tailors; I have had four quarrels, and like to have fought one.' For all the romantic atmosphere of this comedy, with the presence of music and song, there are realistic touches; and these asides are to us more interesting than the love-talk, the baiting and banter, which has usually been regarded as the province of the comic spirit.

Much more of this love-banter occupies *Much Ado*, popular with people who like that sort of thing. I prefer the straight transcriptions from real life of Dogberry, played by the company's brilliant comedian, Will Kemp, and Verges, played by Richard Cowley, who lived in Shoreditch. These were the parish constable and his assistant, the headborough, true to type. Dogberry: 'This is your charge: you shall comprehend [sc. apprehend] all vagrom [vagrant] men. You are to bid any man stand, in the Prince's name.' 'How if 'a will not stand?' 'Why then, take no note of him, but let him go; and presently call the rest of the watch together and thank God you are rid of a knave.'

From the first Shakespeare had got comic effects from lower-class characters misusing the language – what came to be known as malapropisms. The mistress of this idiom was the hostess of the Boar's Head, Dame Quickly, who was put into such tirrits and frights by the menfolk being unable to bear one another's confirmities, and their putting poor Mistress Ford into such a canaries.

The greatest of comic characters in our literature, Falstaff, was developed in the history plays of *Henry IV*, not comedies, though given a further run, by royal command, in *The Merry Wives of Windsor*. This bourgeois farce is the most purely amusing thing Shakespeare ever wrote – straight out of small-town life, as it might be Stratford, though Windsor makes a more reverberating background. The incarnation of the comic spirit, Falstaff, is given yet another aspect, as the would-be seducer of a respectable citizen's wife; and is at last laid by the heels, or, rather, tumbled in a dirty-linen basket into the Thames. Hitherto, he had never been cornered, but got away with everything by the sheer virtuosity of his tongue. In this sphere his inventiveness is infinite. One wonders what he can say next to get out of the fixes he lands himself in, what answer he can possibly think up, what excuse make. He always manages. One realises that the sheer cleverness of the old reprobate is the cleverness of his creator. Rich comic effects in watching the fat old rogue wriggling out of his exposure as braggart, in fact a coward, his expertise in winning the women round when he is in their debt, in letting down his boon-companion by his words behind his back – one wonders how he is going to extricate himself from *that*, when the Prince overhears him. But he does. He is incorrigible, irresistible, invincible – until the wives at Windsor trip him up.

The Merry Wives is something different again from all the other comedies. No romantic lyricism, with the opportunities which that gave for songs and music, as in *Much Ado* and *Twelfth Night*: this play is almost wholly in prose, very rapidly written – traditionally, in a fortnight. Here Falstaff is provided with a whole cast of comic characters. Mistress Quickly is given a larger part in the intrigue; Justice Shallow appears again with a different nitwit for companion; Pistol too with his fantastic, grandiloquent talk, with its parody of lines from Marlowe, Peele or Kyd. New comic creations are Mistress Ford and her jealous husband, a marvellous caricature of a Welsh curate-schoolmaster in Sir Hugh Evans, murdering English, who gives young William his Latin lesson. Virtuous Mistress Quickly is much shocked at his declining 'horum, harum, horum'. Dr Caius 'makes fritters of English' in his own way. The fun is riotous.

The *Merry Wives* is pure farce, as was *The Comedy of Errors* earlier. The word 'farce' originally carried the sense of padding or padding out; there is plenty of that in the *Errors* – to a degree fatiguing to modern taste – where in *The Merry Wives* all is delightful.* Though both are farces, a world of difference, and of experience, lies between them. The earlier – in spite of the metrical variety that bespeaks the poet – is still prentice-work, following a model, that of Plautus; *The Merry Wives* is pure Shakespeare in undress. Though the concept of farce was used in earlier Tudor times for interludes and such, it seems to have lapsed in the Elizabethan age, and Shakespeare never uses it. In any case, he recognised only the three *genres* of history, comedy, tragedy – as does the Folio. The very thought of calling a Shakespeare play a farce has given some ingenuous critics embarrassment. Why should it? It came to mean a short dramatic piece the sole purpose of which was to excite laughter. What is wrong with that?

Comedy had a far more extended sense, especially in the Middle Ages, as we observe from Dante calling his epic a comedy. Even the medievals, in extending the term to narratives, retained the essential kernel of the concept, that all should work out to a happy ending.

Twelfth Night of 1601 is the last of the romantic comedies, offering us something new again in the subordinate characters. The most interesting one, Malvolio, is hardly a comic one, though he is made the subject of mirth in others. His weak spot is a lack of a sense of humour, so that a trick can be played on him to make him think the Countess, his mistress, is enamoured of him. Since he acts dementedly, he is treated as a lunatic, really rather cruelly. I fear that this appealed to the primitive instincts of Elizabethans:

> The cockpit, galleries, boxes are all full
> To hear Malvolio, that cross-gartered gull.

All's Well that Ends Well (1603) and *Measure for Measure* (1604) are sometimes referred to as problem plays and some-

---

*Perhaps we may note here for an example of the frequent foolery of criticism W.H. Auden's description of *The Merry Wives* as Shakespeare's 'worst play'. Even Eliot described *Hamlet*, of all plays, as an 'unsatisfactory play'! Why say such silly things? – better for critics to understand and interpret than to judge.

times as 'bitter comedies'. They are comedies in the sense that they end happily, but they are both essentially serious plays, *Measure for Measure* tragic in tone for most of the time. *All's Well* did not set Shakespeare's imagination on fire, but its intellectual interest is remarkable; perhaps this is why it does not sparkle, because it is overburdened with thought. The dramatist was exploring something new: the *tone* of the play is more like one of Jonson's, having something acrid about it. Bernard Shaw, however – often so silly in his pronouncements about Shakespeare – declared the Countess's 'the most beautiful part ever written'. The women win all round, appropriately for comedy; the men show up badly, except for the King of France, who is noble and ailing. Parolles, the braggadocio soldier, returned from the wars in which he played no very noble part, is a very contemporary type, Shakespeare's most Jonsonesque character: he was being influenced by his junior at this time. The exposure of Parolles provides most of what comedy there is: the young Count, who refuses to marry the girl because she is beneath him socially, is caught by the well-worn bed-trick – unattractive, and unconvincing.

The atmosphere of the play is contemporary – and French; it was at this time that Shakespeare was lodging with the Montjoys in Silver Street. The action is dominated by the French king's sickness; several references to plague occur, and 1603 was a bad plague year, with sickness and death all about. A queasy time in public affairs, the Queen dying in March; a new, unheroic age was opening: a vulgar world, without the dignity the historic figure of Elizabeth I imposed from the top. Everybody on the make, as usual, but too crudely scrambling for favour at the new undignified Court, and in a society where false values, chiefly money-values, prevailed. The spirit of the Jacobean age – with its shocking scramble on the part of everybody to squeeze money out of the easy-going James – is succinctly expressed in the cynicism of Parolles: 'Simply the thing I am shall make me live', and

by foolery thrive:
There's place and means for every man alive.

In Jacobean society class-conflict was opening at the seams

and becoming more evident. This element is touched on, with the dramatist's usual justice of mind:

> Honours thrive
> When rather from our acts we them derive
> Than our foregoers. The mere world's a slave,
> Debauched on every tomb, on every grave,
> A lying trophy, and as oft is dumb,
> Where dust and damned oblivion is the tomb
> Of honoured bones indeed.

We have noticed his observant eye for monuments and tombs as he toured about the country – these becoming grander and more ostentatious in these years. Lord Chamberlain Hunsdon was given the largest monument in Westminster Abbey.

Measure for Measure hovers on the edge of tragedy, until the Duke is brought in as a *deus ex machina* at the end: it is a remarkable play, which has aroused more discussion than any other, always excepting *Hamlet*. The subject is a serious one: the responsibility upon a ruler to govern with even-handed justice; not to be overborne by personal passions; nor to be too strict in punishing personal peccadilloes – getting a girl with child we should think little of. The Elizabethans attached more importance to sexual misdemeanours, perhaps from being more inclined to them, for they were passionate people. Hence the play is dark with guilt; hypocrisy is exposed: no illusions operated with William Shakespeare.

What of comedy we are given is of the lowest of low life – pimps and bawds and murderers in gaol – which gave Victorian critics much embarrassment. Mistress Overdone is another Mistress Quickly, but a professional madam. Elbow, the constable, is another Dogberry, malapropisms and all. A Dickensian inventiveness inspires the names of the company in prison, and a good transcript of contemporary life, as good as Jonson's in its kind.

We can now appreciate the astonishing and prolific variety of Shakespeare's comic inspiration. The greatest of his comic characters, Falstaff, and the most riotous comic scenes, come in the history plays, *1* and *2 Henry IV*. A good deal of farce occurs in several of the comedies, especially in *Love's Labour's Lost*, the very idea of which is farcical. We have the rather bitter satire of *Troilus and Cressida* and an element of Jonsonian realism in *All's Well*, as well as the grim horrors of prison in *Measure for Measure*. But Shakespeare's inner spirit expressed itself more gladly in lyrical romantic comedy, something more gentle and sunny, as in *As You Like It*, or even gentle and melancholy, as in *Twelfth Night*. And this must have spoken more truly for his nature.

Shakespeare's tragedies exhibit quite as much variety as his comedies, and as much of the world's with it, but compassing far greater depths and heights. They are his grandest achievements, at the summit of the world's drama. They not only possess universal appeal, but appeal to the universal, the essential man, in each of us.

Tragedy in its simplest form meant a serious work, with a fatal or disastrous conclusion – the opposite to comedy. In the field of tragedy Shakespeare offers as many varieties of style and treatment as of theme and subject. He began, responding as usual to the demand of the theatre, with what was popular at the time, a revenge-tragedy. His prentice-piece here, *Titus Andronicus*, with its rebarbative theme and blood-curdling horrors, was obviously not in keeping with his nature – he was merely, competitively as usual, going one better than his popular model, Kyd. The third part of *King Henry VI* is essentially another revenge play, written not long after, but more convincing, for it deals with the actual events of the blood-feuds released by the Wars of the Roses.

Something new and deeper entered into his dramaturgy with *Julius Caesar*: here he was responding not only to the grandeur of the subject but to the urgent events of the time, the career of Essex close at hand hurrying towards its catastrophe. *Julius Caesar* is also in part a revenge play, but how much riper and more compelling in its understanding, both political and human, than *Titus*. What development has been achieved! And further again with the very next play, *Hamlet*.

What can be said in short of this universal work, this universe of a play? It originated as a revenge play, too; but how much more there is in it! Even the revenge motive is complex and subtle, complicated by doubt and the necessity to be resolved – hence the self-questioning, the psychological

91

dimension, and the long delay. Love is another element, and of several kinds: Hamlet's love for and loyalty to his father; his love for Ophelia, tormented and embittered by suspicion that she is in the enemy's camp, used as a spy upon him; his love for his mother, turned to bitterness and reproach for her breach of faith to his father. Hamlet has a gift for friendship, like others of Shakespeare's heroes; the loyalty and friendship between him and Horatio form a theme. Politics come in, and naturally ambition with it; for, though this is kept subordinate, Hamlet has a just ambition to gain his rights and succeed his father on the throne of Denmark. Something of the politics of Shakespeare's time is touched on too in the Burghley-like character of old Polonius, with flecks of Essex's personality in Hamlet's.

Several of the plays are political tragedies, with the familiar compounds of politics: ambition, loyalty and disloyalty; party-spirit and treachery; honour and dishonour; patriotism (or the lack of it); even duty. Many of these elements appear in the historical plays, *Henry VI*, *Richard II*, *Richard III* and *King John*. *Julius Caesar* and *Coriolanus* are monolithic political tragedies. Politics naturally come into *Macbeth*, but it is more a tragedy of personal character, of overweening ambition and an overmastering temptation – which was also the trouble with Richard III. Politics appear again in *Antony and Cleopatra*; but it is essentially a love-tragedy – the conflict between the claims of politics and those of love, between public duty and private passion: hence it is a whole dimension richer than the earlier tragedy of love, *Romeo and Juliet*. Love again, but wrecked by jealousy, is the theme of *Othello*; and yet another personal tragedy, of individual character and its consequences, is provided in *King Lear*. In this play, as in *Hamlet*, the psychological motivation leads outward into the exploration of so many further territories of man's nature. Ingratitude is its starting-point and sets the train in motion; but the unawareness of self, the sheer ignorance of reality, gives it its chance with a foolish old man stripping himself of his inheritance. Before the end, the whole world of human nature is portrayed: callous heartlessness, envy and treachery, lust, breach of marriage vows, disgust of sex, but also innocence and goodness, compassion and fidelity. These two tragedies, *Hamlet* and *King*

Lear, are the twin summits of Shakespeare's achievement; yet even they are very different.

What then is so characteristic of his tragedies?

First, the intensity of his imagination, in which he has no parallel, except Racine – or, in his own age, his follower, Webster, and then only in two masterpieces, *The Duchess of Malfi* and *The White Devil*. Perhaps even in those, shattering as they are, one has the impression of their being a little contrived. There is nothing contrived about *Hamlet*: again and again the heart turns over at the simplest sentiments coming straight out of a soul in torment: 'thou wouldst not think how ill all's here about my heart'. Never have words been uttered with such sad force in our language, words that go on echoing in the chambers of our minds all our lives. Even the simplest words: the terrible scene in which Hamlet reproaches his mother with her unfaithfulness to his father, and the mother is forced to see herself in the mirror of her son's eyes – what more tragic human confrontation could there be? The words are forced from her: 'O Hamlet, thou hast cleft my heart in twain!' And then, after the appalling revelation of truth in life: 'Good night, mother.'

There are scenes one cannot behold dry-eyed, today four hundred years after; one has to look away from the stage upon which human anguish is so exposed: Ophelia gone mad with grief, scattering her flowers. 'I would give you some violets, but they withered all when my father died. They say he made a good end'; and singing,

> And will he not come again?
> And will he not come again?
> No, no: he is dead.

Or Lady Macbeth walking in her sleep and uttering what lies on her conscience so that she will never know rest again: 'There's knocking at the gate. Come, come, come, come, give me your hand. What's done cannot be undone.' Or, after all that has happened to Lear, and he regains his wits when he meets once more his younger daughter, whom he had wronged:

> I know you do not love me; for your sisters
> Have, as I do remember, done me wrong:
> You have some cause, they have not.

93

Cordelia replies,

No cause, no cause.

This is among the most heart-rending expressions in the language, simple as it is, when one remembers all that has gone before.

Shakespeare has this unparalleled capacity for knocking us out, not only by the intensity of his imagination but by its truth. Perhaps it is a vulgarism to say that we are knocked out: what it means is that we are faced by a truth about life – what one human being can do to another, the suffering inflicted, the irremediable nature of the ill, the hopelessness, too late, too late, if it were not for compassion and forgiveness – so powerfully that we are shattered by the revelation.

The uncompromising extremism of his imagination serves not only the purpose of dramatic and aesthetic effect – though that enters into it; it has a more potent psychological truth behind it, namely that people reveal their deepest selves, in moments of crisis, in an emergency. Thus Shakespeare stretched the situation, exaggerated the conflict, to plumb the depths of his characters. The original story of Lear, upon which Shakespeare drew, had a happier ending. Not so with Shakespeare, whose instinct told him that the terrible scenes enacted, such heartlessness and treachery, such violence, crime upon crime, could not but have a tragic conclusion – and Lear wanders forth to confront his own fate, bearing his dead daughter in his arms. Dr Johnson, who had a heart equal to Shakespeare's, but not quite his courage, could not bear to contemplate the ending of the play. But it is true to life; such things and worse happen.

Similarly with *Macbeth*. It seems that, historically, Duncan was not all that good, nor Macbeth all that bad; Duncan was not a good king, and Macbeth had a claim to the throne – in fact, ruled for some years with success. Not so in the realm of Shakespeare's imagination: to explore the recesses of the human spirit in Macbeth and his wife, the capability of murder urged on by ambition and superstition, the promptings of the unconscious, the situation needed to be sharpened and concentrated. It is the most concentrated of all the plays, the darkest and most sombre, with almost no relief: it should be played in primeval quasi-darkness, with lurid lights and frightening shadows.

The witches in *Macbeth* may well be seen, by a modern mind, as extrapolations of the unconscious. Shakespeare reaped the reward of trusting to his instinct, instead of following the path of the merely cerebral – and not only in this respect. I note the extraordinary way in which his subconscious, given its head, worked for him day and night; witness the way his imagery clusters together, like seaweed under the surface, to bear out the direction given by the theme.

Similarly the release, the scope, he gave to the promptings of the unconscious enabled him to intuit to an extraordinary degree the corroborative findings of modern psychology. Everyone can now recognise the Oedipal elements in Hamlet, his closeness to his mother, the shock to a son who suspects his mother's fidelity to the father, the hatred of a stepfather inflicted on a son. Or the familiar psychological phenomenon of wanting to kill the thing one loves, who betrays one, or so one is convinced – in the case of Othello. Coriolanus wants to burn the Rome he has loved and served: arson is often prompted to a mind obsessed by resentment, envy or vendetta. The symptoms and workings of schizophrenia are precisely described in the case of Leontes in *The Winter's Tale*: the step-by-step corroboration of a suspicious, unbalanced mind, allowing itself to be convinced by signs innocent and unmeaning in themselves.

An even more powerful exposition of the way jealousy and suspicion can be fostered, to prey upon an obsessive mind, is Iago's treatment of Othello. This is detailed, elaborate and complete: the most convincing portrayal of the process in literature. As one watches Iago's campaign unfolding one cannot but admire the perfection – if only the consequences were not so devilish – with which he can

> Make the Moor thank me, love me and reward me
> For making him egregiously an ass.

For, of course, Othello may be very noble and all that, but he is an ass: on that point even Emilia and Iago are agreed; such simple-natured, credulous types almost ask to be taken in. Whole volumes have been written as to Iago's motivation – by far the most fascinating figure in the play, a Machiavellian in private life. Discussion is superfluous: Iago is obvious enough – he too is an obsessive character, obsessed by hatred. In his way he is as much driven on as Othello, though with Iago the psyche is far more interesting, for with him the working-out of his obsession presents itself as rational. This too is recognisably authentic psychological truth: no problem.

One way and another Shakespeare gives us a whole gallery of studies of obsession, neurosis, mental unbalance, more memorable than the happy contented characters of the comedies who find life good. Richard II is a neurotic; Richard III and Macbeth are obsessed by ambition, the desire for power at all costs – as indeed is that masculine woman, Lady Macbeth. Lear is unbalanced from the start: he has no clear grasp of reality, of what other people are really like or are capable of. Coriolanus is an obsessed character, possessed by pride and a love for his native city to an extreme degree. Antony is a more human, divided character; but he is betrayed by his overpowering love, against common sense, or at least against all political sense. Timon cannot be thought to be normal: profligate in generosity and careless trust, which betray him, he then goes to the opposite extreme of universal misanthropy. Further, too, madness itself is strangely exciting on the stage.

The extremism of Shakespeare's imagination – persuasive as it is from his mastery as a dramatist – opens for us the innermost recesses of the soul. Here is his power. He well knew that, as it has been diagnosed by a critic who is also a real writer: 'in life ... perhaps every person is in some degree dissociated; and this fact of universal significance, which is given gross expression in certain pathological states, often finds a species of covert (and perhaps obscurely cathartic or therapeutic) release in art.'* Before the psychological revolution of our time this was not very well understood – particularly by the Victorians with their mania for seeing everything in systematic ethical terms. Hence much of the criticism of

*J.I.M. Stewart, *Character and Motive in Shakespeare*, 90.

Shakespeare in terms of ethics, and making a system out of it, is beside the mark. William Shakespeare was not a Victorian, but an Elizabethan; he had in truth a firm moral view of life, but it was the comparatively simple, orthodox one of the Elizabethans. The basis is firm and simple enough – in the tragedies ill-doing is rewarded and always comes to a bad end; the complexity, the astonishing richness and ripeness, the variety and the variations, are in the observation, and the forms of expression it took.

We must see him and his work in relation to their time. A governing class that had an Empire to govern, as the Victorians had, needed to impose a control upon itself if it was to control others. The Elizabethans were under no such necessity, and at any rate were before all that in time. Thus they lived life at the coal-face, we may say, more directly and naively, though not without their own sophistication. The great Lord Burghley, very much a Victorian (perhaps this was why the young men disliked him so much), was exceptional in his habit of self-control. Far more characteristic were the uncontrolled – or insufficiently controlled – personalities like Essex and Ralegh and all their following, extravagant peers like Southampton or Oxford, Pembroke or Rutland, the Danvers brothers, Sir Gelly Meyrick, Sir Christopher Blount, or a hundred others. There was nothing these men would not do for power and glory: they were like characters in Shakespeare's plays (and Shakespeare knew a number of them). Men condemned to death, like Essex in the Tower, would bare their own souls, confessing everything, accusing their own fellows as well as enemies. A grandee such as the Duke of Norfolk or Sir Walter Ralegh would turn his last appearance, on the scaffold, into a set scene with speech, appeal to the audience and all.

So Shakespeare's plays are very close to the life of the age, an expression of it in art, none more so than the tragedies.

The overriding concern for control in English life in the past century may have imposed some restriction upon the expressions of passion in our art, to the impoverishment of literature (contrast the Russian novel in the nineteenth century), and notably of painting (contrast French painting in the same period). One might well wonder whether release from the necessity for such control might not be propitious to the arts today; but other factors are so unpropitious as to make it unlikely. The creativeness of the Elizabethans remains: a monument and a memorial.

6

Poetry, Language, Style

WILLIAM Shakespeare was as fortunate in the moment of his entry upon the scene as a poet as he was in his *début* in the theatre proper as a dramatist. For the 1580s had seen something like a poetic revolution, with the flowering of the new poetry of Spenser. The newcomer belonged to no school, was independent, very much on his own – no university man, unlike Spenser, Greene, Nashe; Oxford, Lyly, Sidney, Dyer; Peele, Ralegh, Daniel; or the earlier Sackville and Gascoigne. He had his own way to make, in poetry as in the theatre. He is an outsider, not a professional. His early poetry is very much that of an amateur, trying his hand; it is also of its own kind, defects and all, not mistakable for anybody else's. Naturally, it was influenced here and there by his reading – recognisably by Spenser, the influence of whose recently published *Faerie Queene* (1590) is evident in *Henry VI*. What else would one expect of an outsider, who had no such mentor as Spenser had in Gabriel Harvey, or circle of friends such as the aristocratic Sidney enjoyed, along with his gifted sister?

The desire to recommend himself in the usual way to a patron called into being his first poetic effort, *A Lover's Complaint*. This has often been excluded from his works, on the ground that it is not good enough for Shakespeare – against all common sense: as if an author's earliest work is expected to rank with his most mature. The poem is indeed amateurish, and reveals a promising, though not-so-young poet finding his feet, not yet in full command. Yet it already bears his signature in the liking for grand words that was to be so characteristic of him – words ending in '-ure' or '-ive': prompture, acture, extincture, fluxive; odd words like congest, unexperient; words that were to become favourites with him: credent, perused; odd coinages, like annexions; or the usage of 'pieced' for mended, which occurs later in one of the plays, along with his regular use of the word owe for own.

99

The subject and the tone are complete Shakespeare: it is a serio-comic poem with a smile upon it; an erotic piece about a country lass losing her virginity to a beautiful youth; a merry poem, in the Elizabethan sense of the word merry, where we would say naughty. This was to be characteristic of all Shakespeare's early work, for it was his character: an ebullient, sexy countryman – as Robert Greene saw him – self-confident, with a provincial accent, no urban intellectual. But we shall see that he was prepared to challenge the university wits, the professional poets, on their own ground.

The youth in the poem is recognisably Southampton, who is tactfully praised for his beauty:

> His qualities were beauteous as his form...
> Small show of down was yet upon his chin...

He is pursued by everyone (as was indeed the case):

> That he did in the general bosom reign
> Of young, of old, and sexes both enchanted.

This is the ambivalent lord of the Sonnets, who will not yet respond to women:

> He preached pure maid, and praised cold chastity.

The joke of the poem is that this paragon of youth seduces the country lass. She could not resist his charm any more than anyone else could: she

> Reserved the stalk and gave him all my flower.

A nice way of putting it.

A suggestive word betrays the purpose of the poem:

> Since I their altar, you *enpatron* me.

We may regard the poem as a kind of diploma-piece; for the actor-commencing-poet was received by Southampton as patron. When the Sonnets were brought out into the light of day and published by Thorp many years later, *A Lover's Complaint* was published with them – a significant point: it had been laid by in the same *cache* with the Sonnets.

It is impossible to exaggerate the importance of Southampton's patronage to the actor, of his admission to that circle of young men and to terms of friendship, intimate though always respectful, with its spirited adolescent leader. It meant the entry into an educated, cultivated circle such as his nature could respond to, with its boundless potentiality for development, so far latent, not yet called forth. Caroline Spurgeon noticed, very perceptively, the flowering of his senses and sensibilities observable in his imagery alone. We can observe the flowering of genius from prentice-pieces like *Titus* and *Henry VI* to those plays all of which have their association with this circle: *Love's Labour's Lost*, *A Midsummer Night's Dream*, *Romeo and Juliet* – perhaps even, something of an afterglow, *The Merchant of Venice*. Shakespeare tells us often enough how much he owed to this experience – the cardinal one in his development: it even outweighed in importance his infatuation for his musical mistress, Emilia Lanier. This experience – cultural, intellectual, emotional – was his university.

The rapid development of his powers may be seen in the poems the experience gave rise to, no less than in the plays. He published *Venus and Adonis* in 1593 (with his Stratford schoolfellow, Richard Field, in Blackfriars), as the 'first heir of his invention', a typically grand phrase for his first published work. Dedicated to his patron, it has a no less challenging epigraph from Ovid staking his claim to be regarded as a poet. The poem was written in competition with Marlowe's *Hero and Leander* (Marlowe too was briefly a candidate for Southampton's patronage), complicating the relationship, already sufficiently twisted by the intrusion of a young woman and the inflammable actor's infatuation for her. However, by the time the poem came out, the rival poet had got himself killed – the farewell to him is in Sonnet 86:

> Was it the proud full sail of his great verse,
> Bound for the prize of all too precious you?

Everyone acknowledges that Marlowe's poem, though unfinished, is superior as a work of art: more disciplined and controlled, more concentrated and finished in texture. Shakespeare's poem is undisciplined, even riotously so; it is full of fun, highly erotic, with digressions – one of them describing with enthusiasm (to encourage Adonis) a horse covering a mare; a still longer digression describes coursing the hare, as it might be on the Cotswolds, which looks like a separate poem sewn into the longer one. The poem is a countryman's work, full of rustic lore and descriptive passages; it is too long, but brims over with high spirits and easy inventiveness, spontaneous and natural, full of verbal felicities, headlong as if he cannot stop himself. All this was characteristic of Shakespeare. The poem turned out to be immensely popular, was more frequently printed than any of his other works, and won him fame as the English Ovid.

His involvement with Southampton was obsessive at this time: the theme of the handsome youth who will not (as yet) respond to the love of women occurs again and again. It is the theme of *Venus and Adonis* as also of *Love's Labour's Lost*; of the first section of the Sonnets, and it is glanced at in several lines of *The Shrew*. It occurs also in several of the sugared sonnets – among those passed round among the poet's friends – which Jaggard fortunately for us got hold of. (He annoyed Shakespeare later by using his name without permission – when the name became well known.) Hardly less important than the reluctant but provokingly beautiful youth is the passionately sexy woman in full pursuit of him: awkward as the situation may be in life, it is not without its comic side – and Shakespeare, with his own kind of ambivalence (not sexual, however), sees both sides. Venus, showing the youth where a boar had wounded his predecessor:

> 'See in my thigh,' quoth she, 'here was the sore.'
> She showed hers; he saw more wounds than one,
> And blushing fled, and left her all alone.

Or again when Adonis, standing naked by a pool, catches sight of the lady eyeing him lustfully,

> He, spying her, bounced in whereas he stood:
> 'O Jove!', quoth she, 'why was not I a flood?'

(Where*as*, by the way, is a regular Shakespeare form for where*at*.) And then in another, speaking for himself:

> Ah! that I had my lady at this bay,
> To kiss and clip me till I run away!*

---

* It has not been noticed how this is echoed in the odd, comic Sonnet 143 – a further indication that these sonnets in *The Passionate Pilgrim* are Shakespeare's.

Not to recognise all this for what it is, the perfectly natural eroticism of a highly-sexed heterosexual, and then to slubber it up with a lot of embarrassed priggery, is a double offence: silly in itself and showing an inability to appreciate, or even understand, Shakespeare for what he was.* For it is all part of the *life*, the truth to life, of his writing, which has kept it alive when so much of others' in that age is now dead. (A comparably high sexuality is a preservative in Donne.)

We must not go into a deadening academic analysis of *Venus and Adonis*, all too often perpetrated. We might however point out the originality of the emphasis, implicit as it is in Ovid, upon the woman pursuing the male, which Shakespeare develops with more voluptuous delight than Ovid does, making much more of it. The images throughout are a countryman's, sometimes of a nostalgic beauty:

> Like a red morn that ever yet betokened
> Wreck to the seaman, tempest to the field,
> Sorrow to the shepherds, woe unto the birds,
> Gusts and foul flaws to herdsmen and to herds.

The spontaneous alliteration betokens the born poet; yet he is not very literary – not many signs of other poets, except for an occasional echo, like this from Chideock Tichborne (who would have been known to the Southamptons, a Catholic neighbour):

> But now I lived, and life was death's annoy;
> But now I died, and death was lively joy.

The countryman, we see, was an actor:

> And all this dumb play had his acts made plain
> With tears, which chorus-like her eyes did rain.

We do not need to criticise – though we can see for ourselves phrases that are not effective, or are simply in-filling – still less

---

* cf. *The Arden Shakespeare, The Poems*, ed. by F.T. Prince, xxv, 'Nothing else was likely then, or is likely even now, to win an attentive reading of these poems. For one thing, their eroticism is hardly more acceptable than it was in Coleridge's day; few English or American readers nowadays will respond to such happily wanton fancies as *Venus and Adonis*.'! Or again, xxxvii, 'In both works there is the fascinated contemplation of lust and bloodshed and violated virtue. This is indeed a conception of tragedy which is not only youthful, but vulgar.' After this priggery it is hardly surprising that *A Lover's Complaint* is imperceptively omitted from the edition.

to say, absurdly, that the poem is not successful.* It was highly successful in its own time and has remained alive ever since. All kinds of things are worthy of note: the close parallels with the Sonnets, the common source of inspiration; the parallels with Marlowe; the glimpse of plague in the background; the poet's own country interests, the deer and deerparks, the dabchick and the homely snail, horses and horsemanship, the purblind hare, crows homing over the woods.

Shakespeare fulfilled his promise of some graver labour to his patron with *Lucrece* in 1594, again printed – but not published – by Field in Blackfriars. This is a more elaborate and less inspired poem; it is again too long drawn out, opulent in inventiveness and language, sombre in atmosphere as befits the theme, really rather laboured. The reality behind it, and what gives it its power, is what everyone has noticed, without perceiving the inwardness of it: the close parallel with the Sonnets describing Shakespeare's complex relationship with his mistress, the guilt, the adulterousness, the misery, the helplessness of a highly-sexed man possessed by lust:

> What win I if I gain the thing I seek?
> A dream, a breath, a froth of fleeting joy.

In spite of the enclosed, hot-house atmosphere of the poem, country images bespeak the author: we have country sports, the falcon's bells, bird-liming, the lagging birds before the northern blast, winter meads under melting snow and, as always, hunting the deer:

> As the poor frighted deer that stands at gaze,
> Wildly determining which way to fly...

Once more it is a man of the theatre writing:

> Black stage for tragedies and murders fell.

The actor knows that

> To see sad sights moves more than hear them told,
> For then the eye interprets to the ear

* cf. C.S. Lewis's 'rejection' of *Venus and Adonis, English Literature in the Sixteenth Century*, 499: 'It will not do. If the poem is not meant to arouse disgust it was very foolishly written.' More puritanical priggery. Critics should know their place, or at least have a sense of humour about themselves: not for them to reject but, at least, to try to understand.

104

> The heavy motion that it doth behold,
> When every part a part of woe doth bear.

Evidently he was becoming reconciled to the public profession which supported him, when life had not provided him with the means to live, as he would have liked, as a gentleman.

Again we need not detain the reader with literary analysis or academic 'criticism' – though it has not been observed that, interestingly, it reverts to the seven-line stanza of *A Lover's Complaint*, with the same rhyme scheme, ababbcc; unlike the six-line stanza of *Venus and Adonis*. We may observe the more extended classical references: to the story of Philomel, which he had treated in *Titus*, to the fall of Troy to which his imagination recurred throughout this career, Priam and Hector and Helen, with Hecuba who was to come to mind in a moving outburst of Hamlet's. We may doubt whether the theme of Lucrece's rape moved William Shakespeare very much (any more than it did Britten in his opera, though for opposite reasons). Perhaps his sympathies were on the other side – as in the previous poem they had been with Venus; at any rate, it takes Tarquin an over-long argumentation with himself to screw up his courage to the sticking-point. The Cambridge intellectual, Gabriel Harvey, tells us that *Lucrece* appealed to 'the wiser sort'; to judge from the number of reprints, it was half as successful as *Venus and Adonis*, in which we see the poet more in character with himself.

The Sonnets contain finer poetry, and of a wider range, than the published poems – naturally, for they express the *Paradiso* of his friendship with his young patron, the inspiration and the world it opened to him; the *Purgatorio*, when doubt and suspicion entered in with the woman, the anxious rivalry with Marlowe too; and the *Inferno* of his guilty infatuation, which drove him 'frantic-mad'. This poetry contains a drama which *Lucrece* did not attain for all its promising subject. It is the personal drama of Shakespeare's life in his most significant phase – the unfolding of his genius in the warmth of its inspiration – so intimate that he never published the Sonnets as others did their sonnet sequences, some of them of the nature of literary exercises. That element entered in with some of the less inspired sonnets, naturally, for they were all patronage poems, belonging to the patron – as all his poems were (with the one exception of *The Phoenix and the Turtle*).

To appreciate the drama of the Sonnets one needs to read them as a whole, not pick out one here or there. Though they are usually read this way, they are then unintelligibly out of perspective, without their background. Read as a whole, they range over the whole spectrum of human emotions, from the happy and innocent to the simply sad; from melancholy and longing to regret, to memory and desire, anxiety and doubt, indignation and hope renewed; sexual passion, lust and regret, grief and fear. Everything is in this autobiography of our greatest writer. However, he was a gentleman and he would not publish them, with their candid revelations of others as well as himself. Everything corroborates what Ben Jonson tells us, that his nature was open, free and honourable. No mystery about him; indeed, his very candour in the Sonnets has appeared shocking to the conventional. A perceptive critic has noted that their outspokenness is unconventional.* But, of course, a great writer will say everything: in that his greatness largely consists.

The Sonnets were never published by him, but by the publisher Thorp – much interested in such literary material – who got the manuscript from the only possessor of it, evidently Southampton's stepfather, Sir William Harvey, who inherited all the household goods and chattels from the Earl's mother.

Impossible to do justice in brief to the most personally moving sonnets ever written; we may note merely something of their range, from the purely happy,

> Shall I compare thee to a summer's day?

to the simply sad:

> That you were once unkind befriends me now.

From devastating candour to desolating disillusionment:

> When my love swears that she is made of truth,
> I do believe her, though I know she lies...
> Although she knows my days are past the best...
> And wherefore say not I that I am old?

* cf. M.C. Bradbrook, *Shakespeare and Elizabethan Poetry*, 145.

When he wrote those words his life was in fact more than half over; his situation was the humiliating one of an older man infatuated with a much younger woman.

All the external evidence about Emilia Lanier corroborates that this unvirtuous creature – well educated too – had an exceptionally strong and gifted, as well as tempestuous, personality:

> O, from what power hast thou this powerful might...
> To make me give the lie to my true sight?

And so to the spiritual torment of:

> The expense of spirit in a waste of shame
> Is lust in action...,

the tension between two loves:

> Two loves I have, of comfort, and despair,
> Which like two spirits do suggest me still.

What draughts he had been made to drink, of gall and bitter humiliation, caught as in a vice:

> What potions have I drunk of Siren tears,
> Distilled from limbecks foul as hell within.

Then on to the hopeless end:

> My love is as a fever, longing still
> For that which longer nurseth the disease...
> Past cure I am, now reason is past care,
> And frantic mad, with evermore unrest.

The affair was broken off, with Emilia – perhaps understandably – breaking her vow in bed with him. No wonder he needed to resort to Bath, for cure of 'love's distemper' – and that was probably an element in his anxiety for his young patron.

We should see, from the literary point of view, that the Sonnets, dramatic as many of them are, offer a transition to the poetry of the plays.

In the middle of his dramatic career, in 1601, he wrote, for a special occasion, *The Phoenix and the Turtle*: a strange poem in celebration of married love, which sounds more like a funerary threnody on it. One would say that it is unprecedented in his work, except that these lines recall the theme of the Sonnets:

> So they loved as love in twain
> Had the essence but in one:
> Two distincts, division none.

But of course there had been division in the love celebrated then:

> Let me confess that we two must be twain,
> Although our undivided loves are one.

One might again say that it is almost without parallel; perhaps it comes closest to a song, a dirge like 'Full fathom five'. *The Phoenix and the Turtle* reads like an incantation; magical, mythical, semi-metaphysical, trembling on the edge of nonsense, it is a surrealist poem – like a poem of Mallarmé. An enigmatic, Leonardo-like smile falls across it, such as sometimes rests upon a tragedy like *Antony and Cleopatra*, as who should say: who can compass the complexity, the contradictoriness, of life?

Such ambivalence at the root of his being, reinforced by his profession as an actor and deepened by the tensions of his personal life, constituted a prime qualification for a dramatist. Hence in part his mastery of dramatic justice, his singular capacity for holding a balance between characters so that the scales do not tip up. It is a piece of extraordinary luck that our finest poet, as it turned out, should have been obliged to devote himself to the theatre – and so continues as much alive to the world today as then. Moreover, the challenge of the theatre, the impulse given to his imagination at its sublime moments, brought out his finest poetry.

The literary historian is able to assure us that 'the speed of development in the art of poetry at the time was greater than England has ever known before or since'.* His own practice made its contribution to this, though in the world of the theatre rather than that of books, speaking rather than reading. In one sense he was an unliterary writer; this was what was

* cf. M.C. Bradbrook, *Shakespeare and Elizabethan Poetry*, 77 ff.

probably implied in the continual emphasis upon his being a child of nature – rather than of literary coteries. Not that he was without critical backing in this: the most important work of criticism at the time, Puttenham's *Art of Poesy*, completely chimes with Shakespeare's own practice. We say practice, for he followed his inspiration and intuitions, though he no doubt had his own views, as we have seen in regard to dramaturgy. However, it is true to say that he was 'no theorist, indeed one of the least theoretic minds that could be imagined'. He learned by 'the direct method'. This gave his imagination free rein, where Jonson's was hampered and deadened by theory, particularly in his tragedies. As in the theatre, with regard to acting, so in his poetry Shakespeare followed nature, depicting nature and heightening its effects, not imposing artifice upon it.

As for criticism, our prime authority on the Jacobean drama, G. E. Bentley, points out that Shakespeare's reputation did not stand as high with the critics as Jonson's, 'who in every single decade of the century is praised more often than Shakespeare', mentioned three times more often.* So characteristic of the limitations of critics – Jonson was the kind of writer they could compass better. Shakespeare was more popular – and yet he appealed at every level, from that discerning aesthete, Charles I, to the groundlings – perhaps less to the self-satisfied spirits who prided themselves on being 'intellectuals'. Yet Shakespeare's creations had the far greater vitality of creative life. 'This particular aspect of Shakespeare's genius triumphed over the critical standards which generally blinded the men of the time to his superiority.' Q.E.D.

Actual experiment by the poets themselves was immeasurably more important than the precepts and rules laid down by non-writers: the absurd Gabriel Harvey (who would have misdirected Spenser into alexandrines), or the fatuous Webbe. We may except Puttenham – Shakespeare would have found him a congenial spirit. We need respect only the makers themselves: Philip Sidney on poetry, along with Daniel and Drayton; Shakespeare himself and Jonson (with reservations) on drama.

It has been said that 'where Shakespeare was to break away

* q. Bradbrook, 103.

from his predecessors was precisely in the matter of vocabulary',
and we have seen him, even in his prentice-piece, *A Lover's
Complaint*, addicted to strange words, high-sounding, grandiloquent – and not merely as a matter of experiment. They
were what he liked: this was his nature. To quote again,
'Shakespeare's achievement depends before all else on the
power, range and strength of his use of words.' Before all else?
Surely, it is the range of imagination that comes first, of which
the words are the expression. 'It is well known that his
vocabulary was about ten [?] times that of the average man
of today.' Precisely, his vocabulary was enormous, because
necessary to express his range of imagination. It is well said
that he often had 'difficulty in saying only one thing at a
time'. This is true: he had not only double-mindedness but
triple-mindedness: he often saw two or three images in one
concept; hence the difficulties that sometimes arise in his
poetic style, the extraordinary allusiveness, the ambivalence
of meaning, the obliqueness and indirection that are characteristic, as well as stark simplicity when appropriate.

Such elasticity of mind could respond to any demand made
upon it by any human situation that arose from action in the
theatre. He can express everything. One is sometimes staggered
by the sheer verbal virtuosity, and wonders what he will find
to say next – Falstaff, for example, is never at a loss for an
answer. Just as Flaubert said of Madame Bovary, 'C'est moi',
so one may say – what looks more improbable – Falstaff is
Shakespeare.

Passages of purely descriptive poetry of beauty occur all
through the plays, from early to late, from Mercutio's description of Queen Mab's visitations of the English countryside at
night, to the moonlight at Belmont:

> Look how the floor of heaven
> Is thick inlaid with patines of bright gold...

and on to Prospero's enchanted island:

> Ye elves of hills, brooks, standing lakes, and groves;
> And ye that on the sands with printless foot
> Do chase the ebbing Neptune...

Impossible as it is to illustrate the varieties of his poetic expression, perhaps one may cite it at its furthest boundary, beyond which the language cannot go, in such lines as:

> Not poppy, nor mandragora,
> Nor all the drowsy syrups of the world,
> Shall ever medicine thee to that sweet sleep...

> Tomorrow, and tomorrow, and tomorrow –

the repetition is incantatory, like the knell it is –

> Creeps in this petty pace from day to day
> To the last syllable of recorded time,
> And all our yesterdays have lighted fools
> The way to dusty death.

Or, at the end of *Antony and Cleopatra*:

> O sun,
> Burn the great sphere thou mov'st in! Darkling stand
> The varying shore o' th' world...

> The odds is gone,
> And there is nothing left remarkable
> Beneath the visiting moon.

These are famous passages; many more such are printed unforgettably upon the minds of those who love the English language – which is our country, now that all else has gone.

Yet we might take something simpler to illustrate his magic no less. One day I came upon the lines quoted on someone else's page:

> Thou hast nor youth nor age,
> But, as it were an after-dinner's sleep,
> Dreaming on both –

and suddenly found myself in tears. It was his recognisable voice coming clear across the ages.

People respond most easily to the poetry of the songs; and Shakespeare was the most musical of our poets. (No wonder Emilia had such a hold on him; he well knew that

> music oft hath such a charm
> To make bad good, and good provoke to harm.)

He gave more openings for songs than any other dramatist,

with the widest variety, from simple drinking songs, three-men songs, ballads and catches, to magical incantations. Myself I love the evocations of country life:

> When icicles hang by the wall,
> And Dick the shepherd blows his nail,
> And Tom bears logs into the hall,
> And milk comes frozen home in pail.

Such is the sheer power of these simple descriptive words that one can see it all:

> When all aloud the wind doth blow,
> And coughing drowns the parson's saw –

one can see him in the draughty great church at Stratford in winter.

More magically suggestive are the love songs, that sometimes have a strange melancholy along with their evanescent beauty, perhaps because of its transience:

> O mistress mine, where are you roaming?
> O stay and hear, your true love's coming.

Songs of farewell in his last plays turn the heart over with their spell:

> Full fathom five thy father lies;
>   Of his bones are coral made;
> Those are pearls that were his eyes;
>   Nothing of him that doth fade
> But doth suffer a sea-change
> Into something rich and strange.

It is no wonder that his poetry, his songs and his plays have inspired more music than any writer whatsoever.

Only someone who is familiar with ordinary Elizabethan speech and usage – from reading hundreds of letters, thousands of documents and communications, besides the printed word in books and plays – can fully appreciate Shakespeare's language: not only the richness and variety, but the strangeness, often the difficulty. This is the background against which to see it, the ordinary ambling countryside out of which arise those heights, sometimes hardly accessible to meaning, and those intricate hollows of allusion and indirection.

From the very first, as we have seen with *A Lover's Complaint*, he was addicted to impressive words – evidently this was in his character, as well as in his profession. We note that rare and out-of-the-way words are not a feature of the Sonnets, for they belong to his private world; but they are a feature of his public poems as of his plays. We have mentioned his special liking for words ending in '-ure': expressure, disfeature, rejoindure (for union), repasture (for food, really!), climature, insisture (of which nobody appears to know the precise meaning). These words are not always to be accounted for by the requirements of scansion; for roundure for circle or ceinture for girdle are trochees and all scan alike. He just loved grand words, and usually preferred the more *recherché* word to the expected one. We must allow something here to the taste of the poet. We remember he liked words ending in '-ive': fluxive, plausive, defunctive, forgetive, respective (with various meanings), penetrative, when it was just as easy to use the ordinary word penetrating, which has the same number of syllables.

He does his thinking notably through concrete images, as a poet would, as well as by abstract concepts and argument – he is very clever at arguing – but he uses abstract, latinized words, some of them coined by him, when they occur nowhere else; I do not remember, in forty years of Elizabethan reading, coming across the word exsufflicate. He likes using the latinised past participles: gratulate for gratifying, remediate for remedial, peregrinate. He prefers the abstract form (as more impressive) – at least twice, I find – of ingredience for ingredients, sortance for sorts, suspiration for breathing, abruption for a breaking off, sequestration for the simpler separation; ostentation or ostent for show; excrement several times simply for growth – though that will be for comic effect when it refers to a beard. He uses a word like facinerous for simply wicked, prolixious for prolix, distinguishment for the simpler word, obsequious several times in its more literal latinised sense. Dr Johnson said that he always thought that Shakespeare knew enough Latin to latinise his vocabulary; we now know that it went much further than that – he read Latin, if not so facilely as the university men who continued their study of it from school to college. He is not afraid, however, to compete with them, and in fact he writes like one of them.

Even in the earliest plays, *Henry VI* for example, we find his signature words, commixture, reguerdon for reward; when not choosing a grand word, he will prefer an unobvious one, noontide 'prick' for noontide hour. Already we note his oracular, indirect idiom in a comparatively simple passage such as this:

> Wast thou ordained, dear father,
> To lose thy youth in peace and to achieve
> The silver livery of advisèd age,
> And in thy reverence and thy chair-days thus
> To die in ruffian battle?

Here we have his frequent use of a noun as an adjective.

> Tears virginal
> Shall be to me even as the dew to fire –

this is poetic, but all the same an odd way of putting it. We shall find much odder, until sometimes we do not know what he means. This is especially true of the later plays. In *Cymbeline*, for instance: 'His steel was in debt. It went o' th' backside of the town.' What on earth does it mean? Apparently this: his sword failed to pay, but took a back road, i.e. it just missed. But what a way to put it! By this time the habit of indirection had so grown on him that often he would not put a simple thing simply. One must allow for the need for variation, and also, naturally, he would be sometimes bored.

Perhaps especially with *Cymbeline*, where we find a succession of such passages.

> What makes your admiration?
> It cannot be i' th' eye, for apes and monkeys,
> Twixt two such shes, would chatter this way and
> Contemn with mows the other; nor i' th' judgment,
> For idiots, in this case of favour, would
> Be wisely definite; nor i' th' appetite,
> Sluttery, to such neat excellence opposed,
> Should make desire vomit emptiness,
> Not so allured to feed.

One can make out what he means, but all the same how odd!
It is like no one else. Even a simple sentiment takes this form:

> The love I bear him
> Made me to fan you thus, but the gods made you,
> Unlike all others, chaffless.

He likes also to take a positive word and turn it into a negative
by the ending '-less' – and this is effective – too subtle a matter
to explain why: a matter of verbal instinct. *Cymbeline* is full of
this sort of thing:

> Some jay of Italy,
> Whose mother was her painting, hath betrayed him.
> Poor I am stale, a garment out of fashion,
> And, for I am richer than to hang by th' walls,
> I must be ripped. To pieces with me! O,
> Men's vows are women's traitors! All good seeming,
> By thy revolt, O husband, shall be thought
> Put on for villainy, not born where 't grows,
> But worn a bait for ladies.

We must allow something for carelessness, for we know that
he was a very quick writer who hardly ever blotted his lines,
i.e. corrected them; and we must allow for the pressures upon
him, the deadline for production. We can often tell that he is
thinking of the next play before he has finished the present
one – by the end of *Henry V*, for example, he has *Julius Caesar*
in mind. And we must remember that primarily he *heard* his
lines, so that even the difficult and devious ones become more
direct in speech, pointed up by gesture. This is what his
characteristic grandiloquence had come to.

Cymbeline is not exceptional in style; all the later plays have
passages in this condensed, elliptical style, choosing frequently
indirectness rather than obviousness of statement. What a way
he has come from the simple, linear, end-stopped blank verse
of the early plays to the verse paragraphs of the later! In these
we have breaks coming in the middle of the line, the end
running on with prepositions, 'or', 'and', 'that', 'but', 'O' – as
if he could not be bothered. It is, however, concentrated,
under the pressure of thought, several images combining in a
sentence, not only elliptical, but suggestive, obscure – open-
ended in both senses. It is like the impressionism one observes

in the last phase of great painters, a Titian – to take a contemporary: from the careful, linear art of the beginner to the slapdash impressionism of the later work that contains and suggests so much more.

We anticipate: *Cymbeline* belongs to 1609. Let us illustrate from an earlier play, *King John* of 1596. Here are just as many impressive words as usual. He will use the word expedient for simply swift: 'His marches are expedient to this town'; indigest:

> To set a form upon that indigest
> Which he hath left so shapeless and so rude.

Dispiteous is used for pitiless – I do not remember coming across the word elsewhere.

> And call them meteors, prodigies and signs,
> Abortives, presages, and tongues of heaven –

here the liking for impressive statement is much in place, and note also a favourite ending in '-ive'.

> A whole armado of convicted sail,

has given rise to discussion, unnecessarily, for it is but another latinised formation from the past participle, *convectum*. If Shakespeare were not Shakespeare, an ordinary writer would use, in that place, the more common word concerted: it scans the same. His words indigest, congest are similarly straight from the Latin. Even when they are not, he prefers the rarer word: he almost always uses doom for sentence; nor does he object to an ancient Anglo-Saxon form, like alderliefest. Archaic forms, such as eyne, are earlier taken over from Spenser or Chaucer, or are used for the sake of rhyme.

A poet's instinct naturally directs him to rare words, and Shakespeare often surprises us with special words that have gone out of use: chape, the scabbard of a sword; copatain for a high-crowned hat; chopine, a high-soled shoe; cheveril, soft deerskin for gloves. A glover's son, he knew all about the various sorts of skins and their uses. We know from the Sonnets and elsewhere of his lively interest in horses and horsemanship, natural enough to a touring actor, regularly on the roads between Stratford and London. His trope on the state and diseases of Petruchio's horse in the *Shrew* is a riot of special knowledge, very funny but also a piece of showing off. The poor horse is 'possessed with the glanders and like to mose in the chine, troubled with the lampass, infected with the fashions, full of windgalls, sped with spavins, rayed with the yellows, past cure of the fives, stark spoiled with the staggers, begnawn with the botts, swayed in the back and shoulder-shotten, near-legged before, and with a half-checked bit and a headstall of sheep's leather ... one girth six times pieced, and a woman's crupper of vel*ure*', i.e. velvet. He must have had fun in writing that (note also the alliteration); it is almost like boasting – and that would not have been out of character with Greene's view of the ebullient actor.

Whether Latin or no, he loves the rare words: crants for garland, escoted for maintained, coistrel for knave, neaf for fist, dern for dark, accite for summon, agnize for acknowledge, and so on interminably. I do not know if he was the first to use the deformation of words to raise a laugh which we call a malapropism, but certainly he was the first to use it on such a scale, so frequently and to such good effect. Usually to make fun of the lower orders – Bottom and his workmates, Dogberry and Verges, constable and headborough, Elbow another constable and Pompey, Mistress Overdone's pimp, and Overdone herself in *Measure for Measure*. Mistress Quickly is the mistress of this art whenever she appears. It is also used to make fun of peasants and country folk, or of a Jack Cade. Another kind of deformation of the language for comic effect occurs with Welshmen, Fluellen and Sir Hugh Evans the curate; Dr Caius makes fritters of the language with his French accent.

One hardly knows what to make of Pistol's bombast; it has a literary element in it, for he quotes lines from Peele's plays. Was it intended as a parody of someone in particular? Various elements of literary parody enter into the extraordinary exhibition of linguistic virtuosity that is *Love's Labour's Lost*; one can recognise Antonio Perez' inflated rhetoric in Don Armado, and probably Florio is aimed at in Holofernes. Moth, 'tender Juvenal', is young Nashe – whose own prose comes nearest to Shakespeare in riotous Rabelaisian inventiveness.

Elizabethan English was in a fluid condition, pregnant, we might say (a favourite Shakespeare word, though he uses it to mean the obvious). It was growing hand over fist in the use of new words, expanding with its expansion of mind and experience, exploring new territories, raking in words for special disciplines from Latin and Greek and, among modern languages, chiefly from French, with some Italian and Spanish. Shakespeare was both an annexationist and a coiner. In *Coriolanus* we find a medical term which did not take on: 'the most sovereign prescription in Galen is but *empiricutic* and, to this preservative, is of no better report than a horse-drench'. The whole sentence is very much Shakespeare, and we recall that just at this time he had acquired for a son-in-law the Stratford doctor, John Hall.

Grammar and grammatical usage also were more flexible. It was fairly frequent to use a plural subject with a singular verb; but no one does that so frequently as Shakespeare. Once or twice one catches him out using a singular subject with a plural verb, but that may be an error in transmission of the text rather than his. It is usual enough for Elizabethans to use the impersonal relative 'which', where we should use the personal 'who'; again no one does this so frequently as Shakespeare. Occasionally he even uses the personal 'who' for 'which', but this is rare. Double negatives are very frequent with him and, it must be admitted, effective. The double reflexive is peculiarly characteristic of him: poetic, but it also reflects his duplicity, or duality, of mind, the mirror-effect of a Renaissance self-awareness, like that of Montaigne or Cervantes, in whom he had read.

He is the master of all styles of speech – appropriately for an actor – in verse or prose, from the simplest exchanges to the grandest. We note the conscious stylishness when speaking in his own person to his patron. 'I know not how I shall offend in dedicating my unpolished lines to your lordship, nor how the world will censure me for choosing so strong a prop to support so weak a burden: only, if your honour seem but pleased, I account myself highly praised, and vow to take advantage of all idle hours, till I have honoured you with some graver labour. But if the first heir of my invention prove deformed, I shall be sorry it had so noble a godfather, and never after ear so barren a land, for fear it yield me still so bad a harvest. I leave it to your honourable survey, and your honour to your heart's content; which I wish may always answer your own wish and the world's hopeful expectation.'

There we have him: the antitheses, the balanced clauses, alliteration, subjunctives, the countryman's image from sowing and harvest. The subjunctive, almost lapsed today, was very much alive in Elizabethan English, never more so than with this exponent of its use: he uses it not only after 'if', as we still sometimes do, but after though, till, although, when, whether, lest – whenever there is the least doubt to follow. More important is the tone of the dedication. Everything shows, in his life and in the records, that he was courteous and even courtly, an indispensable qualification for the society he moved into. Thus he became an easy master of courtly speech, the dignified language of kings and courtiers – this was a matter of artistic decorum. He became so familiar with it, from frequent attendance and performances at Court, even apart from his acquaintance with Southampton and his circle, that he could parody it to the life. Here is a young Court fop, as it might be the Earl of Oxford: 'Sweet lord, if your lordship were at leisure, I should impart a thing to you from his majesty. . . . Sir, here is newly come to Court Laertes – believe me, an absolute gentleman, full of most excellent differences, of very soft society and great showing. Indeed, to speak feelingly of him, he is the card or calendar of gentry; for you shall find in him the continent of what part a gentleman would see. . . . Your lordship speaks most infallibly of him.'

Shakespeare emerged as master of the high, low and middle styles in drama. He began with the high rhetorical style of earlier Elizabethan drama, with *Titus* and *Henry VI*, though from the first he showed what he could do with the low style in the Jack Cade scenes which have lived longest and appeal to us best amid so much rodomontade and stichomythia, and so many boring battles. He can hardly be said to have achieved the middle style of easy, natural conversation with his first comedy, for the *Errors* is too artificial, still too much under the influence of his model; he has not yet found himself. *The Two Gentlemen* is more relaxed, and again provides an example of absolute mastery of the low style, a direct transcript from real life observed, in Lance and his dog. That is what we remember best from the play: it is still alive.

We have no priggish embarrassment in confronting the subject of Shakespeare's bawdy language; the difficulty is simply that there is so much of it, it is ubiquitous. What a good thing! For much of it is still amusing, and it all helps to keep the writing alive and kicking. Fortunately there is a whole book devoted to the subject,* so that here we need only point to its function, or functions. It was partly to appeal to the groundlings, though not only to them; and sometimes to liven up the play when the action is at a pause. One can at times catch him dragging it in to wake up the audience or fill a gap. In *All's Well*, Act IV, Sc v, the old courtier Lafew is exchanging banter with the Clown:

LAFEW: Whether dost thou profess thyself, a knave or a fool?
CLOWN: A fool, sir, at a woman's service, and a knave at a man's.
LAFEW: Your distinction?
CLOWN: I would cozen the man of his wife and do his service.
LAFEW: So you were a knave at his service indeed.
CLOWN: And I would give his wife my bauble, sir, to do her service.

Very often the bawdy talk proceeds by innuendo and, with the innocent-minded, may run like water off a duck's back. But the more one understands Elizabethan language, and the better one understands Shakespeare, the more of it is there to uncover, only just under the surface, besides what hits one in the eye.

This is what Robert Bridges objected to, though he also objected to the frequent violence and bloodshed of the action. We need only comment that his own closet dramas are as dead as a doornail. Or consider Coleridge on *Venus and Adonis*: 'Though the very subject cannot but detract from the pleasure of a delicate mind, yet never was poem less dangerous on a moral account.'† The delicacy of Coleridge's mind did not deter him from deserting his wife, and leaving his children to be brought up by others. We detect an element of humbug in Coleridge's moralising.

It is not only a question of words, but of the subject, the action. Like a normal, highly-sexed man, William Shakespeare was excited by sex, the conjunctions and combinations of sex,

* Eric Partridge, *Shakespeare's Bawdy*.
† Quoted in Prince, *ed. cit.*, xxix.

the naughtiness and impropriety – compare old Falstaff's eagerness to get off to bed with the whore, Doll Tearsheet. It really is very funny to hear Dame Quickly give Doll a good character in Prince Hal's words, 'this honest, virtuous, civil gentlewoman'.

HOSTESS QUICKLY: God's blessing of your good heart! And so she is, by my troth.

Nevertheless, when Falstaff and Doll bicker:

HOSTESS QUICKLY: You cannot one bear with another's confirmities. What the good year! one must bear, and that must be you. You are the weaker vessel, as they say, the emptier vessel.

DOLL: Can a weak empty vessel bear such a huge full hogshead?

And then, rather touchingly, for the whore has a good heart:

> Come, I'll be friends with thee, Jack. Thou art going to the wars; and whether I shall ever see thee again or no, there is nobody cares.

Thus we have the bawdiness in keeping with such characters as Falstaff, a matter of artistic decorum, we might say, without paradox.

Thirdly, we have characters whose business is to be bawdy – bawds and whores and pimps – like Mistress Overdone and Pompey; Cressida is hardly any better, her pander Pandarus rather worse; or the bawd and Boult in *Pericles*, where scenes take place in a brothel. We have a whole gallery of contemporary low life – and how incomplete and impoverished a view of the life of the age it would be without them! How true Shakespeare's depiction was to the facts we see from the casebooks and practice of 'Dr' Forman.* The point is that the picture would be *untrue* without this element; what we value in Shakespeare is the quality of life in all its forms, the livingness of it all.

What we have to conclude then is that the essential Shakespeare is as Protean in style as in language; there is no confining him as with lesser writers, Chapman, for instance. Even Marlowe is not master of a simple style, and we cannot say that he had much sense of comedy. Ben Jonson genuinely

* cf. my *Simon Forman: Sex and Society in Shakespeare's Age.*

had, and we see him at his best when he gives rein to it, as in *The Alchemist* and *Volpone*; he had too a pure vein of poetry and fantasy – it is his tragedies, which he set so much store by, that fail to move us. Shakespeare had everything and, appropriately, it was Ben Jonson who concisely summed it up for us:

> how far thou didst our Lyly outshine,
> Or sporting Kyd, or Marlowe's mighty line.

That is, Shakespeare outdid them all in comedy, tragedy, history, and even surpassed Marlowe in poetry.

We have illustrated something of his supreme poetry, and all other poets in the language recognise his supremacy. So perhaps it is not paradoxical to conclude that it is in passages that transcribe the life of his day that we yet feel him most closely in touch with ours. It is the acute sense of life, along with the virtuosity in transcribing it – as with Dickens – that appears again and again. Pompey has in his keeping,

> young Master Rash; he's in for a commodity of brown paper and old ginger, nine score and seventeen pounds, of which he made five marks ready money. ... Then there is here one Master Caper, at the suit of Master Threepile the mercer, for some four suits of peach-coloured satin, which now peaches him a beggar. Then we have here young Dizzy, and young Master Deepvow, and Master Copperspur, and Master Starvelackey, the rapier and dagger man, and young Dropheir that killed lusty Pudding, and Master Forthlight the tilter, and brave Master Shoe-tie the great traveller, and wild Halfcan that stabbed pots and, I think, forty more – all great doers in our trade, and are now 'for the Lord's sake'.

How it must have amused Shakespeare to write that! – we have virtuosity just in the names.

Or passages straight out of the life of the people:

> FIRST CARRIER: Heigh-ho! An it be not four by the day, I'll be hanged; Charles's wain is over the new chimney, and yet our horse not packed. What, ostler!

Or the country clown, preparing for the shearing feast, as it might be in the Cotswolds:

> Let me see: every 'leven wether tods; every tod yields pound and

odd shilling: fifteen hundred shorn, what comes the wool to? ... I cannot do 't without counters. Let me see: what am I to buy for our sheep-shearing feast? Three pound of sugar, five pound of currants, rice – what will this sister of mine do with rice? ... She hath made me four-and-twenty nosegays for the shearers – three-man songmen all. ... I must have saffron to colour the warden-pies; mace; dates – none, that's out of my note; nutmegs, seven; a race or two of ginger, but that I may beg; four pound of prunes, and as many of raisins o' th' sun.

For in such passages speaks the heart of the people still.

7

Shakespeare's Reading

W E FAIRLY certainly underestimate the amount of reading that any literate person does, or did, before radio, television, films and such distractions came in. It is quite certain that we underestimate the amount of reading that William Shakespeare did – we can be sure of that from the evidence of the plays. The subject is, however, a difficult one to deal with; for it falls under several headings and of different kinds, while to provide a list of books that he read, or read in, would be opaquely bibliographical and boring. He was a quick reader, as he was a fast writer; many books he needed only to look into for an idea, a suggestion or a name. We are reminded of Henry James picking up suggestions for his short stories or novels from anecdotes at the dinner-table. James collected names too for his characters, as Dickens did; Shakespeare offers us an extraordinary gallimaufry of names from all over the place.

Further, we must be on guard against the pedantry of source-hunting, reaching back for the origin of a story to the ancient East, the mythology of India or Egypt. Shakespeare took what came to hand, what took his fancy, and as practising actor and dramatist what could most promisingly be turned into a play. As an actor he had a considerable number of plays in his head from acting in them; others he worked on to make them into plays of his own. That already makes a category of its own in his 'reading'.

As for source-hunting, Quiller-Couch, who was a creative writer himself and knew how it was done, gives us a salutary warning. 'When, as with *Twelfth Night*, the story is a primal one, and we have a dozen sixteenth-century versions capable of providing a hint here or a phrase there, the quest may easily turn to a folly of delusion. And after all, for our relief, no one has yet found Shakespeare a debtor to anyone for

Malvolio.'* It has been thought that he looked into William Thomas's well-known *History of Italy* for Prospero's story in *The Tempest*. And so it may be. But the Arden editor comments sensibly: 'More of these names are found in Eden's *History of Travel*; Prospero and Stephano have parts in Jonson's *Every Man in his Humour*, a play in which Shakespeare acted.'† Exactly: something close and ready to hand.

Analogue-hunting is even more a waste of time. Dr Johnson spoke plain common sense, as usual, on this: 'I have found it remarked that, in this important sentence, "Go before, I'll follow", we read a translation of "I prae, sequar". I have been told that when Caliban, after a pleasing dream, says, "I cry'd to sleep again", the author imitates Anacreon, who had, like every other man, the same wish on the same occasion.' To read some of the commentators one would think that Shakespeare was not capable of inventing a situation or a character for himself.

Quiller-Couch also pointed out how often Shakespeare is his own source, and repeats the essentials of a situation in a different context: mistaken identities, which are the stuff of the *Errors*, appear again in *Twelfth Night*. Timon's rejection of Athens is a parallel to Coriolanus' rejection of Rome. The theme of a lost royal child of *Pericles* is repeated in *The Winter's Tale*. An incursion into a chaste lady's bedroom, the subject of *Lucrece*, is made use of in *Cymbeline*, and so on.

To this the historian can add how absurd it is to pile up remote analogues and improbable sources, and to neglect the whole life of the age, which is the necessary background for any writer, and his own experience which is the life-blood of his work. Quiller-Couch saw that the principal stuff of *A Midsummer Night's Dream*, of which there is no identified source, is largely the folklore of his native Warwickshire, which spills over into Mercutio's nostalgic speech about Queen Mab and Robin Goodfellow in *Romeo and Juliet*. At last it is becoming realised how closely *Love's Labour's Lost* – which used to be regarded as a play to which the key was lost – is related to Shakespeare's own experience with Southampton and his circle, and with his mistress Emilia Lanier (born Bassano); as

---

* Quoted in *Narrative and Dramatic Sources of Shakespeare*, ed. G. Bullough, II. 270–1.
† *The Arden Shakespeare. The Tempest*, ed. F. Kermode, lxx.

also are the Sonnets and the related poems. It is as yet not so clearly realised that *All's Well* is in part a reversion to that earlier theme, with which the dramatist had been so much involved.

With these observations in mind we may confront the more elusive subject of his reading, remembering that we must keep as close as possible to the man, inherent probabilities and what is relevant to the work he had in hand. This last will always be revealing, and help to keep us on the rails; but beyond will be the penumbra of an educated Elizabethan's reading, as to which there will be less information. We must, however, always allow for it, and at every point.

We have already seen the basis laid at school of his reading in the classics, not very wide but a sufficient foundation. We know how devoted he was to Ovid and how this was to be reflected forward in his work. Marlowe was similarly devoted to Ovid, and went on to translate the *Amores*: Marlowe was the intellectual, Shakespeare had other things to do – among them, support a family. Otherwise, one does not notice much difference in their joint devotion to the poet of love. And Shakespeare would have continued some classical reading, all the more if the ancient tradition is correct that he taught school in the country for a time.

During those few years of which we have no record, between Stratford and London, he would have been reading as well as acting. When he emerges into public notice with *Henry VI* it is obvious that he has been reading Spenser with enthusiasm, and he is an addict of the new poetry which dominated the young writers of the 1580s. Some plays he knew all the better for acting in them; and, since Elizabethan playing was repertory, this would have meant a considerable number. This partly accounts for the many phrases he picked up from others' work, particularly from Marlowe, who was an important influence. Even to the late 1590s he is parodying lines from Peele's plays, and from the anonymous *Salomon and Perseda*, through the bombast of Pistol. The influence of the foremost playwrights, such as Kyd with the ever-popular *Spanish Tragedy*, is obvious.

The two most influential prose works were Sidney's *Arcadia* and Lyly's *Euphues*. The coming dramatist not only read them but used them in his work. *Euphues* is parodied in *Love's Labour's Lost*, along with others; there are references too to Nashe's Pierce Penniless pamphlets in his literary row with the Harveys. Thomas Lodge's *Rosalynd*, written on his voyage to the Canaries, came out in 1590; it was subtitled, to catch the fashion, *Euphues' Golden Legacy*. It provided the story for *As You Like It*, which also reflected the current popularity of Robin Hood and the Greenwood plays towards the end of the 1590s. Lyly's comedies were written for the boys whom he directed, the Children of the Chapel Royal and those of St Paul's, and they were being published in the 1580s and 1590s. They had considerable influence on Shakespeare's comedies, in their courtly style, their frequent use of proverbial, vernacular sayings, and in the symmetry of their structure as against the rambling shape of popular comedy.

Shakespeare would have known from childhood the old medieval romances the people loved: *Guy of Warwick* (with its additional local interest), *Bevis of Hampton*, *Huon of Bordeaux*. References to these, or characters from them, appear in the plays, and others too helped to stock his mind when young, along with the popular ballads he often quotes. An author much to the fore in the 1580s was Robert Greene, with whom Shakespeare tangled – there must have been dealings in the early years to which we really have lost the key. The Johannes Factotum who could put his hand to anything knew Greene's plays and read his cony-catching pamphlets. He also read his romances, and later based *The Winter's Tale* on the best of them, *Pandosto*; names in the play come from Plutarch, Autolycus from Ovid, some details from Sidney's *Arcadia*. He had already looked into Sir Thomas North's translation of Plutarch's *Lives*, which came out in 1579, for Theseus and Hippolyta in *A Midsummer Night's Dream* came thence.

A revival of interest in Chaucer was noticeable in the nineties, with one or more editions and several issues just before and after 1600. Shakespeare was acquainted with his work, as also with that of Gower, at least with the *Confessio Amantis*. For *Troilus and Cressida* he drew upon Caxton's *Recuyell of the Histories of Troy*, but was also indebted to Chapman's translation of Seven Books of the *Iliad* which had recently come out, in 1598. Shakespeare was obviously making fun of Chapman's heavy heroics in his satire upon them, reducing them to the absurd; mocking them all, not only the foolish Troilus and Cressida, but the blockhead Ajax, the skulking Achilles and his boy-friend Patroclus, exposing Pandarus relentlessly; neither Helen nor Paris is shown in a favourable light. Thersites the misanthrope has the last word on them all. The constipated intellectuality of Chapman with its inflated claims was directly opposite to what Shakespeare stood for.

Nor was he on the same wavelength as Ben Jonson, though he knew his work well from acting in it and, moreover, welcomed his junior to write for his company at the Globe and later at Blackfriars. A closer spirit to Shakespeare's was Samuel Daniel, with whose work he was in sympathy – and he would have known him, for Daniel was Florio's brother-in-law. Their work touched at various points. Daniel's sonnets are not far removed from Shakespeare's in tone. Daniel too was deeply interested in history; his *First Four Books of the Civil Wars* came out in 1595, to be made use of in *Richard II*, along with the anonymous play, *Thomas of Woodstock*, and some reading in Froissart. Daniel's *Cleopatra* was useful too for *Antony and Cleopatra*; after which it is thought that Daniel made a few revisions of his own text. In 1599 he published his fine poem *Musophilus*; Shakespeare immediately adapted the most impressive stanza in it, which struck him, into *Julius Caesar* which he was writing at the time:

> How many ages hence
> Shall this our lofty scene be acted over
> In states unborn and accents yet unknown!

That was the way his mind worked, making use of everything. Another echo shows that he was reading Sir John Davies' philosophic poem, *Nosce Teipsum*, of that year. These were two of the finest long poems of the time: it shows the popular dramatist's instinctive taste.

A common stock of subjects for plays – particularly historical ones – existed, and various authors used the same themes, often competitively: the Chamberlain's Men against the Admiral's, and vice versa. Naturally Shakespeare would read, with exceptional care, earlier plays he was adapting. He may

128

have been re-working earlier material in *Titus*, *1 Henry VI*, and the *Shrew*; he certainly took *The Troublesome Reign of King John* and worked it over for his own *King John*, as he did less closely *The Famous Victories of King Henry V* for *Henry V*. An *Ur*-Hamlet, probably by Kyd, underlies *Hamlet*, while an old play *King Leir* prompted *King Lear*. We may suppose that, busy as he became, much of his later reading had a purpose in view.

Then too there were the various books of stories, usually translated from Italian or French – Bandello, Cinthio, or Boccaccio, sometimes directly or through the French, such as Belleforest – which Elizabethans read avidly and which the dramatists seized upon for subjects. One of the most popular was *The Palace of Pleasure*, by William Painter, a Cambridge man who was rewarded with a job as Clerk of the Ordnance, where he signalised himself – not unusually for a civil servant of the time – by peculation. The story of *All's Well* comes ultimately from Boccaccio mediated through Painter, as that of *Measure for Measure* came from Cinthio, though immediately via George Whetstone's play, *Promos and Cassandra*. The proximate source is always the more likely.

Sir John Harington was another kindred spirit: a clever merry man, full of jokes, liking fun and the flesh, bawdy, disliking Puritans, preferring middle-of-the-road Anglicanism. Shakespeare may have met him, for he was a friend and follower of Essex, and was frequently at Court, as the dramatist also was often enough for performances. Harington vivaciously translated Ariosto's *Orlando Furioso*, at the Queen's bidding. The dramatist drew the story of *Much Ado* from it, so we may suppose that he read the work. We do not need to suppose that he went further afield to find a Beatrice, 'whose name and witty frankness, but nothing else, may come ultimately from Pasqualigo'.* The name Beatrice and frankness are common enough.

Early Elizabethan literature was rather sparse and uninspired; not until the eighties did the new poetry begin, the new drama, the madrigals, the patriotic inspiration of the sea-voyages expressed by Hakluyt (whose epic *Principal Navigations*

* Bullough, *op. cit.* II. 74, 75.

of the English Nation came out in the year after the Armada), the national fervour aroused by the struggle with Spain. Shakespeare caught this tide. A leading writer in the earlier generation was George Gascoigne, a Cambridge and Gray's Inn man. His *Supposes*, adapted from Ariosto, was produced in 1566; its mistaken identities contributed something to the *Errors*, and also again to the *Shrew*. It is interesting that Gascoigne was in attendance at Kenilworth during the Queen's historic visit in 1575, when Leicester outdid everyone in the entertainments offered her – his last attempt to win her hand. We recall that Cupid aimed at 'a fair Vestal, thronèd by the west'; but that his fiery shaft was 'Quenched in the chaste beams of the wat'ry moon' – at that time Kenilworth Castle was practically surrounded by a lake, upon which the water entertainments took place –

> And the imperial Votaress passed on,
> In maiden meditation, fancy free.

It is likely enough that a bright boy of eleven, the alderman's son from Stratford, was present among the Warwickshire folk who attended; and it is not unlikely that the lines incorporate the local tradition as to what transpired behind the scenes. There seems to have been a quarrel between Elizabeth and Leicester.

A popular patriotic poem of the time was William Warner's jog-trot *Albion's England*; a few verbal echoes – always the telltale marks with Shakespeare – in the *Errors* show that he read it, as he would have done in any case. Warner's patron was Lord Chamberlain Hunsdon, patron of Shakespeare's company, also a patron of music and of Emilia Bassano; a number of musical compositions were dedicated to him.

The Elizabethans brought into being a whole new literature of translations alone, mainly from Latin, French and Italian, but also from Greek and Spanish. We may see in it the vigour of an enterprising, up-and-coming people annexing new territories of the mind to itself; a small and hitherto backward people culturally, on the margin of Europe, making astonishingly rapid advances in the propitious circumstances of a flexible and efficient society. The story of *The Two Gentlemen of Verona* seems to have been derived from Montemayor's

Diana, which was not translated at the time. But a play based upon it was given at Court, and the Queen possessed a copy of the Spanish edition. Her lady-in-waiting, Lady Hoby, the Lord Chamberlain's daughter, was praised for her proficiency in Spanish. Bartholomew Young dedicated his translation of it later to Penelope Rich, Essex's sister. This is Shakespeare's grouping: the Chamberlain's Men his professional grouping, Essex via Southampton his personal affiliation.

Lord Treasurer Burghley was the patron of Arthur Golding, in the earlier generation. His translation of Ovid's *Metamorphoses*, of 1565–7, was of much use to Shakespeare, who consulted it again and again, along with, possibly less frequently for a busy man, the original Latin. It was a prime source for classical stories and legends; Shakespeare was also acquainted with others of Ovid's works, the *Fasti* and *Ars Amatoria*. An author pressed for time need hardly read the whole book; Shakespeare would seem to have had the Chestertonian faculty for gutting a work and rapidly absorbing what he wanted. That accounts for quite a large number of passing references to works coming out at the time.

His main historical sources come into a different category: he gave them close attention, and followed them as authorities for several plays. These were above all Holinshed's *Chronicles*, Hall's history of the houses of Lancaster and York, and North's Plutarch. To these he added subsidiary reading relevant to the subject he was writing about. For *King John* he read up the account in John Foxe's *Acts and Monuments*, and consulted it again for *Henry VIII*. Popularly known as Foxe's Book of Martyrs, it was the great best-seller of the age, often placed in churches for people to read. Shakespeare would have read something of this book, if not all of it – everybody did, except Catholics who were mortified by its shocking record of Queen Mary's burnings. Shakespeare took much of his English history – and also the Scottish history for *Macbeth* – from Holinshed, from the second edition which was much expanded from the original compilation. This second edition was under the more scholarly direction of John Hooker of Exeter, the antiquarian uncle of Richard Hooker, philosopher of Anglicanism. Edward Hall's *Union of the Two Noble and Illustre Families of Lancaster and York* was hardly less important and, as we have seen, this developed the theme of national unity achieved with the Tudors.

A book which he could hardly have avoided, even had he wished, was the popular *Mirror for Magistrates*, with a score of stories of the fall of historic figures. This book had some five or six editions in the age; he was able to draw upon it for his portraits of Clarence and Glendower, and for Henry VIII's Buckingham. For the Wars of the Roses, the reigns of Henry VI, Edward IV and Richard III, he had plenty of material. There was Fabyan's *Chronicle* for events in the City of London, the French chronicler Commines had learned that Richard killed Henry VI 'with his own hand, or had him killed in his presence in some secret place', and we have independent confirmation that Richard was in the Tower the night Henry died. The bleeding of his wounds while he lay in St Paul's Shakespeare could have got from Holinshed or Stow, the City chronicler well up in these events. A Renaissance historian, with higher critical standards, was Polydore Virgil, whose patron was Henry VII. Henry himself could have told him who the killers of the young Prince of Wales were at Tewkesbury: Clarence, Richard and Hastings, Edward IV's boon companion whom Richard made away with later when he made his *coup d'état*. Shakespeare was not solely dependent on Sir Thomas More for his information; he seems to have known Lord Henry Howard's *Defensative . . . against Supposed Prophecies*, which came out in 1583; it contains the Howard family tradition as to Richard's 'heinous crime'.

Two books by spirits congenial to Shakespeare were Reginald Scot's *Discovery of Witchcraft* of 1584 and Samuel Harsnet's *Declaration of egregious Popish Impostures* of 1603. Both these men were enlightened and tolerant Anglicans. It is fairly evident that Scot did not believe in witchcraft, and he hated the persecution of poor deluded old women by their no less deluded persecutors. Hundreds of these sad creatures were hounded to death by the usual exhibition of human cruelty; the numbers – which sank to zero under the civilised Charles I and Laud – greatly increased with the growth of the Puritan mania. Scot particularly reacted against the witch-mania exemplified by Bodin, evidently a psychological case (as was James I, hagridden by Calvinism). Scot's book proved useful for the portrayal of the hags who fortified, if they did not suggest, Macbeth's criminal ambition.

Shakespeare took not only the names of the fiends in *King Lear* from Harsnet's book but was indebted to it for many details in the mad world that possessed the minds of Lear, Edgar and the Fool. I have elsewhere gone into the background of Harsnet's exposure of the fantastic handling a group of priests practised in the name of exorcism upon a number of credulous women.* The dramatist had a sensitive ear for what was significant, outrageous or took public fancy at the time – like the sensation made by the Jesuit teaching of equivocation, exposed in the trial of Henry Garnet, who had known about the Gunpowder Plot beforehand.

By the time Shakespeare came to write *Henry VIII* there was the admirable Speed to consult, but he based himself more on a work of the theatre, Samuel Rowley's *When You See Me*. It does not appear that he read the foremost historical work that any Englishman had yet written, Camden's *Britannia*. Camden was Ben Jonson's old schoolmaster at Westminster, who taught him to write poetry by first writing his piece in prose, then turning it into verse – in contrast to Shakespeare's direct method. But Shakespeare certainly read Camden's smaller book, *Remains ... concerning Britain*, which came out in 1605, in time to include Menenius' parable about the belly and the head in *Coriolanus*. Once more we see his quick habit of using something that had recently struck him in his reading. Living on his own in lodgings in London would give him more time for reading than if he had his family around him, like his fellows of the Company. Ben Jonson, who sat loosely to family ties, read even more.

We see that in every respect all through life William Shakespeare was a great one for making the most of his opportunities. When lodging in Silver Street with the Montjoys, we can see him making his way down Wood Street into Cheapside, to the bookstalls which then cluttered up St Paul's Churchyard. Earlier, while correcting proofs of *Venus and Adonis* at Richard Field's in Blackfriars, he read the pamphlets on French affairs which Field was turning out; for

* See my *The Elizabethan Renaissance. The Life of the Society*, 264–72.

133

the names prominent in them appear at once in *Love's Labour's Lost*. The French background of *All's Well* is not far removed from his residence with that French family in Silver Street. It may be no more than coincidence that the name of the French herald in *Henry V* is Montjoy. The dramatist may well have owed something of the French scenes in that play to converse with the family – he was on terms of confidence with Madame Montjoy, for whom he effected the betrothal of her daughter. (Nor is it remiss to recall that Field's interest in French affairs is understandable, since he had married the widow of the French printer, Vautrollier. These things connect up.)

Sir Thomas Elyot's *Book named the Governor* was a classic of Tudor political thinking, widely known and influential. Its influence is reflected at several places in the plays, notably in *Julius Caesar*, its ethical teaching as well as its political. Elyot was an Erasmian – and Erasmus was the chief schoolmaster of Tudor England, after Cicero. Erasmus was no less of an influence upon the English Church, with his Paraphrases and his work on the New Testament, in addition to his general position in favour of moderate reform, with not too much emphasis on sectarian doctrine. Elizabeth I was an entire Erasmian, so was her conception of the Church.

Such too was William Shakespeare's – decidedly un-Puritan, with no sympathy with the inveterate Puritan fixation on Calvinist dogma. He would have known Erasmus' schoolworks, in selection, from schooldays. Erasmus had translated Lucian's dialogue on Timon, though Painter also told Timon's story, and – with Shakespeare – we should always look to the nearer, not the remoter, source. He had also come upon material for his play *Timon* in Plutarch's life of Alcibiades, with which Timon's story was to have been more closely fused. Unfortunate as it is that this play was left unfinished, it is some compensation that from this fact we can detect Shakespeare's method of composition. He did not go straight forward from the beginning, but composed scenes as he visualised them separately – so like an actor – and sketched in the intervals in draft form. The dialogue between the Poet and the Painter owes something to Lyly's *Campaspe*, with all of whose work Shakespeare was familiar.

Pericles, it is well known, poses a difficult problem; for though the play was immensely popular (to Jonson's distaste), the text that has come down to us is most unsatisfactory – apparently a memorial reconstruction by the actors, in part. The announced printing of it in 1608 was probably thwarted by the plague of that year. At any rate the reading that went into it is clear: the story came from Apollonius of Tyre, which Shakespeare had known from earlier classical days, retold by Lawrence Twyne, a Fellow of All Souls, in his *Pattern of Painful Adventures*. Something of Pericles' adventures reflects those of Pyrocles in Sidney's *Arcadia*. Sidney's influence was of the first literary importance, more evident in the Sonnets – as setting a model which so many followed in the 1590s – than in the plays, though the blind Paphlagonian king is echoed in *King Lear*.

A good deal of reading went into *Othello*. The story came from Cinthio's *Hundred Tales*, of which a French version appeared in 1584 (the lodger could have met it at the Montjoys). The story also appeared in Fenton's translation of Bandello – which Shakespeare consulted. Sir Geoffrey Fenton had been one of the Sidney circle, one of the literary folk devoted to Sidney's sister, with her dominant interest in French literature and her translations from the language – through which Fenton's translation came. For Turkish details in the play Shakespeare was indebted to Knolles's *General History of the Turks* recently published (in 1604). For information about Venice he looked into Lewknor's book about foreign cities, published only a few years before, in 1600; and for African colouring the translation of Leo Africanus' *History* by that interesting man John Pory, the traveller, later Secretary to the Virginia Colony.

For his earlier Italian play, *Romeo and Juliet*, Shakespeare based himself largely upon Arthur Brooke's *Romeus and Juliet* – but what a lyrical poem he turned that pedestrian work into, a transformation! Painter had translated the story from the French of Belleforest. In the original, Mercutio was not involved in the duelling and brawls; in the play this is made a feature of his character. The difference is worth noting, since some have thought that Mercutio may carry some characteristics of Marlowe, the passionate addiction to friendship rather than to women, for one.

Military details in various plays are owed to pamphlets and tracts of the time stimulated by the long war. Sir Roger Williams's *Brief Discourse of War* is known to have been used. Shakespeare may well have met him, for he was an intimate follower of Essex, to whom he left his property when he died in 1595. This makes it not improbable that Williams was drawn upon for Captain Fluellen, for he was markedly Welsh and very much of a character. Sir John Smith's tract, *Observations and Orders Military*, came out in 1595, just in time for use in *Henry IV* and *Henry V*. I expect that Shakespeare also knew the military writings of the Diggeses, for he was friendly with the family; a junior member of it, Leonard Digges, wrote two of the poetic tributes to the dramatist's work after his death. No less than four members of this remarkable family were members of University College, Oxford.

The story of *Twelfth Night* came from Barnabe Rich's *Farewell to the Military Profession*: not a military work, though he was a soldier, but a collection of stories, where the dramatist found a suitable one in 'Apolonius and Silla'. We do not need to look further afield, as has frequently been done, to various Italian comedies; for, economical and practical as always, Shakespeare uses tricks that he had played before: identical twins from the *Errors* and sex-disguising from *The Two Gentlemen*.

Though the great heart of the playgoing public remained faithful to old favourites, swift changes of fashion also occurred, particularly with the new developments at Blackfriars. Shakespeare himself set a fashion for Roman plays with *Julius Caesar*. He obviously knew all Marlowe's work, including his translation of the first book of Lucan's *Pharsalia*. Florus' epitome of Livy's *History* he would have known from schooldays. He had used Livy earlier for *Lucrece*; and for *Coriolanus* he used the translation by Philemon Holland, which came out in 1600. Holland was the admirable 'Translator General' of the time, who translated also Suetonius, Ammianus, Xenophon, Plutarch's *Morals*, Camden's *Britannia* and Pliny's *Natural History*. The more exotic details of natural history Shakespeare gained from Pliny, whose work he would also have known in epitome from school, in the usual way.

From the time of the new development at Blackfriars a taste

for historical romance developed, or romantic plays with a flavouring of history: a taste for which the master provided *Cymbeline*. He drew on a new contribution by Thomas Higgins to the expanded *Mirror for Magistrates*, on Holinshed, the old romance, *Sir Bevis of Hampton*, a Boccaccio story, and an anonymous play, *Frederick of Jennen*. It makes a curious mixture: no wonder the play wanders more than a little. A great deal of reading was subsumed, or absorbed, more naturally, in *The Tempest*. From various references in the plays – to the icicle that hung on the Dutchman's beard (Barentz), the new map with the augmentation of the Indies, probably the masque of 'Russians' in *Love's Labour's Lost* and the Russian references in *Measure for Measure* – it is clear that the dramatist was alert to Hakluyt and the travel literature of the time.

The Tempest was suggested by William Strachey's account of the hurricane in which Gates's flagship, the *Sea Venture*, bound for Virginia, foundered on the coast of Bermuda: his letter came to Blackfriars, where he was well known. Other Virginia pamphlets may have provided material, as they had for the gold-digging mania that possessed the colonists, reflected in *Timon*. Shakespeare knew Richard Eden's translation of Peter Martyr's standard work on the New World, from which he took some names.

More important is what Shakespeare gathered from Florio's translation of Montaigne's *Essays*, of 1603. To Montaigne's essay on cannibals Shakespeare owed not only the name Caliban but also much of the atmosphere of primitivism he delineated along with him, as also the description of ideal communism in Gonzalo's 'commonwealth'. Though Montaigne was another kindred spirit in his humanity, scepticism and tolerance, it is significant that Shakespeare has no illusions about primitives in Caliban or about the efficacy of communism.

> No occupation; all men idle, all;
> And women too, but innocent and pure...
> All things in common nature should produce
> Without sweat or endeavour. Treason, felony,
> Sword, pike, knife, gun, or need of any engine
> Would I not have –

137

Soviet Russia offers a sufficient commentary on that idealistic nonsense. When Gonzalo goes on,

> But nature should bring forth
> Of its own kind, all foison, all abundance,
> To feed my innocent people.

Sebastian asks: 'No marrying among his subjects?' Shakespeare answers, in the voice of Antonio:

> None, man; all idle; whores and knaves.

The idealist goes on, incorrigible as idealists are:

> I would with such perfection govern, sir,
> To excel the golden age.

We may see the golden age exemplified in Soviet Russia. William Shakespeare suffered from no illusions about people: he knew human nature for what it is.

With this from Florio's Montaigne – Montaigne and Florio were both half-Jewish, which fact probably drew Florio to translate him – the wheel comes full circle; for Shakespeare had been associated with Florio from early days in the service of Southampton. Florio was his Italian tutor, a ready bridge to Italian culture – and Emilia Bassano was half Italian, both musical and literary.

Though the picture of Shakespeare's reading cannot in the nature of things be complete – I have dealt in an earlier chapter with his constant resort to Bible and Prayer Book – we may say that we have a representative picture of it. On the other hand, we must be on guard against assuming that he read 'only those contemporary works from which he intended to take the plots of his plays. It is hardly too much to credit him with taking a general interest in the thought of his day.'* This is obvious from his familiarity with Renaissance psychology – such books as Timothy Bright's *Treatise of Melancholy*, Thomas Wright's *Passions of the Mind*, Hakluyt or Montaigne's *Essays* – all of which he read, though he was unlikely to get a play out of any of them.

* J.B. Bamborough, *The Little World of Man*, 148.

8

Politics and Society

NINETEENTH-CENTURY criticism and appreciation concentrated largely on Shakespeare's characters – understandably, for he provides a wider range of these and greater diversity than any other writer. In our revolutionary century, in which the foundations of societies all round the world have been frequently shaken and undermined, we have come to appreciate the firmness and truth of his understanding of politics and government, the crucial necessity of order – a concern which also bespeaks his humanity and hatred of cruelty; for the disturbance of social order, its breakdown in civil war or revolution, incurs all the more bloodshed and suffering for people.

The extent of this concern, which recurs frequently in his work, the solidity of his depiction, the penetration of his understanding in these matters, constitute something quite exceptional. One does not find anything like it in any other of the dramatists. Marlowe did not have it – naturally enough: as a homosexual, a non-family man, he was not grafted into society and had no such concern for social responsibility. Nor had Ben Jonson, who was more concerned to criticise and satirise. Shakespeare's situation was more conventional and conformist. He was the son of a Stratford alderman who spent much time on the town's affairs, to the neglect of his own, and of good family on his mother's side. Everything shows that he was keen to rehabilitate the family in his native town. This he accomplished: his daughter Susanna and her husband, Dr Hall, were leading figures occupying the big house; his granddaughter Elizabeth, a titled lady, Lady Barnard.

William Shakespeare, like most Elizabethans, was socially a conservative. Naturally enough again – for the age was filled with the alarms and excursions of civil war abroad. France and the Netherlands were torn in two by their religious and civil wars. The sixteenth century never forgot the threat to society of the Peasants' Revolt in Germany, with its sequel in the fantastic episode of communist anarchism in Münster. England under Elizabeth I was fortunate, and people knew how fortunate they were. Even so the Northern Rebellion of 1569 gave them a shock – at Stratford the town sent its recruits north, and was at charge to equip them for service. The keying-up of the whole country to resist the Armada was a different matter – an inspiration to national unity.

Patriotism is much to the fore in those early years after the Armada; that and the insistence on national unity helped to make for the success of the history plays. Love of country and pride in its achievement in successfully resisting the might of Spain, with the resources of its world empire, are expressed in passages which have become famous but bear their date and the circumstances of the time:

> This fortress built by nature for herself...
> This precious stone set in the silver sea,
> Which serves it in the office of a wall,
> Or as a moat defensive to a house,
> Against the envy of less happier lands.

They had indeed reason to think that, with their nearest neighbours, France and the Netherlands, devastated; nor could Scotland or Ireland be described as happy.

The moral was drawn in another well-known passage, the final words of *King John*:

> This England never did, nor never shall,
> Lie at the proud foot of a conqueror,
> But when it first did help to wound itself –

i.e. by disunity and dissension.

> Nought shall make us rue,
> If England to itself do rest but true.

The message is carried over into the most patriotic of all the plays, which continued to inspire as recently as the liberation of Europe from the Germans: D-Day 1944 put many of us in mind of Henry V's speech before Agincourt:

> This day is called the feast of Crispian:
> He that outlives this day, and comes safe home,

Will stand a-tiptoe when this day is named ...
He that shall live this day, and see old age,
Will yearly on the vigil feast his neighbours,
And say, 'Tomorrow is Saint Crispian.'

As the war with Spain dragged on for some twenty years, disillusionment set in and questioning began; the inspiration of Armada days was lost, the patriotic note no longer heard. But in Shakespeare's last play, when the age was over of which in time to come he would be regarded as the chief ornament, he paid tribute to it in the form of prophecy at the infant Elizabeth's baptism:

she shall be ...
A pattern to all princes living with her,
And all that shall succeed ...
She shall be loved and feared; her own shall bless her;
Her foes shake like a field of beaten corn....
In her days every man shall eat in safety
Under his own vine what he plants, and sing
The merry songs of peace to all his neighbours.

That is, internal peace would be maintained, of which the condition was national unity. Such was the consistent message, the consequence – 'they are a people such that mend upon the world'.

The inveterate ambitions of politicians are portrayed in all these plays: in *1 Henry VI* the main conflict was between the popular Humphrey Duke of Gloucester – 'good Duke Humphrey' in the people's eyes – and the politic Cardinal Beaufort, who favoured peace with France. The latter was unpopular and is unfavourably depicted; Duke Humphrey was sabotaged by his wife, who went in for sorcery, was made to do public penance and exiled. Those were medieval times, but politicians since then have been known to give their women as hostages to fortune.

The *locus classicus* for political ambition is the long speech of Richard of Gloucester forecasting the future for himself, which ends with the Marlovian lines, promising that he will

set the murderous Machiavel to school.
Can I do this, and cannot get a crown?

There stood between him and the crown the rightful king, Henry VI, and his son Edward, Prince of Wales, both Richard's brothers, Edward IV and Clarence, and their sons. Henry, his son, and Clarence had already been disposed of when Edward IV unexpectedly died. Politicians must make the most of the opportunities that befall them; but, though it was the regular thing in the Wars of the Roses to kill one's male opponents, it was not done to kill women or children. The latter was what turned the country's stomach against Richard III.

Political ambition, if of a less murderous kind, is again portrayed in Hotspur, its epitaph spoken by Prince Hal:

> Ill-weaved ambition, how much art thou shrunk!
> When that this body did contain a spirit,
> A kingdom for it was too small a bound;
> But now, two paces of the vilest earth
> Is room enough.

The motives of the holy fool of a clergyman, Archbishop Scrope, for joining in rebellion are not very clear; he paid the price – and in consequence was venerated by the people as a martyr. In these circumstances it is rather ironical, in a moment of truth, that the Archbishop should thus characterise them:

> An habitation giddy and unsure
> Hath he that buildeth on the vulgar heart.
> O thou fond [foolish] many, with what loud applause
> Didst thou beat heaven with blessing Bolingbroke
> Before he was what thou wouldst have him be.

But of course. When Oliver Cromwell was setting forth to subdue Scotland cheered by the populace, he commented to his companion that they would cheer as loudly if they were on their way to be hanged – 'to be baited with the rabble's curse', Shakespeare put it.

He penetrated to the essence of the leader of the Welsh resistance, Glendower, who had something of the *mage* about him. He possessed undoubted charisma such as the leader of a people fighting for existence needs to have. This was a factor in their devotion to him and their undying memory of him (anyway, for centuries afterwards – one can hardly expect a demotic society to remember anything of value out of the past). Shakespeare's treatment of the Welsh is markedly sympathetic, of the Irish not – but that was usual with Elizabethans and in accordance with their experience.

The word 'politician' had disagreeable connotations to Elizabethans: they meant by it what we should mean by Machiavellian, an intriguer, someone on the make at all costs. And Shakespeare's idea is in keeping: 'Am I politic? am I subtle? am I a Machiavel?' A servant of Timon's, confronted by the meanness of one of the lordly flatterers who refuse to come to Timon's help when he had been so generous to them, comments: 'The devil knew not what he did when he made man politic – he crossed himself by it.' King Lear, forced to learn the facts of life by adversity, says with bitterness to the blinded Gloucester:

> Get thee glass eyes,
> And, like a scurvy politician, seem
> To see the things thou dost not.

Honest Sir Andrew Aguecheek hates 'policy: I had as lief be a Brownist as a politician'. We can appreciate what a hateful alternative a Puritan would be to such merry men as he and Sir Toby Belch.

We have seen from Shakespeare's trope on Commodity, the bias of the world, his observance of political expediency and how it operated. Francis Bacon said contemporaneously: 'All rising to great place is by a winding stair' – as he knew from his own experience – 'and it is sometimes base, and by indignities men come to dignities. The standing is slippery, and the regress is either a downfall, or at least an eclipse.' He himself experienced all of these; he also said that there was little friendship between men at the top. Ben Jonson said of Robert Cecil, the ablest politician of them all, that he 'never cared for any man longer than he can make use of him'.

Shakespeare sums up as pithily from his own observation:

> the art o' the Court –
> As hard to leave as keep: whose top to climb
> Is certain falling: or so slippery that
> The fear's as bad as falling.

The modes and habits of the denizens of the Court are as clearly seen by the sharp eyes of the uncommitted observer:

> 'Tis certain greatness, once fallen out with fortune,
> Must fall out with men too. What the declined is
> He shall as soon read in the eyes of others
> As feel in his own fall. For men, like butterflies,
> Show not their mealy wings but to the summer...

And then, when fortune fails them,

> when they fall, as being slippery standers,
> The love that leaned on them as slippery too,
> Doth one pluck down another and together
> Die in the fall.

So much for political friendship; it is even more bitterly expressed, as Shakespeare grew older, in *Coriolanus*:

> O world, thy slippery turns! Friends now fast sworn,
> Whose double bosoms seem to wear one heart...
> Unseparable, shall within this hour,
> On a dissension of a doit, break out
> To bitterest enmity.

Since this is what one finds at the top, one can hardly expect to find better at the bottom.

William Shakespeare's opinion of the people in the mass is uniformly unfavourable. One could say that his was an upper-class view, except that it was that generally held by Elizabethans. The commons are fair game to provoke mirth, and so they are used from the first. As early as *Henry VI* we have Jack Cade's rebels, exchanging wisdom one with another:

> O miserable age! Virtue is not regarded in handicrafts men.
> The nobility think scorn to go in leather aprons.
> Nay, more, the king's Council are no good workmen.
> True; and yet it is said, 'Labour in thy vocation'; which is as much to say as, 'Let the magistrates by labouring men'; and therefore should we be magistrates.
> Thou hast hit it; for there's no better sign of a brave mind than a hard hand.

And so on.

Jack Cade, however, was no laughing matter: he meant business, like the revolting peasants of 1381 who burned down

John of Gaunt's palace of the Savoy, with all its treasures of tapestry, furniture, books and illuminated manuscripts. Cade and his followers got as near as London Bridge to sacking the City. Perhaps it was understandable that these rebels, like the Peasants before them, should make bonfires of legal records, for they symbolised their servitude; but they were in any case enemies of learning and cultivation. 'Thou hast most traitorously corrupted the youth of the realm in erecting a grammar school; and whereas, before, our forefathers had no other books but the score and the tally, thou hast caused printing to be used ...' A great deal of fun is made of this. However, it was not all fun. The rebels got hold of the Lord Treasurer, Lord Saye and Sele. 'Away with him! He has a familiar under his tongue: he speaks not a' God's name. Go, take him away, I say, and strike off his head presently [instantly]. And then break into his son-in-law's house, Sir James Cromer, and strike off his head, and bring them both upon two poles hither.' And so they did. 'The proudest peer in the realm shall not wear a head on his shoulders unless he pay me tribute. Men shall hold of me *in capite* [by the head, i.e. as tenants]; and we charge and command that their wives be as free as heart can wish or tongue can tell.'

Social disturbance was the concomitant of weak government. When the forces of order gathered strength and regained the initiative, the name of the mighty Henry V was enough to daunt the rebels: 'Only my followers' base and ignominious treason makes me betake me to my heels,' said Cade. He was a stout fellow, but like all such stout fellows was undermined by the appeal to order, the *mystique* of the King's name, and deserted by his followers. In his estimation of them he is at one with the King: 'Was ever feather so lightly blown to and fro as this multitude?'

This is the same image that Henry uses, when he has been found wandering on the Borders betrayed by two keepers. They had sworn oaths to him as king:

> I was anointed king at nine months old;
> My father and my grandfather were kings –

nevertheless, the keepers proposed to break their oaths, like a great many more important persons. Why? They have their answer:

For we were subjects but while you were king.

This is the ordinary person's answer to all the boloney of political theories, rights and duties, divine or otherwise: power is what ultimately counts in politics. In the dazed and confused 1930s much nonsense was talked by idealists and doctrinaires about, and against, 'power-politics'. What was their alternative, 'weakness-politics'? Apparently so, for it was to that that they succumbed – like Henry VI.

In 1593, as at some other times during Elizabeth's reign, agitation mounted against immigrants, mainly from the Netherlands and France. These were useful immigrants, bringing in higher skills in various trades, particularly the woollen industry, sail-making, printing, glass- and paper-making, along with their capital. They increased the wealth of the country, made admirable citizens in the areas where they settled, especially East Anglia, Kent, Sussex and London, and the government wisely encouraged immigrants of that sort. The ignorant people objected and made riots, as in London on 'Evil Mayday' in 1516, when it fell to Sir Thomas More as sheriff to deal with it.

This suggested a play on More to a group of dramatists who collaborated on it, and Shakespeare was called in to handle the awkward riot-scenes. This he did with his usual aplomb; but the subject was too ticklish to be permitted on the stage, any more than it would be today, and it was censored. Shakespeare's scenes exhibit his characteristic combination of comedy at the expense of the people, with the assertion of authority and due obedience. One sees that *he* never gave any trouble to the government, as other dramatists did, even though the deposition scene of *Richard II* was not allowed to be printed until James I was safely on the throne.

One wiseacre objects against the immigrants: 'Our country is a great eating country; argo [ergo], they eat more in our country than they do in their own.' Another objects: 'They bring in strange roots, which is merely to the undoing of poor prentices, for what's a sorry parsnip to a good heart?' Parsnips were just being introduced from abroad. Venereal diseases were becoming more prevalent, and immigrants were held responsible by uninstructed persons: syphilis was known as the French disease; the plays have numerous references to it.

Shakespeare's answer to the rioters was what his argument against social disorder constantly reiterated: it had worse consequences:

> For other ruffians as their fancies wrought,
> With self-same hand, self reasons and self right,
> Would shark on you, and men like ravenous fishes
> Would feed on one another.

Their duty was obedience to lawful authority – in their own interest and in the interest of humanity:

> What would you think
> To be thus used? This is the stranger's [foreigner's] case
> And this your mountainish [barbarous] inhumanity.

The mutability of the mob is more fully portrayed in *Julius Caesar* and again in *Coriolanus*, where in both the citizens of Rome form practically a character in the action, appropriately for its history. In the first scene the people are out in the streets to celebrate Caesar's victory over Pompey and cheer the great man, though they had often enough done the same for Pompey. For this they are rated by an aristocrat, though one hardly sees why – with them anything for a day off work!

> And do you now put on your best attire?
> And do you now cull out a holiday?
> And do you now strew flowers in his way
> That comes in triumph over Pompey's blood?

One can hardly blame them for their lack of concern about the conflicts of their betters.

Nor would one blame them for their sycophancy towards the winner: they have to live, and the grandees are no better. Cassius is motivated by sheer envy of Caesar – a familiar feature in politicians – but he at least has no illusions, which means that he has better judgment than the doctrinaire Brutus, with his fixation on liberty. (To a visiting European Communist who ventured to think that perhaps there was insufficient liberty in Soviet Russia, Lenin replied: 'Liberty? What for?') The people's attitude towards liberty is realistically depicted in the famous Forum scene, where Mark Antony twists the mob round his finger with his emotional oratory.

Brutus, like the noble mind we are constantly reminded he is (historically, he was a great reader), appeals to their reason. 'Censure me in your wisdom, and wake your senses, that you may the better judge.' He gets what he deserves: they have no understanding of his appeal to principle, and respond with, 'Let him be Caesar!' That should have taught him; but such idealists are unteachable: Brutus never did learn, up to the end. One can sympathise more with the mob, rather than with such a type, who had had all the benefits of education, culture, aristocratic upbringing, the personal favour of Caesar, etc.

What one cannot sympathise with is the mob's credulity, their falling as suckers for the sob-stuff ladled out by Mark Antony – he was well known in ancient Rome for his 'Asiatic', i.e. flowery, oratory. 'Poor soul! his eyes are red as fire with weeping,' says a common man. He makes no fatuous appeal to reason: he goes straight to their emotions, plays upon them, arouses their sympathy for the murdered leader, rubs in Caesar's generosity towards them – 'bread and circuses' – reveals to them his intention of further largesse by his will, and so stimulates their cupidity. That settles them against the conspirators and turns the tide.

The result is what might have been expected: Rome was divided in two by a long civil war, until the cool and politic Octavian eventually won and imposed his Augustan peace – under an empire in fact. No people's party could rule an empire – no democracy can. Meanwhile the good citizens of Rome ran amok. They took to fire and slaughter, and killed Cinna the poet by mistake because he had the same name as Cinna the conspirator. Never mind: what matter? We are treated to a mob lynching, not unknown in democracies. So much for Brutus' rule of reason. I detest such types in politics: they probably do more harm then real cynics. At any rate they open the way to them – like the ineffective liberals of the Weimar Republic dealing with Hitler.

Shakespeare's view of the mob is no less unfavourable in *Coriolanus* – in fact it has hardened with the years. It was not objected to in his own time, for it was what everybody thought

– everybody who had a mind to think with. I do not recall any democratic sympathies expressed in the Elizabethan age; and, though Shakespeare would have been the last man to express them, he was not singular in his attitude. Once more he was in keeping with the general opinion.

The tragedy of Coriolanus is that of a leader whose nature is in conflict with his people: he stands out by his eminent services to the state, which he has saved in war. He is a soldier and a patrician; we might say – as used to be said of Churchill – that he was the man to lead in war, but not in peace. (Similarly, after his eminent services to his people in the war, Churchill was as resoundingly turned down in 1945 – and much resented it.)

Shakespeare says less for the people than might be said for them; after all, they were suffering from dearth of corn, even if their idea of remedying it – by confiscating stocks – was wrong. (The people, given their head, will eat the very seed-corn; during the appalling communisation of agriculture in Soviet Russia, for which millions died, the peasants slaughtered their cattle on a vast scale, and consumed corn stocks necessary for sowing, rather than yield them up to the Party bureauc-racy.) *Coriolanus* is a play that has a lot to say to us today, perhaps not so much in its main theme as in the penetrating reflections Shakespeare makes in dealing with it.

The main theme is curiously topical today, more so than in the Elizabethan age, when elections were confined to a small number of people in the boroughs and not a wide franchise in the counties. Since Coriolanus stands out by his capacity for leadership in war, he is pressed to stand for election, especially by that Roman matron, his mother. (Essex had been pushed on by two beautiful but intolerable women, his mother – whom Elizabeth I detested – and his sister, Penelope Rich, Sidney's 'Stella'.) But Coriolanus has not got the qualities that make for electoral success: he cannot and will not talk humbug; he will make no concessions to the people, or only with obvious disgust. So far from commanding popularity, he prefers unpopularity. In that case, he should not have submitted himself for popular election. We must blame him, as Shake-speare does not; something is to be said for the people: they must have something in return for their votes – if only the kisses with which the beautiful Georgiana, Duchess of Devonshire, rewarded electors in the celebrated Westminster election, when a gallant Irishman said that he could light his pipe at her eyes.

Coriolanus asks for a rebuff in submitting himself to popular election – not so much because of his view of the people, for many (perhaps most) successful politicians share it – but because of the uncompromising candour with which he expresses his contempt. He is a man of integrity – of excessive integrity for a politician – and will not lower himself to 'a most inherent baseness'. We, in democratic days, should be able to understand the situation. Shakespeare sums up in the words of an officer of the Senate, as it might be a Parliamentary observer: 'There have been many great men that have flattered the people, who ne'er loved them; and there be many that they have loved, they know not wherefore: so that if they love they know not why, they hate upon no better a ground.'

Coriolanus was rejected and driven into exile with the enemies of Rome. He has a consuming love for Rome; rejection, with such a man, turns to passionate hatred. He wants to destroy what he loves and burn Rome – a penetrating intuition on Shakespeare's part, in keeping with modern psychological findings (I know that impulse). Coriolanus is betrayed by his one weakness, his love for his mother, who prevails upon him not to destroy his native city which had had the ingratitude, the insolence, to reject him (one rather wishes that he had: that would have taught them).

All this might be thought remote from the actualities of politics. It is not. It is more or less what Hitler did do, in the deliberate *Götterdämmerung* he brought down upon Germany in his defeat. He too had a Coriolanus-like arrogance and contempt for humanity in the mass.

Shakespeare's play is no less topical in its reflections on society, for they are of perennial relevance, a society

> where gentry, title, wisdom
> Cannot but conclude but by the Yea and No
> Of general ignorance – it must omit
> Real necessities.

We see that today in democracies that will not think of their long-term interest, but simply in terms of present consumption – of petrol, in the United States and Canada, for example. In consequence, such societies will not think ahead, as authoritarian societies do, to effective purpose. With democratic, consumers' societies

> Purpose so barred, it follows
> Nothing is done to purpose.

This is all too true, and with such societies it is regarded as eccentric, if not worse, to question their arrangements,

> And manhood is called foolery when it stands
> Against a falling fabric.

Shakespeare's views on society are to be read throughout his plays, but are perhaps at their most conveniently concentrated in his satirical comedy, *Troilus and Cressida*. Behind this is the bitter faction-fighting of Elizabeth I's last years and the disaster that overwhelmed the popular hero, Essex, which the dramatist observed from close at hand. He specifically condemns, in his own words, 'fools on both sides'. We need not subscribe to that: actually the Queen and her government were in the right, as against Essex, Southampton and their gang. Shakespeare's personal affections were, however, with them; nothing could be more embittering than the irresponsible foolery of his friends, for his head told him that authority was in the right. This added to the tension and the edginess obvious in the play – and perhaps to the urgency with which he speaks out about the necessity of order in society.

After all, he had said the same thing consistently from the beginning. The main theme is disillusionment with both love and war; we need not enter into those here, though the reflections on war have their relevance. The war with Spain had been going on too long, and had fought itself to a standstill. The heroic period of the Armada years, which had been such an inspiration earlier, was long over; the war had entered into a static phase (like the Trojan war in the play), though peace was not yet in view.

Reflections on society, its nature and exigencies, are put in the famous speeches of the wise Ulysses, who sees things rather from the outside. The prime necessity, the very condition by which civilised life exists, is order:

> The heavens themselves, the plants and this centre,
> Observe degree, priority, and place;

and when order is undermined, society is shaken, all 'enterprise is sick'. We see that borne out today. A society that is organised vertically is naturally more efficient, because it gives direction – without which ordinary folk cannot operate – and stimulates incentive. Damage the working of incentive, and it eats through a society like a fungus, consuming its heart-strings. Nor is it efficient to organise society horizontally, as Communist countries have found from experience: it does not work. Any more than a wall made up of thousands of pebbles of equal size can be expected to stand up as well as one of stones of different shapes and sizes. The Cotswold dry-walling familiar to Shakespeare will stand up even without cement.

Shakespeare goes deeper. He feared, as the sixteenth century did, that the undermining of order would lead to the dissolution of society. Terrible things were happening outside happy England. Considerable areas of France were devastated by the prolonged civil wars; so too with the Netherlands: Antwerp lost many thousands of its citizens in and after the Spanish Fury of 1576, and never recovered its primacy. Spain itself was impoverished and exhausted, in spite of the precious metals from America. Undermine order, take away degree and differences of function, level everything down – and brute force prevails, no justice or right, no cultivation or much that deserves to be called civilised society. (Shostakovich did not regard Soviet Russia, under 'the extermination machine', as a civilised society.)

> Then everything includes itself in power,
> Power into will, will into appetite;
> And appetite, an universal wolf,
> So doubly seconded with will and power,
> Must make perforce an universal prey,
> And last eat up itself.

How relevant Shakespeare is to our revolutionary time! Revolutions have a way of eating themselves up, and revolutionaries each other, when societies are reduced to the naked struggle for power. I do not suppose that Hitler or Stalin cared much for anything other than power. It is symptomatic that when Stalin was embarking on his last murderous purge, beginning with Jewish doctors, he took to drawing wolves again. Shakespeare's imagery is infallible.

Egalitarian society releases envy to a notorious degree. In an hierarchical society people know their place and are less uneasy, not for ever worrying about their status or looking over their shoulders at the next man, wage-rates, hours of work, or whatever. Shakespeare expresses something of this in

> So every step
> Exampled by the first pace that is sick
> Of his superior, grows to an envious fever
> Of pale and bloodless emulation.

Actually he has his own conception of equality, that which is held by all the best people: not one determined by social status or external rank but by the inherent quality of the man or woman. This is the theme of *All's Well*, where the Count, who refuses to marry a deserving woman because she is beneath him socially, is shown up and exposed. Shakespeare's conviction is this:

> From lowest place when virtuous things proceed,
> The place is dignified by the doer's deed.
> Where great additions swell us and virtue none,
> It is a dropsied honour....
>
>> Honours thrive
> When rather from our acts we them derive
> Than our foregoers.

And that obviously spoke for himself, *Non sans droit*!

9

Contemporary Life

THE whole of Elizabethan life is portrayed in Shakespeare's plays, with one large and important exception. That was religion, with its disputes and controversies, which filled such a part in public life and the time with sound and fury. This kind of thing was not permitted on the stage – a merciful relief; one certainly doesn't miss it. Nor was it the kind of thing that appealed to the mind of William Shakespeare, sensible man, any more than it did to the Queen. For the rest we have the entire spectrum of contemporary life, from the Court at the top, through country and town life, that of the City of London, down to brothel and prison at the bottom. No one but an actor could have compassed it so well, with his opportunities of looking in on every kind of life, the country at his feet when on tour, and to all of it he gave the form and pressure of the time.

Many plays have Court-life as their background, not only the historical plays where it is a main subject. We are not here concerned with the political role of the Court, though then it was the centre of government, the plane upon which the national life was most intensely projected and as highly lighted as any stage. Several kinds of Court are illustrated, ducal as well as royal; they range from the melancholy charm of the Duke's in *Twelfth Night* to the sinister horror of *Macbeth*. The most brilliant and telling depiction is in *Hamlet*, in which one see the falseness, the insincerities and treacheries underlying the external glamour; but we find also faithful friendship and love, the amusements of plays and tourneys, betting and gaming, if turned to sinister purpose.

One characteristic all Courts shared – envy. Since they were the centre of power and life was competitive, Shakespeare's observation was much to the point: the 'envious Court'. He frequently contrasts the dubious sophistication of Court life with the kindly simplicity of the pastoral, of shepherds and country folk, from *Henry VI* at the beginning to the end. Never more fully than in *As You Like It* with its autobiographical touches – life in the forest of Arden: 'Are not these woods more free from peril than the envious Court?' The Court jester, Touchstone, was a privileged person who could say what he liked – as Tarleton, most famous of Elizabethan clowns, had been privileged to say to the Queen's face things no one else would have dared to do.

Touchstone and a country shepherd put the opposing points to be made. 'If thou never wast at Court, thou never sawest good manners.' Well, 'those that are good manners at Court are as ridiculous in the country as the behaviour of the country is most mockable at the Court. You told me you salute [kiss] not at the Court, but you kiss your hands.' Courtiers' hands were perfumed with civet – 'the very uncleanly flux of a cat'. The Queen was highly sensitive to smells – as Shakespeare became, it has been noted from his imagery, after his introduction into the Southampton circle.

Naturally, sophisticated courtiers could appreciate jokes at their own (and others') expense, and quite a bit of fun is deliberately aimed at a Court audience. Autolycus the thief puts on Court airs to bemuse the shepherd: 'Seest thou not the air of the Court in these enfoldings? Hath not my gait in it the measure of the Court? Receives not thy nose Court-odour from me? Reflect I not on thy baseness Court-contempt?' It is given to a jester again to jest with the Countess of Rosillion: 'Truly, madam, if God have lent a man any manners he may easily put it off at Court. He that cannot make a leg, put off his cap, kiss his hand, and say nothing has neither legs, hands, lip, nor cap; and indeed such a fellow, to say precisely, were not for the Court.'

Life was apt to be empty for hangers-on who had not a post or a job to perform, as opposed to busy ministers like Robert Cecil, Secretary of State, observed going in to the Queen, his arms full of papers and documents. The hours were filled up with 'quarrels, talk, and tailors' – like the quarrels in the Presence Chamber and on the tennis court with which Southampton won the Queen's disfavour. There were also 'mirthful comic shows, such as befits the pleasure of the Court', especially the plays which filled the holidays from Christmas eve to

Twelfth-night, and again at Shrove-tide. Tournaments and jousts celebrated the Queen's Accession day. Flattery was the familiar language, 'Court holy water', and all round the Queen the language of love and adulation: Cynthia, 'the mortal moon', the 'terrene' moon, 'dear empress of my heart', the 'fair vestal throned', etc.

Artistic patronage was a feature. Lord Chamberlain Hunsdon had his players and musicians (as well as a musical mistress), and was the poet Warner's patron. Leicester and Essex had a much wider field of patronage; Southampton followed in their footsteps with his poet and dramatist. Sir Thomas Walsingham befriended Marlowe, who was aiming higher at Southampton when he threw his life away.

The insincere side of patronage is caricatured later in *Timon*. A poet and a painter attend upon him in his waiting-room:

PAINTER: You are rapt, sir, in some work, some dedication
To the great lord?

POET: A thing slipped idly from me.
...What have you there?

PAINTER: A picture, sir. When comes your book forth?

POET: Upon the heels of my presentment [presentation], sir.
Let's see your piece...
                                        Admirable. How this grace
Speaks his own standing! What a mental power
This eye shoots forth! How big imagination
Moves in this lip!

PAINTER: It is a pretty mocking of the life.
Here is a touch; is 't good?

POET: I will say of it
It tutors nature. Artificial [artistic] strife
Lives in these touches, livelier than life...

PAINTER: How this lord is followed!

We discern a good deal in those exchanges: the artistic doctrine of the time, which Shakespeare held, that art should follow nature; the pressure of needy artists upon noble persons for their patronage; the bogus modesty of some about their work, the mutual flattery.

Some judicious flattery necessarily entered into Shakespeare's relationship with his patron; and it was not without its tedium at times. It is expressed in the Sonnets, which are, we must always remember, essentially patronage poems, addressed by poet to patron:

> Being your slave, what should I do but tend
> Upon the hours and times of your desire?
> I have no precious time at all to spend,
> Nor services to do, till you require.
> Nor dare I chide the world-without-end hour
> Whilst I, my sovereign, watch the clock for you,
> Nor think the bitterness of absence sour,
> When you have bid your servant once adieu....

As usual with Shakespeare *every*thing is put to the service of his writing: all of life is in it, his dependence during those plague years, his having to wait about, though Heaven forfend

> I should in thought control your times of pleasure...
> Being your vassal, bound to stay your leisure!
> ...being at your beck,

he is ready to 'bide each check', with 'patience, tame to sufferance'.

Soon, the formation of the Lord Chamberlain's Company gave him independence and security. This then took up all his time, so that he now has to accuse himself of neglecting Southampton:

> Accuse me thus: that I have scanted all
> Wherein I should your great deserts repay;
> Forgot upon your dearest love to call,
> Whereto all bonds do tie me day by day.

He has 'frequent been with unknown minds' – naturally enough, for he was fully engaged in his occupation. The patronage episode, so important in his life and development – it may even have saved his life, as he avers, in those years of plague and crisis in his fortunes – was ending. Its nature is clearly summed up in its concluding sonnet:

> Were 't aught to me I bore the canopy,
> With my extern the outward honouring....

That means that his attitude to his young Lord had never been one of outward form, paying respect to the peer, the person of state; it was one of inner affection, 'obsequious in thy heart'. At its ending, he offered his 'oblation, poor but free', no art

> But mutual render, only me for thee.

Here was a real equality between the patron and his poet: that of love.

It was not altogether exceptional at the time. Shakespeare's fellow-Warwickshire man, Drayton, spent much of his life with his patrons, the Gooderes. Daniel was on kindly terms both at Wilton with the Pembrokes and with the Countess of Cumberland, who put up his monument we see in the church at Beckington in Somerset. Marlowe spent time with Sir Thomas Walsingham at Scadbury, and Jonson years with Sir Robert Cotton. Young Southampton's patronage came at the most opportune and needed time; then the theatre gave his poet the independence that was exceptional.

Italy set the model for Renaissance Europe in manners and fashions as well as in the arts. The northern nations were well aware of their backwardness in these matters, and sent hundreds of young gentlemen thither to school:

> Report of fashions in proud Italy,
> Whose manners still our tardy apish nation
> Limps after in base imitation.

This was not approved of by old-fashioned persons like Lord Burghley or Roger Ascham, who feared the effects of Italian sophistication upon the young men's religion and morals – and, indeed, it had some scandalous effects, witness the career of Burghley's son-in-law, the Earl of Oxford.*

The objects of foreign travel were familiar:

> Some to the wars to try their fortune there,
> Some to discover islands far away,
> Some to the studious universities.

The young men were encouraged to take note of 'any rare noteworthy object in their travel'; or departed

> Rash, inconsiderate, fiery voluntaries,
> With ladies' faces and fierce dragons' spleens –

* See my *The Elizabethan Renaissance. The Life of the Society*, 160.

Have sold their fortunes at their native homes,
Bearing their birthrights proudly on their backs.

It was a commonplace of the time, when upper-class clothing
was so gorgeous and so expensive, that often men bore whole
manors on their backs. When they returned it was to be
expected that they would 'lisp and wear strange suits, disable
the benefits of your own country ... or I will scarce think you
have swam in a gondola'. One detects a certain home-keeping
prejudice in that; it is fairly clear that the circumstances of
Shakespeare's life kept him at home.

The time was full of wars and rumours of wars abroad;
hence war in various aspects and soldiers of different sorts
recur, even apart from the historical events that are the subject
of the earlier plays.

Now thrive the armourers, and honour's thought
Reigns solely in the breast of every man.
They sell the pasture now to buy the horse.

We hear of the armourers again:

The armourers, accomplishing the knights –

'accomplishing'!, a very Shakespeare word –

With busy hammers closing rivets up,
Give dreadful note of preparation.

The armourers were located in the eastern part of the City,
where the Tower was the main arsenal of the nation. 'I'll to
the Tower with all the haste I can, to view the artillery.' The
later Artillery Yard lay out beyond Bishopsgate. Drilling and
mustering took place in St George's Field, where Justice
Shallow as a lad lay all night in the windmill; or at Mile End,
where the little quiver fellow was very good at managing his
piece, with a 'Ra-ta-ta'. Or there was the archer who could
'clap in the clout', i.e. hit the mark, 'at twelve score, and
carried you a forehand shaft a fourteen and fourteen and a
half'. Archery was encouraged, even enforced, in early Elizabethan days, before war became modernised with improvements in gunnery and artillery.

The war in the Netherlands was a hard slog for decades, in
the course of which the English learned the art of modern

warfare, particularly infantry discipline, from the Spaniards. Essex's youthful expedition to Normandy in 1591, to help Henry of Navarre, was another matter: it was hardly serious, as the Queen complained – an exhibition of foolhardy gallantry in which his youthful following displayed themselves. Southampton ran away at seventeen to join him and was recalled. He was a spirited youth for all his feminine appearance, and showed that he never wanted courage. He was not like the young lord who displayed his 'silken dalliance' on the battlefield, though there were such:

> Came there a certain lord, neat and trimly dressed,
> Fresh as a bridegroom, and his chin new reaped
> Showed like a stubble land at harvest home –

there speaks Shakespeare the countryman.

> He was perfumèd like a milliner,
> And twixt his finger and his thumb he held
> A pouncet box, which ever and anon
> He gave his nose, and took 't away again.

It is a speaking likeness of someone Shakespeare had observed, always watching men's 'humours' as John Aubrey had heard.

> He made me mad
> To see him shine so brisk, and smell so sweet,
> And talk so like a waiting gentlewoman
> Of guns and drums and wounds...
> And telling me the sovereignest thing on earth
> Was parmaceti for an inward bruise;
> And that it was great pity, so it was,
> This villainous saltpetre should be digged
> Out of the bowels of the earth –

to destroy many a good tall fellow by 'these vile guns'. Saltpetre was a constituent of gunpowder; the government awarded patents for its production.

Serious-minded professional soldiers are portrayed in the Welsh, Scotch and Irish captains, Fluellen, Jamy and Macmorris; they are given their respective lingos, and Fluellen was well up in the disciplines of war, familiar even with ancient Roman practice. The seamy side of war was more actual to William Shakespeare; this would have been borne home to him in the streets of London from the mid-nineties, with the wounded and crippled, the seedy and skulking, the ragtag and bobtail (or, as he said, the 'tag-rag') thronging town and country.

Here they are, swashbucklers and camp-followers:

Bardolph, he is white-livered and red-faced; by the means whereof 'a faces it out, but fights not. Pistol, he hath a killing tongue, and a quiet sword; by the means whereof 'a breaks words, and keeps whole weapons. . . . They will steal anything, and call it purchase [i.e. prize]. Bardolph stole a lute-case, bore it twelve leagues, and sold it for three ha'pence –

just as the ordinary soldier's or sailor's way has always been with what they pick up. 'Nym and Bardolph are sworn brothers in filching, and in Calais they stole a fire-shovel.' Bardolph was to be hanged for robbing a church in France. Pistol would return:

To England will I steal, and there I'll – steal;
And patches will I get unto these cudgelled scars,
And swear I got them in the Gallia wars.

Plenty of such fellows were about in the later nineties.

Such a rogue now and then goes to the wars to grace himself at his return into London under the form of a soldier. And such fellows are perfect in the great commanders' names, and they will learn you by rote where services were done: at such and such a sconce, at such a breach, at such a convoy; who came off bravely, who was shot, who disgraced, what terms the enemy stood on. . . .

Shakespeare evidently observed this kind of thing with interest, for he repeats it in the person of the braggart Parolles, whom he makes the very type of it. 'Good sparks and lustrous, a word, good metals. You shall find in the regiment of the Spinii one Captain Spurio, with his cicatrice, an emblem of war, here on his sinister cheek; it was this very sword entrenched it. Say to him I live, and observe his reports for me.'

All's Well is not a popular play, but it is more revealing of contemporary life than most. It came at the end of Elizabeth's reign, after the Essex catastrophe, with Southampton condemned and in the Tower. This brought back Shakespeare's intimate involvement ten years before in trying to get the young lord properly married, and his refractoriness. Not only is this situation made the theme of the play, but more recent events are recognisably touched on in it. Youthful Count Bertram is made a general of horse – which was precisely what Essex made Southampton in Ireland, to the Queen's displeasure. In the play this was thought 'a charge too heavy' for the young Count, with his adolescent frame of mind – precisely what the Queen thought of the young Earl. Nevertheless Count Bertram did 'most honourable service', as Southampton had done in Ireland – to set against their faults. Count Bertram incurred the King's 'everlasting displeasure' in the play, as Southampton incurred the Queen's in real life. The Count's mother pleads for him,

> I beseech your majesty to make it
> Natural rebellion done i' th' blade of youth.

This was exactly the plea the old Countess, Southampton's mother, made for her son's life: it was his youth that made men pity him at his trial.

Count Bertram had his Parolles, who called him 'sweetheart'; Southampton had his braggadocio Captain, Piers Edmonds, with whom he would lie culling in his tent in Ireland. Shakespeare had observed from close at hand Southampton and his mother, the Countess, a charming woman like Bertram's mother, the Countess of Rosillion, both anxious to see their sons safely married and settled.

Ireland was a chronic headache to the Elizabethans, who could neither afford to let the island become a strategic threat, a base for the Spaniards, nor be expected to sympathise with a pre-medieval, Celtic culture breaking down in chaos and decay. The Elizabethans were shocked by it, and could not understand why the green island could not become a settled country like England, with squires and villages, tenant farmers, farms and orchards – progressive, if not Protestant. Shakespeare was not involved in the mess, as Spenser intimately – and in the end, tragically – was. And his point of view was that of the ordinary Englishman of the time. When Essex went over in 1599 to quell the Ulster resistance, Shakespeare wished, like everybody else –

Were now the General of our gracious Empress –
As in good time he may – from Ireland coming,
Bringing rebellion broachèd on his sword,
How many would the peaceful City quit
To welcome him!

They had gone out in their hundreds to give him a good send-off – Simon Forman, one of them, describes it. In fact, the General made a disastrous failure – and no more characteristics of his are favourably reflected.

Earlier characteristics are described with sympathy: 'his courtship to the common people' was 'observed',

How he did seem to dive into their hearts
With humble and familiar courtesy...
Wooing poor craftsmen with the craft of smiles...
Off goes his bonnet to an oyster-wench;
A brace of draymen bid God speed him well
And had the tribute of his supple knee,
With 'Thanks, my countrymen, my loving friends';
As were our England in reversion his,
And he our subjects' next degree in hope.

Essex's innate courtesy was part of his charm, but it was also politics. As the nineties progressed and his popularity increased, so the Queen's suspicions of him grew. He had discussed the question of the succession to her throne with her grand rebel, the O'Neill, at an interview in Ulster with only Southampton present. The day before his outbreak into the City, his followers got Shakespeare's company at the Globe to put on *Richard II*, who had been deposed. 'I am Richard II. Know ye not that?', Elizabeth said angrily, and that the play had been performed forty times in public places.

Ireland was as fatal to Richard II as to Essex. Richard hoped that the lining of John of Gaunt's coffers would make coats 'To deck our soldiers for these Irish wars'. 'Coat-and-conduct' money was the regular phrase for the provisioning of recruits, and in the late nineties the Irish war engulfed men and money. O'Neill's strength was due to his modernising his forces, equipping and training them with guns. Hitherto Irish forces, apart from horsemen, consisted largely of gallowglass, i.e. the tribal followers of their chiefs, and kern, or swift-running footmen. Several references occur to these. 'A mighty

power of gallowglasses and stout kerns is marching hitherward.'
The kern were not impeded by trousers: 'You rode, like a
kern of Ireland, your French hose off.' They are described as
'rough, rug-headed', 'shag-haired and crafty'; they wore their
matted hair down over their eyes in 'glibs', so that they could
not be recognised. In *Macbeth*

> the merciless Macdonald...
> from the Western Isles
> Of kerns and gallowglasses is supplied.

This leads us straight into the contemporary situation: the
Gaelic-speaking Celts of the Scottish Western Isles and of
Ulster formed one culture, could see, support and fight each
other across their narrow strip of water, and were much
intermingled. The Scottish Macdonalds were the same folk as
the Irish MacDonells, and the Scots had originally come out
of Ireland. It was not until James of Scotland came to the
English throne that some order was introduced into Ulster
with the plantation of Lowland Scots (not English). *Hinc illae
lachrymae!*

To the Elizabethans the general barbarity of Irish conditions
was signalised by the survival of wolves, which had become
extinguished in England: 'Tis like the baying of Irish wolves
against the moon.'

It has often been put forward that Shakespeare was not
interested in the topical – as if he were not interested in the
world about him! This mistaken idea springs from an inade-
quate knowledge of the life of the time – though it is true that
he was not a dramatist of the kind of Shaw, making plays out
of journalistic material. Progress of the war abroad is registered.
We have seen how the *Henry VI* plays were a response to the
campaign of 1591 in Normandy, arousing historic memories.
Essex's triumph – at any rate that for which he got all the
credit, and where his chivalry made a noble impression on the
Spaniards – was his capture of Cadiz in 1596. The Spaniards
had run their vice-admiral, the *St Andrew*, on the sands of the
inner harbour to prevent her being captured:

> I should think of shallows and of flats,
> And see my wealthy *Andrew* docked in sand,
> Vailing her high-top lower than her ribs.

That autumn Spain followed up with a second Armada, which was disastrously dispersed by tempest – as in *King John* (and this gives us the dating for the play):

> So, by a roaring tempest on the flood,
> A whole armado of convicted sail
> Is scattered and disjoined from fellowship.

In 1600 began the ding-dong struggle for tiny Ostend. The English army under Vere proved its maturity at last by a victory at Nieuport over seasoned Spanish troops, and proceeded to occupy a strip of their territory in and around Ostend.* Digging themselves in, they were surrounded by a large Spanish army; and the siege went on for many weary months:

> We to gain a little patch of ground
> That hath in it no profit but the name.

This is from *Hamlet* of just that year.

Othello has a reference to a carrack:

> he tonight has boarded a land carrack:
> If it prove lawful prize, he's made for ever.

Carracks were the great Portuguese ships that brought home to Lisbon the treasures of the East Indies: spices, silks, porcelain, jewels. The richest prize of these was the *Madre de Dios*, captured in 1592. A kitchen-wench is caricatured, her appearance likened to America or the Indies. Why? 'O, sir, upon her nose, all o'er embellished with rubies, carbuncles, sapphires, declining their rich aspect to the hot breath of Spain, who sent whole armadoes of carracks to be ballast at her nose.' The humour is forced, for it is an early play; the interest is that it is from the *Comedy of Errors* and gives it its dating, the year of the capture of the Great Carrack, 1592.

Recruiting the forces is handsomely caricatured when Falstaff assembles the men whom Justice Shallow has provided for him: Mouldy, Shadow, Wart, Feeble, Peter Bullcalf of the green. They are a seedy lot; it is given to Feeble to repeat the familiar commonplaces of the time: 'We owe God a death. A man can die but once'; and 'No man is too good to serve's

* cf. my *The Expansion of Elizabethan England*, 410–13.

prince.' Falstaff had had no better luck when he sent Bardolph ahead to recruit for him, along the road to Coventry through Sutton Coldfield. 'I press me none but good householders, yeomen's sons; inquire me out contracted bachelors, such as had been asked twice on the banns' – or so he said; but he was not above accepting a bribe to let one or other of them off. So he ended up with 'discarded serving-men, younger sons to younger brothers, revolted tapsters, and ostlers trade-fallen.... If I be not ashamed of my soldiers, I am a soused gurnet. No eye hath seen such scarecrows.' He wound up, 'I'll not march through Coventry with them, that's flat' – a note of respect for Warwickshire's cathedral city. Anyone who is familiar with Elizabethan recruiting and mustering will recognise the fidelity of the caricature.

Warwickshire is given a good show from the earliest play, *Henry VI*. Here is Sir William Lucy, of the leading family near Stratford, out at Charlecote; and we have neighbouring places, Southam, Dunsmore, Daintry (the old pronunciation of Daventry). 'Here Southam lies; the drum your honour hears marcheth from Warwick.' Neighbouring Gloucestershire features with Justice Shallow's garden, his orchard and his pippins; and so to Dumbleton and Berkeley Castle. More references occur to the neighbouring Cotswolds, once with an old pronunciation: 'How does your fallow greyhound, sir? I heard say he was outrun on Cotsall.' Banbury cheese appears, 'and how a yoke of bullocks at Stamford Fair?'

Much around and about Stratford comes in the talk of Christopher Sly, old Sly's son of Barton-on-the-Heath: this was where the Lamberts lived, Shakespeare's uncle and aunt, to whom his father had mortgaged a piece of his wife's property – and he and William could never get it back. Marion Hacket was 'the fat ale-wife of Wincot', the old pronunciation of Wilmcote, whence Shakespeare's mother came. Old John Naps was of Greet, not far away, misprinted by the London printers of the Folio as Greece – and many subsequent editors have been silly enough to adhere to the misprint out of mere textual pedantry.

The consequences of the prolonged war are written into the progressive disillusionment of the plays noticeable in the years just before and after 1600. Some of them are put concisely by Mistress Overdone, bawd and brothel-keeper: 'What with the war, what with the sweat [plague or epidemic], what with the gallows, and what with poverty, I am custom-shrunk.' One gentleman admits, 'I have purchased as many diseases under her roof as come to ... three thousand dolours a year.' We have an enormous amount of talk about brothels, an intimate glimpse into the interior of one in *Pericles*, and about the diseases picked up in them – it is rather surprising to us that the Elizabethans would joke about syphilis – numerous references to the pox and its effects, to loss of noses (Sir William Davenant lost his, and he was supposed to have been an Oxford by-blow of Shakespeare's by a buxom vintner's wife there), puns on French crowns (*morbus gallicus* was supposed to induce baldness).

All this – and there is a great deal of it – much embarrassed prudish Victorians. Robert Bridges, no historian, fiercely disapproved of it as an artistic offence, thinking it was put in to please the groundlings. Naturally, it did; but an historian knows that it is true to the life of the time, which was much more disreputable and diseased than ours – as the extraordinary revelation of it in Simon Forman's case-books has now brought home to us.*

We hardly need to go into it here in depth, merely point out how true to London life was the low sex-life portrayed. *Measure for Measure* has sex, in various aspects, as its prime subject, with government a secondary theme. In *Pericles* the chaste Marina is placed in a brothel. There 'the poor Transylvanian is dead that lay with the little baggage. She quickly pooped him.' Marina's virginal charms were cried through the market. 'There was a Spaniard's mouth watered, and he went to bed to her very description.' It was observed at the time how many of the Spanish Armada's drowned were affected by syphilis – the disease raged through Europe in the sixteenth century in a particularly malignant form. 'Mistress,' the pimp inquires, 'do you know the French knight, that cowers in the hams?' 'Who, Monsieur Vérole?' (i.e. French for pox). 'Well, well, as for him, he brought his disease hither; here he does but repair it [i.e. by giving it to someone else!].

* cf. my *Simon Forman: Sex and Society in Shakespeare's Age.*

I know he will come in our shadow to scatter his crowns of the sun.' All this was very familiar – actually the South Bank stews were conveniently next door to the theatres there. To omit this aspect of common life would do an injustice to the experience of the time.

Hot-houses similarly: I suppose they were bathing establishments, conveniently provided, where assignations were made. 'Now she professes a hot-house, which I think is a very ill house too.' Garden-houses – such as that where the wicked Deputy, Angelo, thought to seduce the pure Isabella – were places of assignation also, as we know from Forman's experience and the information of the puritanical Stubbes.

Doctors are sufficiently represented. It is natural that Shakespeare should cite Galen, for he was revived as the leading medical authority of the Renaissance; but he knows also of Hippocrates and the controversial Paracelsus, while his classical foundation comes out in casual references to Aesculapius, the ancient god of medicine. *All's Well* is very interesting from the medical point of view. The King is sick, apparently beyond all hope,

> When our most learnèd doctors leave us, and
> The congregated college have concluded
> That labouring art can never ransom nature
> From her inaidible estate.

On the other hand, he did not wish

> To prostitute our past-cure malady
> To empirics...

In *Coriolanus* a character says, on receipt of good news, 'I will make a lip at the physician. The most sovereign prescription in Galen is but empiricutic.'

Empirics were doctors who practised without authority and were regarded as cranks, or worse. Simon Forman was an empiric, constantly pursued by the College of Physicians, whom we recognise in the reference above. He was something of a herbalist, and he did not hold with the excessive bleeding which was a practice of the time, nor did he attach as much importance to urinology as was usual. What an irreparable loss that Shakespeare did not appear to consult Forman – as his former mistress, Emilia Lanier, did a few years after their affair. But the theatre-folk, probably much too busy and frequently away on tour, were not among his clients.

Richard II advises the quarrelling Bolingbroke and Mowbray:

> Let's purge this choler without letting blood.
> This we prescribe, though no physician;
> Deep malice makes too deep incision...
> Our doctors say this is no month to bleed.

For bleeding was under the control of the planets: certain times were ruled propitious, others ruled out as unpropitious. Falstaff inquires of his page, 'What says the doctor to my water?' Page: 'He said, sir, the water of itself was a good healthy water; but, for the party that owed it [always Shakespeare's word for 'owned'], he might have moe [more] diseases than he knew for.' When teasing Malvolio as either bewitched or mad, his tormentors say, 'Carry his water to the wise woman', i.e. a beneficent white witch.

It has been thought that Shakespeare's later plays show a more inquiring interest in medicine after his daughter Susanna's marriage to Dr John Hall. In *Pericles* we read:

> 'Tis known, I ever
> Have studied physic, through which secret art,
> By turning o'er authorities, I have,
> Together with my practice, made familiar
> To me and to my aid the blest infusions
> That dwell in vegetives, in metals, stones;
> And can speak of the disturbances
> That nature works, and of her cures.

In *Cymbeline* Dr Cornelius plays a part in the action through his drugs.

It is something to set against our disappointment that Shakespeare did not consult Forman, so far as we know (some of his case-books are missing), yet Dr Hall kept his and published his *Select Observations*.* Among the prescriptions of his which we have, are those for his daughter, Shakespeare's granddaughter Elizabeth, the poet Drayton and his patrons, and Forman's old friend, Bishop Thornborough of Worcester.

As for the law and lawyers Shakespeare is so familiar with them that it has been argued – quite unnecessarily – that he

---

* cf. Harriet Joseph, *John Hall: Man and Physician.*

must have known the inside of a lawyer's chambers. It is true that some of his plays had special performances in the Inns of Court: the *Comedy of Errors* at Gray's Inn, *Twelfth Night* in Middle Temple hall, and fairly certainly *Troilus and Cressida*. The Inns were near neighbours of Blackfriars, and just across the river from the Globe; the 'termers' were devotees of plays. Gray's Inn, Clement's Inn and the Temple are mentioned. It is no more likely that he had any such apprenticeship than that this home-keeping man – with a family to support from the age of nineteen – travelled abroad, simply because so many plays and scenes are supposed to take place abroad.

Any and every Elizabethan property-holder was better acquainted with the law than we are. He had to be, partly because of the law's uncertainties, partly because of the ubiquitous litigiousness of the age (Shakespeare characteristically kept out); but mainly because of dependence on title-deeds, documents, parchments, leases, rentals, quittances, and so on. Hamlet's word 'quietus' is simply the phrase 'quietus est', i.e. paid, or quit, which appears on thousands of documents to survive. 'I have neither the scholar's melancholy, which is emulation [true of academics at all times], nor the lawyer's, which is politic.' With whom does time stand still? 'With lawyers in the vacation, for they sleep between term and term.' When lawyers feel Robin Goodfellow tickling their fingers at night, they straightway dream of fees; or, 'like the breath of an unfee'd lawyer, you give me nothing for 't'. 'These nice sharp quillets of the law' – of a dead lawyer, a skull in a graveyard – 'where be his quiddities now, his quillets, his cases, his tenures?'

Not much justice was done in the case of Dr Lopez which made such a sensation in the winter of 1593-4. A Portuguese Jew, he was the Queen's doctor; he was also an intelligence man – a dangerous duality. Moreover, he was not a wise man, and his position went to his head. He blurted out that Essex was infected with a venereal disease, and Essex determined to ruin him. The trouble was that Lopez *was* in correspondence with Spain and in the receipt of gifts, hoping he would poison the Queen. She, sensible woman, did not believe this for a moment, and there was no likelihood of its being true. However, in Elizabethan England, as in uncivilised countries today, a man charged with treason was held guilty unless he could prove his innocence, and this the unfortunate doctor was unable to do.

Essex staked his prestige on running him down, raised a clamour and ultimately – the chief prosecutor! – headed the tribunal that condemned the man. Disgraceful anti-Semitic feeling was aroused by the case, which hung fire over London for months, for the Queen refused to have the sentence executed until her hand was forced by public clamour. With this encouraging background Marlowe's play, *The Jew of Malta*, was successfully revived.

A more immediate reaction was that of Southampton's poet, who as usual shared the popular point of view:

> The mortal moon hath her eclipse endured,
> And the sad augurs mock their own presage.

That is, the Queen has come through the shadow upon her, and prophets of ill have been proved wrong: she is safe. More nonsense has been written about these lines than any others in the Sonnets, by people who do not know the contemporary scene – as one needs to, from month to month. The dating is corroborated by the concurrence of the next two lines:

> Incertainties now crown themselves assured,
> And peace proclaims olives of endless age.

This refers simultaneously to the surrender of Paris to Henri IV in May 1594, with which he crowned his victories; this at last gave promise of an end to the civil wars that had racked France all Shakespeare's lifetime hitherto. The concurrence of the two events makes the date quite certain – early summer 1594. Those who do not know the history of the time should at least refrain from confusing the public mind by ignorant conjectures.

Marlowe's play sparked off *The Merchant of Venice*; Marlowe's Barabas became Shylock. Shakespeare, with his popular leanings, began with the usual anti-Jewish prejudice:

> thy currish spirit
> Governed a Wolf [Lopez = lupus = wolf],
> who hanged for human slaughter,
> Even from the gallows did his fell soul fleet...

Disgraceful as it is to us, we must remember that to the Elizabethans the Jew was a comic character – as in uncivilised Germany in our time. But Shakespeare did not get very far into his character before – so like him – he saw the other side: 'Hath not a Jew eyes? hath not a Jew hands, organs, dimensions, senses, affections, passions? Fed with the same food, hurt with the same weapons, subject to the same diseases, healed by the same means, warmed and cooled by the same winter and summer, as a Christian is?' Before the end one's sympathy is won for Shylock – as mine wholly is. He dominates the play, its most memorable character.

We are not yet at the end of what we can learn about Shakespeare, as with any writer, by the proper method of exploring the contemporary experience that went into his writing, when scraping the barrel of textual minutiae or suggesting remote and ineffectual 'sources' has ceased to yield any worthwhile returns. A new possibility has recently been suggested,* which may throw some light on the incubation of the combined Italian–Jewish theme of the play – namely, that the Bassanos, the talented musical family to which Shakespeare's Dark Lady belonged, were Jewish, as was Florio. This would mean that Emilia Lanier was half-Jewish – and indeed her Poems and her personality alike suggest certain Jewish characteristics. Till we know which Bassanos were Jewish (some would have been, others not) this must remain conjectural, though the identification of the Dark Lady is clear from the complete concurrence of all the evidence, internal and external.

The life of contemporary London is recognisable in many of the plays. Even in this, which opens with the merchants of Venice,

> Plucking the grass to know where sits the wind,
> Peering in maps for ports and piers and roads,

speculating where their argosies are at sea: it is of course the Pool of London, exactly as the river-life of London is portrayed in Forman's autobiography and case-books. Further down the Thames went the ships: 'Her husband's to Aleppo gone, master o' the *Tiger.*' Several ships of that name existed, and Aleppo occurs in merchants' enquiries of Forman as to their

* Roger Prior, 'Shakespeare and his Dark Lady', *Books and Bookmen*, February 1980.

172

ships' whereabouts. It was either, 'My ships have all miscarried, my creditors grow cruel'; or, 'Here I read for certain that my ships are safely come to road.'

We cannot hope to do justice to all the London life crowded into the plays – the hostelries and taverns, St George's hostelry and the Elephant (near the present Elephant and Castle), above all the Boar's Head in East Cheap with its merry and improper goings-on – the plays themselves are the thing. Or the prison-life, as depicted in *Measure for Measure* – to us horrid, but to the Elizabethans a subject for comedy – Abhorson the executioner and his prisoner perpetually drunk, who doesn't care what happens to him. Foreigners at the time noted that the English exhibited a devil-may-care attitude towards hanging – they preferred to be done with it, rather than have a man broken on the wheel, as abroad.

We do not have a play devoted to apprentices and lower-middle-class life, like Dekker's *A Shoemaker's Holiday*; for that was his background, not Shakespeare's line. He saw the citizens' life rather from the outside:

> Many a time and oft
> Have you climbed up to walls and battlements,
> To towers and windows, yea, to chimney-tops,

to see some show passing in the streets. Battlements and chimney-tops – this is not ancient Rome, but Elizabethan London, tradesmen and all: carpenters signalised by leather apron and rule, cobblers living by the awl. Shakespeare knew the smell of Bucklersbury 'in simple time'. John Stow tells us that the whole street there was entirely occupied by grocers and apothecaries, so 'simple time' was when the herbs were brought in.

> They say this town is full of cozenage –
> As nimble jugglers that deceive the eye...
> Disguised cheaters, prating mountebanks,
> And many such-like liberties of sin.

It was indeed – and Robert Greene devoted his journalistic talents to uncovering their tricks, with which he was well acquainted, for he shared their disreputable life, Shakespeare not. However, he knew very well about cony-catching, the subject of Greene's pamphlets; several references bear witness to that.

Plague always rumbled away in the background of the rat-infested City; every ten years or so it broke out in a severe epidemic, and killed off about a tenth of the population. Too many references to plague occur to enumerate; but what is significant is that they are most frequent in what he was writing at the time of the outbreaks. This is to be expected, but their importance is that it helps to corroborate dating. Severe outbreaks occurred in both 1592 and 1593: several references occur in the Sonnets, the poems, and *Love's Labour's Lost*, written in just those years. In this play, 'Thus pour the stars down plagues for perjury,' expresses the contemporary view that the plague was due to planetary influences. The notion occurs again, 'When the planets in evil mixture to disorder wander, what plagues!' This is one of many references in *Troilus and Cressida* of 1603, which was again a bad plague year. So too in *Timon*: 'Be as a planetary plague, when Jove will o'er some high-viced city hang his poison in the sick air.' *Timon* of 1608 has a number of such references, for 1608 was another plague year.

All this but illustrates the main themes of this book: that a writer writes from his experience, and not only his inner experience; that he reflects the world around him, and that, if only one knows enough about it, this illuminates his work.

To the City tradesmen we have a country parallel in Bottom the weaver, Quince a carpenter, Snug a joiner, Flute a bellows-mender, Snout a tinker, Starveling a tailor – all more affectionately delineated, for William Shakespeare remained always a countryman at heart. And though the performance they put on is made fun of, a charming apology is made for them: 'The best in this kind are but shadows; and the worst are no worse, if imagination amend them.' There he speaks, out of his own heart, on his profession.

The Merry Wives of Windsor – though it has plenty of Windsor lore and the dramatist is familiar with the place from Court performances there – depicts just the kind of bourgeois town life he knew so well at Stratford. Respectable citizens like Master Ford and Master Page might well be aldermen of Stratford, with their wives and daughters; nor is Sir Hugh

Evans, the Welsh schoolmaster-cum-curate, at all remote. The play presents a jolly picture of social life in an Elizabethan town, for all the grand presences of the Castle, St George's Chapel and Eton in the background. It too has its own medieval lore, such as Shakespeare loved, in Herne the Hunter and Herne's Oak.

As a comedy of contemporary social life – thus a rarity – it has many touches of the time. We have the tiresome Count Mömpelgart, of Württemberg, who had paid the Court an expensive visit, taken up horses and failed to pay for them. Ralegh's recent voyage to Guiana and his book about it provide some fun – which would have pleased the Queen, for she did not put much credit in either. Nor would she object to a depreciatory reference to a Knight of Cales, i.e. Cadiz; for, whenever Essex was in command, he cheapened the order by creating too many knights.

Even more endearing are all the touches of country life – the woodlands of Arden, places in the Cotswolds, coursing the hare, hunting the deer across hill and valley, the voices of the hounds, and all the flowers he always notices; fairs and Whitsun pastorals and the shepherds' shearing feasts. We note something particular in this picture of country hospitality:

> When my old wife lived, upon
> This day she was both pantler, butler, cook;
> Both dame and servant; welcomed all, served all;
> Would sing her song and dance her turn; now here,
> At upper end o' th' table, now i' th' middle;
> On his shoulder, and his; her face o' fire
> With labour, and the thing she took to quench it:
> She would to each one sip.

It is a loving observation.

As he toured the countryside he had an eye not only for the bare ruined choirs of the dissolved monasteries (which disfigured London at the time) and the ripped-up brasses in the churches, but a special eye to the monuments which were such a feature of the age: indexes to the family sense of the rising (and risen) gentry, in place of the altars and shrines of the saints. Some of the monuments he looked at were old ones – 'this monument five hundred years hath stood', or 'on your family's old monuments hang mournful epitaphs', or there was John Gower's dominating tomb in the neighbouring church at Southwark to suggest *Pericles*. In that play

> her monument
> Is almost finished, and her epitaphs
> In glittering golden characters express
> A general praise to her, and care in us
> At whose expense 'tis done.

It was a matter of frequent comment at the time when 'rich-left heirs let their fathers lie without a monument'. 'He shall live no longer in monument than the bell rings and the widow weeps.' Alabaster or marble monuments and tombs are much mentioned. The references in a couple of sonnets are particularly interesting:

> Not marble nor the gilded monuments
> Of princes shall outlive this powerful rhyme;

it will survive unswept stone, overturned statues, and the work of masonry. Whether he lives to make his patron's epitaph, or his young lord survives when he is in the earth, 'Your monument shall be my gentle verse.' These sonnets belong to 1594, which was precisely when the contract was made to build the splendid monument at Titchfield upon which Southampton figures with his parents and grandparents. He does not 'sit like his grandsire cut in alabaster', but is portrayed kneeling. We may be fairly sure that Shakespeare gave instructions for his own monument looking down upon his grave in Stratford church.

With the accession of James I the sensitive can detect a new atmosphere, new figures dominate the scene, a new generation comes to the fore. *All's Well* of 1603 registers it at once. The old King shared the values of the young Count's father:

> He had the wit which I can well observe
> Today in our young lords, but they may jest
> Till their own scorn return to them unnoted
> Ere they can hide their levity in honour.
>   ... Such a man
> Might be a copy to these younger times;

Which, followed well, would demonstrate them now
But goers backward.

Macbeth made its bow to the new dynasty, which received
a rude shock with the Gunpowder Plot. Of the trial of the
Jesuit Superior, who had known something was afoot and
suppressed his knowledge – though he had been allowed to
live peaceably in England, in spite of the laws – there are
disapprobatory notices, again in keeping with popular feeling.
The play also registers James I's resolve to resume the
sacramental healing of the King's Evil, an attribute of
his medieval ancestors, which had lapsed in unsacramental
Edinburgh:

strangely visited people,
All swollen and ulcerous, pitiful to the eye,
The mere despair of surgery, he cures,
Hanging a golden stamp about their necks
Put on with holy prayers.

This was religious duty, an outward and visible sign of royalty.
On the other hand, *Measure for Measure* records his dislike of
being pressed upon by crowds – unlike his predecessor, a gifted
actress, who always played up to them.

With the peace with Spain in 1604 the way was at last clear
for settlement in North America: a new phase indeed opened
for the English people. At once it is reflected in the work of
the most sensitive register of the time, as we have come to
expect. Jamestown was founded in 1607. Public interest was
much aroused. The colonists, instead of planting and making
sure of food supplies, went crazily digging for gold. News came
back from Virginia in 1608: 'No talk, no hope, no work but
to dig gold, wash gold, refine gold, load gold.' This became
a major theme in the next play, *Timon of Athens*. The last two
acts are mainly about Timon's finding gold by the seashore;
he combines this with digging for roots for food – as the
colonists were reduced to do in Virginia.

We have a typical address to gold, like those examples of
rhetorical *oratio* we have seen to run all through his work from
apprentice days:

Thus much of this will make black white, foul fair,
Wrong right, base noble, old young, coward valiant....

> This yellow slave
> Will knit and break religions, bless the accursed,
> Make the hoar leprosy [pox] adored, place thieves
> And give them title, knee, and approbation
> With senators on the bench.

'Thou visible god' – money was the visible god of the Jacobean age, with its characteristic note of inordinate ostentation.* Standards were slackened, with no Elizabeth I or Burghley to keep an eye on peculation and graft, and a Lord Treasurer could build a vast palace like Audley End out of embezzlement from the state.

Timon is a play of utter disillusionment – no wonder it was never completed. Timon at the end has his grave

> Upon the beachèd verge of the salt flood
> Who once a day with his embossèd froth
> The turbulent surge shall cover.

It is the situation of low-lying Jamestown on the verge of the great tidal estuary of the Chesapeake.

The Tempest of 1611 is still more devoted to these new themes – indeed it was suggested by the wreck of the Governor's flagship, going out to Virginia in 1609, in a tornado. Its strange phenomena, with St Elmo's fire running along the rigging, are described in William Strachey's letter home to Blackfriars. Shakespeare had been reading the translation of Montaigne's *Essays* made by his old acquaintance, John Florio. Interestingly enough, Southampton was closely interested in Virginia and American settlement – places along that coast, Hampton river, Hampton Roads and former Southampton Hundred were all named for him – and ultimately became Treasurer of the Virginia Company in its last years, 1620–4.†

In the play, particularly in the person of Caliban, Shakespeare confronts the issue Montaigne had touched on, the relation between civilised man (so called) and primitive societies. Here again Shakespeare has not ceased to be topical and has his relevance to today with its racial issues and conflicts between societies at widely differing cultural levels.

---

* A good study of this is Lawrence Stone, *Family and Fortune. Studies in Aristocratic Finance in the 16th and 17th Centuries.*

† See my *Shakespeare's Southampton. Patron of Virginia,* c. XII.

He does not suffer from Montaigne's illusions about primitive peoples and man in a state of nature, illusions which were to have a long forward development in political theorising right up to the paranoiac Rousseau. Not that Shakespeare is wholly unsympathetic to the idea of primitive man. After all, the island was Caliban's before Prospero came; when he first came he took care of the savage – as all Elizabethans called the American Indians – and gave him 'water with berries in it', and

> would teach me how
> To name the bigger light, and how the less,
> That burn by day and night.

This was how it was, as we know from the accounts in Hakluyt, which Shakespeare read. Civilised whites have always taught the natives how to drink; it was a Hariot, the best mathematical mind of the time, who astonished the Indians by showing them the sun and moon through his optical glass when in Virginia in 1585–6. On the other hand, primitive man was a man, and therefore a brute (like civilised man): Caliban tried to kill Prospero and to rape his daughter. All that was authentic too. William Shakespeare was no utopian.

10

Ethics and Religion

IT USED to be largely thought that one could not give an account of Shakespeare's beliefs, his outlook on life, simply because he was a dramatist, stating the views of his characters, not his own, and putting both sides of any question. The question is rather a subtle one, but there are certain assumptions in that position that are not wholly justified. Ben Jonson, though a dramatist, had no reluctance to state in downright terms exactly what he thought. In *Every Man in his Humour*, as in other plays, Jonson lays down his doctrine on various subjects, analysing and diagnosing – 'humours' for example. Shakespeare knew well what Jonson thought, for he acted in that play. He does not comment, he does not take it up, merely used Jonson's 'humours' for a joke several times over; he does not discuss it.

This is completely characteristic. Jonson made his characters fit in with his intellectualist theory, Shakespeare never. His nature was that of an observer, his outlook pragmatic, rather sceptical. He thought life more important than theory; human beings, the extraordinary varieties of character, their passions and conflicts and inconsistencies, were all in all. He has always been recognised as the greatest master and delineator of character, of all writers. We must go more deeply into this; for the moment it is enough to say that here is good reason why he, who was content to search and probe, observe and describe, is not outmoded – as Jonson is, preaching doctrines that have had their day, or even Milton with his theological preconceptions no one any longer believes in.

Something is to be said for that older conception of Shakespeare. As a dramatist he was concerned to keep a balance between conflicting characters, to say something on both sides. Beyond that is something more significant: on controversial questions it was habitual with him not to commit himself. That may be regarded as a good line for a dramatist, but it clearly represented his own nature. He knew that a lot of people's certainties – about religion, for example – were uncertain:

> In religion
> What damnèd error but some sober brow
> Will bless it, and approve it with a text?

One can hear strong personal feeling in that dismissal of people's prejudices.

So with the law:

> In law, what plea so tainted and corrupt
> But, being seasoned with a gracious voice,
> Obscures the show of evil?

Again, we can recognise real feeling. Or there is his habitual scepticism about appearances, the dichotomy between seeming and being, which is touched on so often, of which a lifelong actor would be peculiarly aware. One can never be sure of a man's character simply from his face: a young man

> Hath not yet dived into the world's deceit:
> No more can you distinguish of a man
> Than of his outward show which, God he knows,
> Seldom or never jumpeth with his heart.

'Jumps' is a favourite, personal word with Shakespeare, like 'entreats', all through his plays and recurring again in his Will. Both words are indicators. 'Jumps with' means chimes with. 'Countenance' could cover many unlikely things – notably 'evil, which is wrapt up in countenance'. One can never be sure. Ben Jonson and Marlowe were all too self-confident and sure – and in consequence were caught out. William Shakespeare was a wary man: he was never caught out – except by infatuation for a woman, which in earlier years he thought beyond one's control.

The uncertainties of appearance, what lay behind countenance, the fine line between seeming and being, had greater urgency for the Elizabethans than for us.

> There's no art
> To find the mind's construction in the face.

And of course ordinary people can hardly ever tell what is behind appearances:

> ... the fool multitude that choose by show,
> Not learning more than the fond [i.e. foolish] eye doth teach.

The question is rendered difficult for us not only by the assumptions of Renaissance psychology, which Shakespeare shared – an important part of the outlook of the time – but also the conventions of the stage. These were much more expressive: actors put on the 'countenance' of the part they acted, indeed they became those characters. Hypocrisy and deceit were both more familiar, sharper and more strongly resented in a society where passions were stronger and life was lived 'at the coal-face', as I have expressed it – more directly, more eagerly and naïvely.

William Shakespeare was a subtle man, all too aware of the uncertainties life holds. Jonson and Marlowe, in their different ways, were all too certain. It was Shakespeare's *nature*, not merely stage expediency, to leave disputed questions open. As has been well said, 'like Cicero, he reports all attitudes';* observe that Cicero was sceptical on fundamental questions, on the nature of the gods, for example. At the time there was much controversy as to the nature of the soul. Various opinions were reported in Sir John Davies' fine philosophic poem, *Nosce Teipsum*, which came out in 1599. Shakespeare read it and, as usual with him, left a mark of his current reading in the play he was writing only the next year or so. *Twelfth Night* belongs to 1600–1. In it the matter is turned to a joke when Malvolio's tormentors tease him with questions about Pythagoras' doctrine of metempsychosis and the flight of the soul into 'wild fowl', birds and such. The question is shrugged off with, 'I think nobly of the soul, and no way approve his opinion.'

The word 'soul' is used scores of times, just in the way ordinary people would conventionally use it; never once does William Shakespeare enter into discussion on the matter. How wise he was, and also not interested to pursue such a question, philosophically non-sense. Jonson and Marlowe were both interested, committed, and are thus outdated. A certain

* D.C. Allen, *The Star-Crossed Renaissance*, 167.

modesty entered into Shakespeare's attitude: he was not an academic, and we have seen his expressed respect for the 'learned'. He was content to leave these matters to theologians – and how lucky for him!

Similarly with other such matters, the influence of the stars, the nature of ghosts, or witchcraft. He shared the ordinary conventional views of his time on these matters. In accordance with the habit of his mind, he puts both views: here was his real ambivalence, not at all sexually. Naturally we hear much about the stars, for they are the subject of poetry and useful metaphorically. But it is their influence that is at question. When it was obvious that the sun and moon govern physical conditions on the earth, it was natural enough that people of his time should think that the stars did also. Relics of this thinking are familiar to us today in the concepts 'jovial', 'mercurial', 'saturnine', 'venereal', 'martial' or in the word 'influenza'.

We have heard Shakespeare mention the stars as responsible for plagues and disasters; we also hear of the influence of the stars upon human fate and character: some are born under an auspicious or a charitable star; with others their stars were opposite, their fate or their love 'star-crossed'. What of their influence on one's fate? This was the subject much debated at the time, i.e. that of 'judicial astrology'. We hear at one time:

> It is the stars,
> The stars above us, govern our conditions:
> Else one self-mate and -make could not beget
> Such different issues.

On the other hand,

> Men at some times are masters of their fates:
> The fault ... is not in our stars,
> But in ourselves.

His last word on the subject is:

This is the excellent foppery of the world that, when we are sick in fortune – often the surfeits of our own behaviour – we make guilty of our disasters the sun, the moon, and stars. As if we were villains on necessity, fools by heavenly compulsion, knaves, thieves and treachers [treacherous] by spherical predominance; drunkards, liars and adulterers by an enforced obedience of planetary influence.

We have a personal statement of what Shakespeare was thinking on the subject in 1592, in Sonnet 14:

> Not from the stars do I my judgment pluck,
> And yet methinks I have astronomy;
> But not to tell of good or evil luck,
> Of plagues, of dearths, or seasons' quality ...
> Or say with princes if it shall go well
> By oft predict that I in heaven find.

This indicates that, like the more intelligent and sceptical intelligences of the time, he did not subscribe to 'judicial astrology', i.e. the strict foretelling of events from horoscopes and such – a sufficient reason for not consulting Forman. (What Emilia wanted to know from him – 'high-minded' as ever – was whether her husband would be knighted, and she become a titled lady.) Shakespeare left open what 'the stars in secret influence comment' on the shows that this huge stage, the earth, presents.

No necessary contradiction can be assumed in these diverse statements – even apart from the fact that we must allow for change in a man's thought with the years (one more pointer to the importance of chronology). In Shakespeare's view evidently both positions could be urged. There were people who, however excellent their qualities or arduous their efforts, could achieve nothing against the external conditions adverse to them: these made their fate. Equally it happens that the fault is in ourselves, and not in external conditions, that we fail or have ill fortune – as we are still apt to put it. Men are not responsible for their heredity:

> As in their birth wherein they are not guilty,
> Since nature cannot choose his origin;

and it may be one defect only that, without self-control, may overmaster and ruin a man. The implication is that he agreed with Aristotle – 'Aristotle's checks' – in regarding moderation as the best and safest rule in life; and this he exemplified consistently in his own conduct.

An Elizabethan would certainly have believed in ghosts, but neither is this matter so simple as it seems. It is understandable even to us today that Hamlet could not be certain whether his father's ghost was not the projection of his own imagination, disordered by grief, resentment, suspicion. Richard III and Macbeth are haunted by the apparitions called up by their guilty consciences, and Brutus is visited by Caesar's ghost. And no wonder – for they were all three murderers: the same might happen to us, if we were murderers. A different aspect of the question is opened up by Hamlet's doubt whether the ghost was not the devil leading him on. Though we have ceased to believe in the devil, the psychological phenomena of 'possession' make it easy for us to understand why people have believed in the existence of evil spirits: some obsessions are so powerful that, even though the extrapolation of an internal psychological state, they appear to have objective external existence. However different our explanations, the phenomena observed by Shakespeare are authentic. Even the witches in *Macbeth* – they are not actually called such: we may see them easily as extrapolations of Macbeth's unconscious – certainly expressed his desires, only half recognised, hitherto withheld.

Quite undoctrinally Shakespeare shares the view, taken from the ancient Greeks, which everybody held of the four elements.* These constituted nature and man: the heavy elements of earth and water, the light elements of fire and air. 'Does not our life consist of the four elements?' The Dauphin's horse in *Henry V* is 'a beast for Perseus: he is pure air and fire; and the dull elements of earth and water never appear in him'. Cleopatra, dying, is 'fire and air: my other elements I give to baser life'. It was the harmonious combination of the elements that made the best kind of man – like the too favourable summing up given to Brutus:

> the elements
> So mixed in him that nature might stand up
> And say to all the world 'This was a man.'

Drayton is referring to this commonplace of the time in his

---

*cf. J.B. Bamborough, *The Little World of Man*, 83 ff.

tribute to Marlowe: 'his raptures were all air and fire'. In the same poem he greets his countryman:

> Shakespeare, thou hadst as smooth a comic vein,
> Fitting the sock [stage], and in thy natural brain
> As strong conception and as clear a rage
> As anyone that trafficked with the stage.

He describes the harmony of the elements in a man in terms similar to Shakespeare's:

> He was a man ...
> In whom so mixed the elements all lay
> That none to one could sovereignty impute
> As all did govern yet all did obey ...
> As that it seemed, when nature him began,
> She meant to show all that might be in man.

It was indeed the common view, accepted by everybody, and dismissed by Shakespeare with 'I might say "element", but the word is overworn'.

Unhampered by doctrine, let alone dogma, he was free – markedly freer than any other writer in the age, except possibly Montaigne – to go further than anyone into that exploration of man's nature which was of the essence of the Renaissance experience. Since religion had lost its universal validity with the breakdown of medieval Catholicism, and the security of one faith with the rise of the sects, the elect intelligences of the age were faced by the problem of man's nature in itself – not without God, or independent of God, but nevertheless a microcosm in himself. This was another commonplace of the age: it led to the glorification of man on the one side, of his marvellous potentialities, 'the world, the power and the glory'; on the other hand it sharpened the sense of the evil in him, such potentialities as were nowhere more powerfully realised than in Macbeth or Richard III, or Iago.

On the one hand, 'What a piece of work is a man! How noble in reason! how infinite in faculties! in form and moving how express and admirable! in action how like an angel! in apprehension how like a god! the beauty of the world! the paragon of animals!' There speaks the Renaissance: it is doubtful if any medieval person could have written that. On

186

the other hand is what Thersites and Apemantus, Lear and Timon have to say about man, in terms no less scathing, and searing, than Swift. Both views of humanity are true, and Shakespeare – so like him – states them both, with equal power, as well as depicting every variety of human character in between, every variation of normal and abnormal (subnormal with Caliban), ordinary happy men and women, comic, inflated or absurd, gifted, sparkling, remarkable, all up and down the spectrum, in every sphere and at every level from king to peasant.

It is his grasp of character – along with the poetry in which it is expressed – that is most astonishing. Again, what an advantage he had as an actor! Only Molière had a comparable advantage. An actor has to put himself inside the skin and into the minds of any number of men or women, average or above and below. The tragic and the abnormal give the deepest glimpses into human nature, and the reason is not far to seek. A short-story writer of genius in our own time, Flannery O'Connor, has pin-pointed it: it is in moments of emergency and crisis that a man or woman's character most truly reveals itself and is lighted up, often in lurid lights.

Shakespeare accentuated the conflicts of character and deliberately made situations more extreme, not only for dramatic effectiveness, though that was a motive too; but to give deeper glimpses into the recesses of the human soul he was bent on exploring. For his was an exploring, ever-experimenting mind that knew no bounds to his intellectual and artistic ambition. (Robert Greene had caught a glimpse of that, and it infuriated him – as it might a second-rate man confronted by such serene self-confidence, as yet not justified by achievement. But it was to be!)

William Shakespeare trusted always to his intuition and followed it wherever it led – unlike Ben Jonson, who disapproved. But it was Shakespeare who had a far deeper intuition of the monster in man – he is nearer to Dostoievsky than to Ben Jonson. This does not mean that William was not a clever man, really cleverer than Ben, for all the latter's airs as an intellectual. But the natural Shakespeare – this is what is meant by people speaking of him as 'the child of nature' – used his cleverness to smooth the way for his imagination to work freely, not get in the way of it and frustrate his creativeness. Of course he was a more skilful dramatist than Ben or any of them;* he used his brain to make the way clear.

How mightily in consequence he reaped the rewards of trusting his intuition! I once observed that his subconscious worked for him night and day; one can see that in the Sonnets no less than in the plays, in the image-clusters that well up from his subconscious at any moment to illuminate the concept in the forefront of his mind. These have been studied – without perhaps an understanding of where they come from and how they work.

Similarly with his exploration of character. A real writer, who creates not merely criticises, writes: 'He is always ready to follow his intuition behind and beneath life's visible and tangible surfaces, and at any time he will shake hands with probability and even possibility when beckoned from some further border of consciousness by an imaginative truth.'† The Elizabethans were not bothered by considerations of probability, nor hampered by an unimaginatively restricted realism; and they were not afraid of the passions – as we are. We are too self-conscious to allow them free run. We may have happier, or rather more orderly, lives in consequence: it is doubtful if normally we know the heights and depths, the glory and the horror, that they did. Some of the revelations therefore that he brings before us on the stage – Lady Macbeth's sleep-walking, Hamlet's torturing Ophelia, Leontes' realisation of what he has done to wife and child and to ruin his own life – are almost more than we can bear to see enacted. Shakespeare's imagination was unsparing of us; it so searches the recesses of our hearts as to arouse our own complexes of guilt and remorse and unassuageable grief for what we are and have done, or failed to do.

For there are things in our minds and hearts that consciousness will not acknowledge, motives that we will not avow, even when half-aware of them. It is not merely that we are not so rational as we think we are – that is obvious enough – but that our unknown selves are more potent than the

* I would recommend for the study of his stage-craft, Nevill Coghill, *Shakespeare's Professional Skills*, and Granville Barker, *Prefaces to Shakespeare*.
† J.I.M. Stewart, *Character and Motive in Shakespeare*, 107.

known, that we are moved by the will, not only when we do not understand what we are doing, but even when we do – against reason, self-interest, our own profit or advantage, *against* self-knowledge. For we are not all of a piece; our very personalities are often fragmented, dissociated, with elements in conflict with each other. Even the most self-aware persons have the greatest difficulty in achieving consistency; it is doubtful if the average human being tries, or is aware of the problem. As Eliot has said, 'I do not believe that any writer has ever exposed the human will to see things as they are not, more clearly than Shakespeare.' It is notable how many of the careers of his characters are progresses in self-discovery: not only a Lear, an Othello, a Timon, a Leontes, a hypocrite like Angelo or a braggart like Parolles, a young Count Bertram (Southampton came to terms with himself in the Tower), but even a Macbeth at last:

> for now I am bent to know
> By the worst means the worst ...

>   I am in blood
> Stepped in so far that, should I wade no more,
> Returning were as tedious as to give o'er.

Of Lear it is said, 'he hath ever but slenderly known himself'; of Timon,

> The middle of humanity thou never knewest,
> But the extremity of both ends.

Neither of those things could have been said of William Shakespeare.

These themes are archetypal, deeply embedded in human nature – hence their undying power, however much overlaid. They may be more truthfully conveyed by myth or fable, or something resembling a fairy-tale – like the myth of the sick king healed by a virgin at the back of *All's Well* – than by the superficial realism of a Shaw. Though Shakespeare's plays are not realistic, they are none the less true to human nature.

> Lovers and mad men have such seething brains,
> Such shaping fantasies, that apprehend more
> Than cool reason ever comprehends.

So, he goes on to say, does the poet.

Shakespeare is the most musical of all dramatists; music plays a great part in the plays and there are numerous references to it. We are not here concerned with the subject in and for itself, but rather with what he thought of its place in life and what it has to say to man's nature. It had many uses and differing effects, but also it spoke for that harmony within which he so much valued.

> The man that hath no music in himself,
> Nor is not moved with concord of sweet sounds,
> Is fit for treasons, stratagems, and spoils;
> The motions of his spirit are dull as night,
> And his affections [inclinations] dark as Erebus.
> Let no such man be trusted.

An Iago would certainly not be moved by music.

This speech in *The Merchant of Venice* – the whole of the last act of which is suffused by music – has a countryman's tell-tale observation of a group of young colts, suddenly brought to a stand by a trumpet or sound of music.

> Therefore the poet
> Did feign that Orpheus drew tears, stones and floods;
> Since nought so stockish, hard and full of rage,
> But music for the time doth change his nature.

Hence its varying effects – to express imagined happiness or assuage melancholy, to comfort weary spirits or arouse the dead, or one assumed dead like the Queen in *The Winter's Tale*: 'Music, awake her; strike! 'Tis time: descend: be stone no more.'

Music is the associate of love. We have a self-portrait of him standing by his musical mistress while she plays to him:

> How oft when thou, my music, music play'st
> Upon that blessed wood whose motion sounds
> With thy sweet fingers, when thou gently sway'st
> The wiry concord that mine ear confounds,
> Do I envy those jacks that nimble leap
> To kiss the tender inward of thy hand.

Music can arouse the passions as well as lower their tension, chiming with the listener's mood, perhaps the sadness of Olivia's love-sick Duke; or, 'I am never merry when I hear sweet music.' Even before the disturbing presence of his musical mistress broke into the harmony of his early relations with Southampton, he is writing to him,

> Music to hear, why hear'st thou music sadly?...
> Why lov'st thou that which thou receiv'st not gladly?

He uses the image of the concord of well-tuned sounds married in union to reproach the young man for his single state, when he should be doing his duty by himself and his family by marrying:

> Mark how one string, sweet husband to another,
> Strikes each in each by mutual ordering.

It is true that the music of the time commands an extraordinary, haunting sadness, a note of inner passion, a plangency like no other. And then, when discord breaks in,

> How sour sweet music is,
> When time is broke and no proportion kept!
> So is it in the music of men's lives.

Often the power of music is equated with that of poetry: 'If music and sweet poetry agree, as they must needs'; or 'Music and poesy use to quicken you', i.e. to stir one up. And then,

> In sweet music is such art
> Killing care and grief of heart.

This is from the song in *Henry VIII*:

> Orpheus with his lute made trees,
> And the mountain tops that freeze,
> Bow themselves when he did sing.

(And this would seem to corroborate Shakespeare's authorship of the play.)

The songs themselves play an important part, usually to punctuate some juncture in the action, as well as offering their own felicity. Here we are concerned to note only that they sometimes bring home some ethical thought:

> Blow, blow, thou winter wind,
> Thou art not so unkind
> As man's ingratitude ...

Freeze, freeze, thou bitter sky,
That dost not bite so nigh
　　As benefits forgot;
Though thou the waters warp,
Thy sting is not so sharp
　　As friend remembered not.

He seems to have been singularly sensitive about ingratitude
– we have seen him reproaching himself for forgetting the
benefits received from his patron. Three times he describes
ingratitude as monstrous. 'I hate ingratitude more in a man
than lying, vainness, babbling.' It is interesting that he should
not like vanity or babbling: a prudent, good-humoured man,
but with a control upon his tongue, not bumbling about the
town like loquacious Jonson; able to keep his own counsel,
another reason why there is little gossip about him. 'Ingratitude, thou marble-hearted fiend!' 'Filial ingratitude! Is it not
as this mouth should tear this hand for lifting food to it?' He
specifically calls ingratitude a sin; filial ingratitude was thought
far worse of by the Elizabethans when family obligations were
so strict. With his time so fully pre-empted, under continual
pressure of work for the theatre and his writing, he yet accepted
his obligations to society – if ever you have

　　... been where bells have knolled to church,
　　If ever sat at any goodman's feast,
　　If ever from your eyelids wiped a tear,
　　And know what 'tis to pity, and be pitied ...

'Under the greenwood tree' counterpoints the charm of
country life and the woodlands, shunning ambition and loving
to live in the sun. And where is fancy bred? In the heart or
in the head? The answer is in keeping with the accepted
psychology of the time: in the eyes, fed by gazing, rather than
in the heart or anywhere else.

　　The error of our eye directs our mind.
　　What error leads must err: O, then conclude,
　　Minds swayed by eyes are full of turpitude.

This was in keeping with his own experience with his black-
eyed, black-haired young mistress:

　　O me, what eyes hath love put in my head,
　　Which have no correspondence with true sight!

Or, if they have, where is my judgment fled,
That censures falsely what they see aright?
If that be fair whereon my false eyes dote,
What means the world to say it is not so?

Here in his personal experience we have the dichotomy
between seeming and being, between appearance and reality,
that comes so often into the plays. Even in the songs, 'what's
to come is still [i.e. ever] unsure'. Until the end, when death
closes up life's uncertainties:

Fear no more the heat o' the sun,
    Nor the furious winter's rages;
Thou thy worldly task hast done,
    Home art gone and ta'en thy wages.

We have seen all along Shakespeare's extraordinary openness
of mind, his intellectual ambivalence, his capacity for holding
in his mind opposing thoughts, not necessarily so mutually
exclusive as superficial minds, addicted to a too rationalist
logic, are apt to think. For he saw always the uncertainties,
the duplicity of life. This does not at all mean that he had no
convictions: he certainly had. They are the normal convictions
of a normal family man, a good member of society – the
converse of the outrageous (and more intellectually excited,
and exciting) Marlowe. Nor is it so difficult to know what
William Shakespeare thought or felt. A writer, Logan Pearsall
Smith, had the perception to see that a personal tone of voice
enters when Shakespeare is telling you what he thinks, sometimes almost a raised voice; it is more obvious again when he
urges the same point over and over.*

His wary, sceptical view of the uncertainty of things, the
unreliability of people and appearances, the frailty of man's
nature, the uncertainty there is in external circumstances, in
one's fate and fortune however fair it may look – all this was
based on his own experience as registered by the most sensitive
of recorders. Jonson tells us that his nature was open, candid
and free, 'honest', i.e. honourable, though we should not need
Ben to tell us, it is so obvious. No writer could be more candid
than he is about his long struggle upwards, the crosses he

* cf. L. Pearsall Smith, *On Reading Shakespeare*.

endured, his discontent with his lot in life – from the beginning
of the Sonnets in 1592, when he was no longer young, his life
in fact more than half over, though almost all the work by
which he is remembered was yet to come.

> Let those who are in favour with their stars
> Of public honour and proud titles boast,
> Whilst I, whom fortune of such triumph bars –

in fact, must look for patronage, lucky to find such a patron.

So far he had not had much reason to be pleased with his
luck in life, his 'outcast state', though there was no use in
troubling

> deaf heaven with my bootless cries,
> And look upon myself, and curse my fate,
> Wishing me like to one more rich in hope,
> Featured like him, like him with friends possessed,
> Desiring this man's art and that man's scope.

However, there is no point in crying – his eye 'unused to flow'
– over 'precious friends' now dead, the griefs of love, or even
of 'grievances foregone'. The extreme good fortune of his
friendship with his patron had its load of anxiety and grief;
for Southampton succumbed to the temptation of Shakespeare's mistress, and the poet had to put up with it – needs
must. Even when this crisis, and that of the rivalry with
Marlowe for favour, was surmounted, he still had reason to
gird at 'the spite of fortune',

> if ever now,
> Now while the world is bent my deeds to cross.

This, from Sonnet 90, would be 1593–4, before the foundation
of the Lord Chamberlain's Company, which was to solve the
problem of a livelihood for him: in the most fortunate way –
but when life was half over.

So he had plenty of experience of both sides of life to equip
him with what he had to say about it, and with the ambivalence
which was second nature to him. One may compare it with
the kindred spirit of his contemporary, Montaigne – *divers et
ondoyant*. Such an outlook meant few illusions – as Montaigne
had few – least of all with regard to opinion, other people's
opinions, let alone their doctrines, preconceptions and

prejudices. Shakespeare uses the word 'opinion' most commonly to mean fancy; their opinions are but fancies. One saves a lot of time by disregarding them. 'A plague of opinion! A man may wear it on both sides, like a leather jerkin. Whiles others fish with craft for great opinion, I with great truth catch mere simplicity.'

Thus his ethical ideas are simple and tried ones, those held by the consensus of common sense and found to work best. But they are held with an uncommon degree of observation as to how they do work with people, and allowing a wide margin for uncertainty. One can never be sure how things will work out. There is ambivalence in fortune itself, not only in people:

> We, ignorant of ourselves,
> Beg often our own harms, which the wise powers
> Deny us for our good: so find we profit
> By losing of our prayers.

Sometimes 'our mere defects prove our commodities'; occasionally in this earthly world

> to do harm
> Is often laudable, to do good sometime
> Accounted dangerous folly.

That is not necessarily so in itself, merely what people think; in truth, one sees in a moment of illumination,

> There is no shuffling, there the action lies
> In his true nature.

We have been told often enough that

> Opinion's but a fool, that makes us scan
> The outward habit by the inward man.

It is also true that

> men's judgments are
> A parcel of their fortunes, and things outward
> Do draw the inward quality after them
> To suffer all alike.

Is there a levelling process at work in our fates? He suggests – and this is very characteristic of him – that just where we may expect nothing but good, an ill blow often befalls us; conversely, out of ill often good unexpectedly comes. One never can tell. The moral of this is clear: not to entertain expectations, not to hope too much from life; on the other hand, not to grieve too much either – he says that several times, not only in the Sonnets. The Sonnets and the plays agree and cohere; so do the poems: they are all one man, though the point of view sometimes shifts, with the subject undertaken – a *Troilus*, a *Timon*, a *King Lear*, *Macbeth* or *Othello* offer us extreme cases – or, naturally, with increasing years.

Consistency is clear in recurrent notes: 'Use every man after his desert, and who shall scape whipping?' Or,

> Why dost thou lash that whore? Strip thy own back,
> Thou hotly lusts to use her in that kind
> For which thou whip'st her.

No point in pretending to be better than one is: the candid confession in the Sonnets is at one with the plays: 'I am that I am,' he says.

> ... Why should others' false adulterate eyes
> Give salutation to my sportive blood?
> Or on my frailties why are frailer spies,
> Which in their wills count bad what I think good? ...
> No: I am that I am: and they that level
> At my abuses reckon up their own.

So – one doesn't live one's life in the light of other people's eyes, in accordance with what they think. And there occurs a charming admission, which is very much Shakespeare, put into the mouth of a good woman, forgivingly:

> They say best men are moulded out of faults,
> And, for the most, become much more the better
> For being a little bad.

One must not expect too much of human beings. He evidently did not like the 'unco guid', the cold-blooded and puritanical – Angelo, Iago, Richard III all had a streak of the puritanical – they were hypocrites, deceivers, seemers, not what they put out they were. By a twist of irony he puts the point into the mouth of Iago: 'Men should be what they seem'; for Shakespeare knew (as Hitler did) that if you want to take fools in, tell them the truth for they will not believe it. As an historian of morals, Lecky, summed up: 'Men will believe contrary to the evidence, they will believe in spite of the evidence, but hardly ever because of the evidence.' The whole history of religions shows that humans prefer to believe nonsense rather than sense.

Once more the inflexion given in the plays is corroborated by that in the Sonnets, out of his own experience: they

> That do not do the thing they most do show,
> Who, moving others, are themselves as stone
> Unmoved, cold, and to temptation slow –

they are 'the lords and owners of their faces', in control of themselves and others – more so than one of 'sportive blood' and warm feelings.

What kind of things did Shakespeare hate most? Can we discern a particular personal inflexion?

A highly civilised and sensitive man, he clearly hated cruelty. But this again is not as simple as it looks. Some forms of cruelty are general, almost impersonal. In war the individual is not held to blame, unless he breaks the 'rules of war', in killing prisoners for example. Or a man may kill in an outburst of passion when he is completely out of control and regarded as hardly responsible; or in self-defence. Shakespeare is in keeping with common opinion in holding cold, calculating evil as worst, an Iago or an Edmund, those monsters of heartlessness, Goneril and Regan.

The worst of the seven deadly sins, according to Catholic morality, is pride, as the nourisher of all the others. Pride is not so ill thought of by Protestants, indeed a proper pride is rather a Protestant virtue. Nor is it badly spoken of by Shakespeare – 'he's proud, and yet his pride becomes him', etc. Vastly more is said of honour, and that is appropriate to the time, when the Elizabethans thought of themselves as reviving medieval ideas of chivalry – 'the Honour of the Garter' and all that (the title of Peele's poem, with a tribute to young Southampton).

Honour is 'bright', honour is 'shining', and so forth, and 'if I lose mine honour I lose myself'. It was a time when the concept of honour sanctioned a perfect mania for duelling, and many were the good lives thrown away, like Mercutio's, for this nonsense.* We may wonder whether that prudent man, William Shakespeare, who saw through everybody and never involved himself in any *fracas* as his colleagues did, was not expressing himself in the voice of Falstaff:

Honour pricks me on. Yea, but how if honour prick me off when I come on? Can honour set to a leg? No. Or an arm? No. Or take away the grief of a wound? No. What is honour? A word. What is in that word? Honour. What is that honour? Air. Who hath it? He that died o' Wednesday. Doth he feel it? No. Doth he hear it? No. 'Tis insensible, then? Yea, to the dead. But will it not live with the living? No. Why? Detraction will not suffer it. Therefore I'll none of it. Honour is a mere scutcheon [an outward sign]. And so ends my catechism.

It is a singularly searching catechism, especially when one looks at it from the perspective of the time, which attached an exaggerated importance to the concept. One would say that Shakespeare did not, and, though he was no cynic, neither did he entertain vain illusions.

Our virtues must be given outer expression – we have seen that Shakespeare was no solitary, let alone a misanthrope, but a man fully accepting the obligations of society. His last will and testament fully corroborates this. When he made it on Lady Day, 25 March 1616, he was 'in perfect health and memory, God be praised', though he was to die rather unexpectedly only a month later, on St George's Day, 23 April. It is a generous and neighbourly document, all his family provided for, poor relations and friends remembered; his sword – every gentleman carried a sword – to neighbour Combe out at Welcombe, money for mourning rings to several neighbours and to three of his Fellows of the Company in London, Burbage, Heming and Condell. The last two have put us for ever in their debt by pushing through the Folio collection of his works, an exceptional undertaking and no easy task, as an extraordinary tribute to their already famous colleague. Nor were the poor of Stratford forgotten, a generous £10, when many richer bequeathed less; '20s in gold to my godson, William Walker'.

* cf. my *The Elizabethan Renaissance. The Life of the Society*, 197–9.

He was defeated in his aim of perpetuating his family in his
name by the death of his little son, Hamnet, at eleven in 1596.
We have already seen that *King John* was written that year;
turning to the play we find,

> Grief fills the room up of my absent child,
> Lies in his bed, walks up and down with me,
> Puts on his pretty looks, repeats his words,
> Remembers me of all his gracious parts,
> Stuffs out his vacant garments with his form.

The touching simplicity of it bespeaks personal grief; it is
completed with a thought such as has often consoled bereaved
parents: the hope, not a certainty,

> That we shall see and know our friends in heaven:
> If that be true, I shall see my boy again.

> Heaven doth with us as we with torches do,
> Not light them for themselves; for if our virtues
> Did not go forth of us, 'twere all alike
> As if we had them not.

For,

> ... no man is the lord of anything ...
> Till he communicates his parts to others.

We have a vast deal about love and friendship in the plays
– naturally when love is the staple fare of romantic comedy.
More significant is the conflict between love and friendship
recorded in the Sonnets and contemporaneously in *The Two
Gentlemen*.

> Friendship is constant in all other things
> Save in the office and affairs of love –

he observes, in accordance with his experience. In his relation
with Southampton friendship had to come first, the affair with
Emilia was inconstant and undependable anyhow – besides
being adulterous (the tell-tale word 'adulterate' occurs). In the
contemporaneous *The Two Gentlemen* one of the two sacrifices
his love, his young woman, to his friend – to the eternal
disapprobation of critics taking the matter *au pied de la lettre*,

without knowing what was behind it. One must not shake off a friend:

> I am not of that feather to shake off
> My friend when he must need me.

Little enough is said about religion, though that is not only because its discussion was prohibited, but because he was not interested in futile discussion. He accepted undogmatically what a conforming member of the Church accepted at the time. He was neither Puritan nor Papist, and used their senseless disputes to make fun of them both: 'If men could be contented to be what they are, there were no fear in marriage; for young Charbon the Puritan and old Poysam the Papist, howsomever their hearts are severed in religion, their heads are both one: they may jowl horns together like any deer in the herd', i.e. may be cuckolded alike. Even his references to Puritans are not very hostile though he did not like them. (Who could?) 'But one Puritan amongst them, and he sings psalms to hornpipes.' 'The devil a Puritan he is, or anything but a time-pleaser.' We are given no satirical portrait of a Puritan such as Jonson's of a hypocritical sectarian, Ananias the deacon, in *The Alchemist*. (Jonson was a Catholic convert for a time, while in prison.)

Shakespeare's conception of religion is a conventional one: it is religion that makes vows to be kept – and he hates a promise-breaker; religion puts people in fear of doing wrong, and gives them a conscience. Even his concept of conscience is not very searching; it is taken for granted, and is sometimes used to turn a joke. 'It is a dangerous thing: it makes a man a coward; a man cannot steal, but it accuseth him; he cannot swear, but it checks him ... It fills one full of obstacles: it made me once restore a purse of gold that I found; it beggars any man that keeps it.' Thus conscience makes cowards of us all, if we have any – as most normal people have. Richard III was hardly normal, physically or mentally, and he considered conscience 'but a word that cowards use, devised at first to keep the strong in awe'. Nevertheless, he felt agonies of guilt, and was visited by the phantoms of his victims.

William Shakespeare had reason enough to know guilt in his own life, and to be conscience-stricken: a highly-sexed man, he could not resist the urge of sex when confronted by a seductive young woman, gifted and (we now know) remarkable in her own right, for all her ill character. His sexual passion was a fever, 'longing still for that which longer nurseth the disease', in the end driving him 'frantic-mad', his impulses in rebellion against what he knew to be right, the evidence of what people told him, and of his own eyes. Hence the bitterness of his candid confession:

> The expense of spirit in a waste of shame
> Is lust in action ...
> Enjoyed no sooner but despisèd straight;
> Past reason hunted and, no sooner had,
> Past reason hated, as a swallowed bait ...
> Mad in pursuit, and in possession so ...
> Before a joy proposed, behind a dream.

Perhaps only a passionate man could have reacted so violently – the one area where he could not control himself – and only a sensitive and honourable one would reproach himself in such terms.

With this humane and civilised man it is natural that we should have a notable amount about pity and mercy – he knew that he would need the latter, if not the former, himself, as we all do. Most of the references are just the words as used in common discourse; but the concept of mercy itself is a leading theme in both *The Merchant of Venice* and *Measure for Measure*, besides occurring elsewhere. The idea of mercy in and for itself appears in

> Not ... the deputed sword,
> The marshal's truncheon, nor the judge's robe,
> Become them with one half so good a grace
> As mercy does.

And then, after pardon:

> Mercy then will breathe within your lips
> Like man new-made –

the religious idea, familiar from baptism. We hear of 'a man of truth, of mercy', and of 'the infinite and boundless reach of mercy'. The *locus classicus*, however, is the celebrated speech:

> The quality of mercy is not strained;
> It droppeth as the gentle rain from heaven ...
>> It is twice blest:
> It blesseth him that gives and him that takes.

Mercy is to be rated higher even than the justice which is the prerogative, as well as the duty, of sovereigns and rulers:

> It is an attribute of God himself,
> And earthly power doth then show likest God's
> When mercy seasons justice.

It is not in the course of justice that we see our salvation: we all have reason to pray for mercy –

> And that same prayer doth teach us all to render
> The deeds of mercy.

As for pity – 'where no pity, no friends, no hope; no kindred' – it is a characteristic turn of thought. 'Say "Pardon" king; let pity teach thee how: the word is short.'

The one really a-moral man to be depicted – and he is a fascinating study as such – is Iago in *Othello*. When women betray their husbands, 'their best conscience is not to leave it undone, but to keep it unknown'. Usually, however, conscience is connected with guilt and remorse; the image that springs naturally to Shakespeare's mind is the common one of the worm that gnaws at the conscience.

Angels are frequently referred to, usually in a metaphorical sense or a sense implying nothing very specific. There are good angels and bad angels overlooking one, as one might still refer to such without meaning much. The brightest of them fell – that is all: William Shakespeare was not the man to write *Paradise Lost*. It was a commonplace that they were ministers of grace, and 'grace is grace despite all controversy'. I think we may fairly say that he would never have entered into controversy – he would not have thought it worth it; whereas the author of *Paradise Lost* was never out of controversy.

Again, and finally, this did not mean that he had no belief, that he was so sceptical that he did not think right was right, and wrong was wrong. He had a firmly moral view of life, an 'honest' one, i.e. honourable; it was comprehensive but simple, conventional and conforming. And by it he was well capable of judging – 'their ways I judge, and much condemn' – but a tenderer and more merciful man than the author of that line. He had a belief in a Judge and judgment beyond that of men, and wrote in some of his most moving lines:

> Why, all the souls that were forfeit once,
> And He that might the vantage best have took
> Found out the remedy. How would you be,
> If He, which is the top of judgment, should
> But judge you as you are? O think on that!

One more fleck of personal religious feeling occurs when Henry IV announces his wish to go on crusade to recover Jerusalem, across

> those holy fields
> Over whose acres walked those blessed feet,
> Which fourteen hundred years ago were nailed
> For our advantage on the bitter cross.

He uses the word 'vantage' and 'advantage' in these two places: i.e. Christ died for us. It is in keeping with the words of his last will and testament: 'I commend my soul into the hands of God my Creator, hoping and assured by believing through the only merits of Jesus Christ, my Saviour, to be made partaker of life everlasting.' There is nothing Catholic in this, it is the regular formula of the English Church at the time, in conformity with which he died as he had lived: gathered with his family in the chancel of the church where he and his had been baptised and are buried.

Index

AESOP, 26
African coast, 35
Africanus, Leo, 135
Alleyn, Edward, 39, 43
America, U.S. of, 151
Anglican Church, 131, 134, 203
Antwerp, 152
Arden family, 3, 36
Arden, Forest of, 28
Ariosto, 129, 130
Aristotle, 22, 184
Armada, Spanish, of 1588, 18, 140,
    141; of 1596, 165
Armin, Robert, 40, 41
Arscot family, 84
Ascham, Roger, 158
Aubrey, John, 40, 45, 57
Auden, W.H., 88
Audley End, 178

BACON, Francis, 1, 81, 143
Bale, John, 74
Banbury, 166
Bandello, M., 129, 135
Barentz, W., 137
Barton-on-the-Heath, 166
Bassano family, 44, 172
Bath, 41, 107
Beaufort, Henry, Cardinal, 69–70,
    141; Lady Margaret, 67
Beaumont, Francis, 52
Belleforest, F. de, 129, 135
Bermuda, 137
Bible, the, 7
Blackfriars, 55–6, 61, 101, 104, 133,
    137, 138
Boccaccio, G., 129
Bodin, J., 132
Bosworth, Battle of, 67
Bridges, Robert, 7, 80–1, 120, 167

Bright, Timothy, 138
Britten, Benjamin, 105
Brooke, Arthur, 135
Brothels, 167–8
Brutus, Marcus, 20, 30–1, 148
Buckingham, Henry Stafford,
    duke, 71
Burbage family, 45, 51–2; James,
    36; Richard, 36, 39, 42, 198
Burghley, William Cecil, Lord, 40,
    92, 97, 131, 158, 178

CADIZ, 164, 175
Caesar, Julius, 11, 20, 30–1, 67
Cambridge, 19, 49
Camden, William, 133
Canada, 151
Canterbury, King's School, 3
Caxton, William, 33, 127
Cecil, Sir Robert, 61, 143, 155
Chapman, George, 2, 21, 23, 29,
    33, 121, 127–8
Charles I, 73, 109, 132
Chaucer, Geoffrey, 127
Chettle, Henry, 37
Chichele, Henry, archbishop, 74
Churchill, Sir Winston, 149
Cicero, 18, 20, 31, 134, 182
Cinthio, G., 129, 135
Cobham, Lord, 43–4
Coleridge, S.T., 120
Commines, Philippe, 132
Communism, 137–8, 140, 152
Companies, theatre: Boys', 11,
    46–7, 51; Lord Admiral's, 41,
    43; Lord Chamberlain's
    (afterwards, King's Men), 37,
    39–40, 41–3, 47, 53, 157,
    194
Condell, Henry, 19, 52, 198

Cooper, Thomas, bishop, 12
Cotswolds, the, 13, 60, 102, 122,
    152, 166
Cotton, Sir Robert, 158
Coventry, 166
Cromwell, Oliver, 73, 142
Cumberland, Anne Clifford,
    countess, 158

D-DAY 1944, 140
Daniel, Samuel, 69, 73, 109, 129,
    158
Dante, 88
Danvers–Long feud, 25
Davenant, Sir William, 167
Daventry, 166
Davies, Sir John, 128, 182
Dekker, Thomas, 1, 47, 173
Democracy, 150–1
Dickens, Charles, 32, 124
Digges, Leonard, 135
Donne, John, 103
Dostoievsky, F., 187
Dover, 41
Drayton, Michael, 1, 8, 158, 169

EDEN, Richard, 125, 137
Edward IV, 67
Edward VIII, 75, 132
Eliot, T.S., 16, 188
Elizabeth I, 15, 27, 40, 48, 53, 62,
    67, 74, 75, 76, 83, 84, 85, 89,
    129, 130, 131, 134, 149, 151,
    155, 156, 160, 162–3, 170–1,
    175, 178
Elizabeth, princess, James I's
    daughter, 53
Elizabethan age, 1, 14, 15, 26, 32,
    35, 53–4, 62, 88, 97, 98, 117–
    18, 149
Elyot, Sir Thomas, 134
Epicurus, 22
Erasmus, 20, 134
Essex, Robert Devereux, earl, 23,
    27, 33, 40, 48, 75, 83, 88, 92,
    97, 149, 151, 156, 160, 161,
    162–3, 170–1, 175
Eton, 2, 175

FABYAN's *Chronicle*, 132
Fenton, Sir Geoffrey, 135
Field, Richard, 55, 101, 104, 134
Flaubert, G., 110
Fletcher, John, 52
Florio, John, 21, 23, 25, 83, 128,
    137–8, 172
Folklore, 125
Fool, rôle, 41–2, 84–5
Forman, Simon, 83, 121, 163, 167,
    168, 169, 172–3, 184
Foxe, John, 131
France, 73–4, 77, 79, 139, 140,
    141, 146, 152
Froissart, J., 73, 128

GALEN, 27, 118, 168
Garnet, Henry, 133
Gascoigne, George, 130
Gates, Sir Thomas, 137
Gaunt, John of, 73, 145
Germany, 140, 150
Gibbon, Edward, 69
Glendower, Owen, 142–3
Gloucestershire, 166
Golding, Arthur, 16, 131
Gower, John, 55, 127, 176
Greene, Robert, 2, 15, 18, 24, 25,
    33, 37, 81, 127, 173–4, 187
Greet, 166
Guiana, 175
Gunpowder plot, 177

HAKLUYT, Richard, 18, 129–30,
    137, 179
Hall, Edward, 68, 131–2
Hall, Dr John, 118, 169
Hardwick Hall, 15
Harington, Sir John, 129
Hariot, Thomas, 179
Harsnet, Samuel, archbishop, 132–
    3
Harvey, Gabriel, 99, 105, 109
Harvey, Sir William, 106
Hastings, William, lord, 132
Hatfield House, 15
Heming, John, 19, 52, 198
Heneage, Sir Thomas, 24

Henri IV, and as Navarre, 25, 74, 83, 160, 171
Henry IV, 27, 72, 75–6
Henry V, 27, 64, 69, 77, 79
Henry VI, 69–70, 71, 132
Henry VII, 67, 68, 132
Henry VIII, 67
Henslowe, Philip, 43, 44
Hippocrates, 28
Hitler, Adolf, 150, 153, 196
Hoby, Lady, 131
Holinshed's *Chronicles*, 18, 68, 72, 131, 132
Holland, Philemon, 136
Homosexuals, 1, 23, 81
Hooker, John, 131
Horace, 8, 17
Howard, Lord Henry, 67, 132
Hunsdon, 1st lord, Lord Chamberlain, 36, 43, 44, 55, 156; 2nd lord, Lord Chamberlain, 55–6, 130, 131

IMMIGRANTS, 146
Inns of Court, 130, 170
Ireland, 33, 40, 72, 140, 162–4
Italy, 158

JAGGARD, William, 102
James I, 37, 84, 89, 132, 176, 177
James, Henry, 124
Jamestown, 177, 178
Joan of Arc, 70
Johnson, Dr Samuel, 34, 80, 83, 94, 113, 125
Jonson, Ben, 1, 3, 8, 9, 12, 17, 29, 33, 37–8, 44, 45, 46–7, 48–51, 54, 57, 81, 106, 109, 121–2, 128, 133, 135, 139, 143, 158, 180, 181, 182, 187–8, 200

KEMP, Will, 39, 41, 45, 48
Kenilworth Castle, 130
King's Evil, 177
Knolles, Richard, 135
Kyd, Thomas, 1, 17, 91, 122, 125

LANGLEY, Francis, 43

Lanier, Emilia, b. Bassano, 5, 21, 23, 31, 44, 55, 82, 101, 107, 111, 138, 168–9, 172, 184, 192–3
Laud, William, archbishop, 132
Lecky, W.E.H., 197
Leicester, Robert Dudley, earl, 130, 156
Lenin, 147
Lewknor, Sir L., 135
Lily, William, 1, 9, 27
Livy, 11, 136
Lodge, Thomas, 127
London, 35–6, 44, 55, 71, 132, 133–4, 145, 146, 159, 161, 172–4
Lopez, Doctor, 170–1
Lucian, 32, 134
Lucy, Sir William, 166
Lyly, John, 11, 122, 127, 134

MANTUAN, 9
Margaret of Anjou, queen, 70
Marlborough, John Churchill, duke, 64
Marlowe, Christopher, 1, 2, 3, 8, 12, 21, 25, 28, 29, 43, 44, 54, 73, 81, 86, 101, 105, 121, 122, 136, 139, 156, 171, 181, 182, 193, 194
Marston, John, 46
Martyr, Peter, 137
Merchant Taylors' School, 11
Meres, Francis, 34
Midlands, risings in, 32
Milton, John, 13, 180, 202
Mirror for Magistrates, 68, 132
Molière, J.B.P., 187
Mompelgart, Count, 175
Montaigne, M., 137–8, 178–9, 194
Montemayor, J. de, 130–1
Montjoy family, 55, 89, 133, 134
Montherlant, H. de, 29, 42
Moorfields, 55
More, Sir Thomas, 69, 71, 132, 146
Mulcaster, Richard, 11

NASHE, Thomas, 19, 44, 50, 83, 117, 127
Netherlands, 139, 146, 152, 159–60
Normandy, 160, 164

O'CONNOR, Flannery, 187
Oldcastle, Sir John, 43
O'Neill, Hugh, 163
Ostend, 105
Ovid, 7, 10, 12, 16, 20, 21, 22, 24, 28, 34, 48, 101, 103, 125, 131
Oxford, 13, 19, 136, 167
Oxford, Edward de Vere, earl, 158

PAINTER, William, 129, 134
Palingenius, 10
Paracelsus, 168
Paris, 32, 171
Patriotism, 18, 140–1
Patronage, 156–8
Peele, George, 19, 126, 197
Pembroke, William Herbert, earl, 37
Perez, Antonio, 23, 83–4, 117
Plague, 174
Plautus, 9, 12, 17, 21, 61
Plays, other than Shakespeare's:
    The Alchemist, 48, 122, 200;
    Cynthia's Revels, 47, 48; *The
    Duchess of Malfi*, 93; *Edward II*,
    73; *Every Man in his Humour*,
    45, 46, 180; *Every Man out of
    his Humour*, 45, 47, 48; *The
    Famous Victories of Henry V*,
    129; *Frederick of Jennen*, 137;
    The Isle of Dogs, 61; *The Jew
    of Malta*, 9; *King Leir*, 129;
    The Parnassus plays, 49; *The
    Poetaster*, 46–7, 48–9; *A
    Shoemaker's Holiday*, 173; *The
    Spanish Tragedy*, 17; *Thomas of
    Woodstock*, 128; *The
    Troublesome Reign of King John*,
    129; *The Two Noble Kinsmen*,
    52; *Volpone*, 122; *The White
    Devil*, 93
Pliny, 20, 136

Plutarch, 24, 29, 31, 32, 34, 69, 127, 134
Politicians, 141–2, 143–4
Polydore Virgil, 68, 132
Pory, John, 135
Prayer Book, the, 4, 5–6
Puritans, 35, 132, 200
Puttenham, George, 109

QUILLER-COUCH, Sir Arthur, 124–5

RALEGH, Sir Walter, 97, 175
Renaissance, the, 15, 32, 118, 158, 168, 182, 186–7
Rhetoric, School, 10
Rich, Barnabe, 136
Rich, Penelope, Lady, 131, 149
Richard II, 64, 73, 163
Richard III, 64, 67, 71–2, 92, 132, 141–2, 200
Romances, popular, 127
Rome, 148–50
Rousseau, J.J., 179
Rowley, Samuel, 133
Russell, Anne, Lady, 61
Russia, Soviet, 32, 138, 147, 149
Rutland, Francis, earl, 36

ST PAUL'S SCHOOL, 11
Sallust, 11
Scot, Reginald, 132
Scotland, 140, 142, 164
Scrope, Richard, archbishop, 142
Seneca, 9, 12, 17, 61
Shakespeare, Edmund, actor, 55, 58
Shakespeare, William: on acting, 81–3; as actor, 4, 36–40, 54, 61–3; and astrology, 183–4; and audience, 45–6, 57–8, 64–6; and bawdy, 120–1; and the Court, 40, 44, 53, 75, 89, 119, 143–4, 154–6; and farce, 88, 90–1; and friendship, 21, 82, 199–200; as gentleman, 3, 36, 47–8, 53, 67; and ghosts, 30, 185; and honour, 197–8; and law, 170; and love, 22, 82,

199–200; and monuments, 41,
175–6; and music, 111–12,
190–1; and opinion, 194–5;
and the people, 62, 144–51;
self-portrait, 5, 24, 80–1;
his daughter, Susanna, 139;
granddaughter, Lady Barnard,
139; son, Hamnet, 199;
Plays: *All's Well*, 85, 88–9, 91,
120, 134, 153, 161–2, 168,
176–7, 189; *Antony and
Cleopatra*, 29, 31, 64, 128; *As
You Like It*, 29, 31, 64, 128;
The Comedy of Errors, 12, 17,
119, 125, 165; *Coriolanus*, 17,
29, 31–2, 57, 82, 118, 125,
144, 148–50, 168; *Cymbeline*,
29, 53, 114–16, 125, 137, 169;
Hamlet, 30, 33–4, 40, 47, 49,
59, 61–3, 87, 88, 91–3, 94, 95,
136, 154, 165; *Julius Caesar*,
17, 29–30, 91, 128, 147–8;
King Henry IV, Parts I and II,
10, 48, 65, 74; *King Henry V*,
5, 40, 55, 57–8, 60, 65, 69, 77–
8, 134, 136; *King Henry VI*,
Parts I, II, III, 9, 18, 19, 32, 56,
57, 65, 70–1, 73, 74, 91, 99,
114, 119, 141–2, 144–6, 166;
King Henry VIII, 52, 53, 60,
66, 131; *King John*, 3, 26, 69,
73–4, 116, 131, 140, 165, 199;
King Lear, 41, 92–4, 133, 135;
King Richard II, 26, 40, 72–3,
128, 146, 163; *King Richard
III*, 3, 20, 25–6, 69, 71–2;
Love's Labour's Lost, 3–4, 20,
21, 22–3, 83–4, 85, 90, 117,
125, 137, 174; *Macbeth*, 33, 92,
94–5, 131, 164, 185; *The
Merchant of Venice*, 42, 59, 86,
171–2, 201; *The Merry Wives
of Windsor*, 28, 44, 50, 76, 87,
88, 174–5; *A Midsummer
Night's Dream*, 24–5, 42, 58,
125, 127; *Much Ado*, 4, 28–9,
42, 86, 129; *Othello*, 10, 56–7,
92, 95–6, 135, 165, 202;

Pericles, 51, 55, 64, 121, 134–5,
167, 169, 176; *Romeo and
Juliet*, 64, 92, 125, 135; *The
Taming of the Shrew*, 13, 41,
60–1, 82–3, 116–17; *The
Tempest*, 53, 56, 125, 137–8,
178–9; *Timon of Athens*, 29,
31, 96, 134, 174, 177–8; *Titus
Andronicus*, 8, 12, 17, 91;
Troilus and Cressida, 21, 29, 32–
3, 40, 49–50, 58, 91, 150–2;
Twelfth Night, 41, 42, 65, 84,
87, 88, 91, 124–5, 136, 182;
The Two Gentlemen of Verona, 3,
21, 56, 82, 119, 130–1; *A
Winter's Tale*, 53, 95, 127;
Shakespeare's part in *Sir
Thomas More*, 146–7;
Poems: *A Lover's Complaint*, 22,
99, 103, 105, 109; *The Phoenix
and the Turtle*, 106, 107–8; *The
Rape of Lucrece*, 16, 34, 55, 104,
105; *Sonnets*, 5, 34, 41, 62, 82,
83, 99, 102, 105–7, 113, 157–8,
184, 196; *Venus and Adonis*, 10,
13, 16, 23, 34, 55, 101, 102,
103, 105

Shaw, Bernard, 89, 109
Shoreditch, 35, 44, 54
Shostakovich, D., 152
Sidney, Sir Philip, 99, 109, 125–6,
127, 135, 149
Smith, Sir John, 135
Southam, 166
Southampton, Henry Wriothesley,
earl, 2, 21, 22, 23, 25, 37, 40,
42, 82, 83, 84, 99, 100–1, 118–
19, 138, 151, 155, 156, 157–8,
161–2, 178, 189, 197; his
mother, 24, 106, 162, 176
Southwark, 35, 55, 168
Spain, war with, 18, 53, 130, 141,
151, 164–5
Spencer, Gabriel, 44
Spenser, Edmund, 89, 125, 162
Stalin, J., 153
Stow, John, 173
Strachey, William, 56, 137, 178

Stratford-upon-Avon, 4, 9, 13, 14–15, 35, 47–8, 54, 101, 130, 139, 140, 198; grammar school, 12
Sturley, Abraham, 11
Syphilis, 167–8

TARLETON, Richard, 155
Terence, 9, 12
Theatres: Blackfriars, 38, 46–7, 51–4, 55, 136–7; Curtain, 35, 43, 45, 54–5; Globe, 35–6, 45, 47, 48, 53, 63, 163; Rose, 36, 43, 45; Swan, 36, 43, 45; the Theatre, 35, 43, 54–5; War of, 46–50, 51, 61
Thomas, William, 125
Thornborough, John, bishop, 169
Thorp, Thomas, 100, 106
Tichborne, Chideock, 103
Titchfield, 25, 176
Troy, fall of, 32–3
Twyne, Lawrence, 135

UNIVERSITY WITS, 19, 25

VAUTROLLIER, T., 134
Venice, 42

Victoria, Queen, 85
Victoria and Albert Museum, 15
Victorian age, the, 7, 84, 96–7
Virginia, 135, 137, 177–9
Virgil, 18, 27

WALSINGHAM, Sir Thomas, 156, 158
War, the Civil, 6, 68
Warner, William, 130, 156
Wars of the Roses, 6, 67, 69, 71, 91
Warwickshire, 3, 125, 166
Watson, Thomas, 44
Webster, John, 1, 93
Welsh, the, 142–3, 160
Westminster Abbey, 77; school, 3, 133
Whetstone, George, 129
Williams, Sir Roger, 27, 135
Wilmcote, 166
Windsor, 87, 174–5
Witchcraft, 132–3
Wollaton Hall, 15
Wright, Thomas, 138

YARMOUTH, 44
Young, Bartholomew, 131